Wittgenstein and Gadamer

Forthcoming from Continuum:

Deconstruction and Democracy, Alex Thomson (Continuum Studies in Continental Philosophy)
Hegel and Critical Theory, Alex Thomson (Continuum Studies in German Philosophy)

Wittgenstein and Gadamer

Towards a post-analytic philosophy of language

Chris Lawn

Continuum Studies in German Philosophy

continuum
LONDON • NEW YORK

Continuum
The Tower Building
11 York Road
London SE1 7NX

15 East 26th Street
New York
NY 10010

British Library Cataloguing-in-Publication Data
A catalogue record for this book is available from the British Library.

Library of Congress Cataloguing-in-Publicaton Data
A catalog record for this book is available from the Library of Congress.

ISBN: HB: 0-8264-7529-9

Typeset by Acorn Bookwork Ltd, Salisbury, Wiltshire
Printed and bound in Great Britain by Biddles Ltd, King's Lynn

Contents

Preface

For many years now the thought that the later writings of Wittgenstein have received far too restrictive a treatment by analytic philosophers has haunted me. Countless excellent studies find their way into print but I felt, and I see little recent evidence to persuade me otherwise, the focus of attention is frequently sharp but excessively narrow and restricted to the analytic idiom. At bottom my reservations about much recent exegetical work stems from antipathy to the treatment of the *Philosophical Investigations*, and the other posthumous writings, as though they exclusively address issues in the analytic tradition and, further, are best interrogated in the same style. The issues pervading much modern Anglophone philosophy spring from a basic interest in philosophy of mind and a desire to locate all philosophical themes, including that of language, within its limited purview. In his later writings, Wittgenstein, if anything sought to move well away from this now familiar terrain, as his work became progressively broader and more obviously defined by the cultural and social practices undergirding language-games. Admittedly much of the later work illuminates aspects of mind, but throughout the primary concern is the way we *talk* about these things, and further, it is always within the context of the practices and ceremonies we daily enact within the mundanities of everyday life. The motif of language, explorations in the uses and misuses of words, and language's capacity to infiltrate, illuminate, and frequently mislead every aspect of our social lives seem to me to be the key issues treated with great urgency in the later writings. To read the *Philosophical Investigations* as a narrow forensic exploration of mental concepts misses the enormous richness of this and subsequently published works. Whether Wittgenstein focuses on minds, souls, or duck-rabbits he constantly attests to the inventiveness of language and the central part it plays in the various forms of life.

I get a strong sense of the later work as a laboratory of experimentation in ideas, styles of writing and approaches to the familiar and the unfamiliar. Throughout this work we witness an attempt to escape the rigidity and formalism of the early work of the *Tractatus Logico-Philosophicus*, a struggle to free up language and see it in its broadest light, in its inventiveness, its endless diversity. What is daring and bold – and occasionally misguided – on the actuality of language is often tamed and neutralized by reducing his work to a sequence of arguments about other minds and private languages.

The omnipresence of the written and spoken word, the extent to which we are totally immersed in linguisticality, is a key feature of the later Wittgenstein. This thought came back to me with increased intensity when I worked on Hans-Georg Gadamer for my MA thesis. I began to read Gadamer because he addressed, in interesting ways, concerns I had about the history of philosophy and how a coherent historiographical narrative could be constructed. The question of historicality always seemed to me to be inadequately explored in Wittgenstein whereas it takes centre stage in Gadamer's philosophical hermeneutics. On general questions of the nature of language Gadamer seemed to be working the same street as Wittgenstein, and yet his explorations of the historical, or rather temporal, dimension to communication exposed a blind spot to history one senses in Wittgenstein. For all his widening of the domain within which ordinary language is encountered this failure to reckon with the historical is a glaring lacuna.

Beyond a general failure to confront questions of history and temporality there is a problem about linking up Wittgenstein to the body of work called the history of philosophy. Reading the philosophical canon as a dialogical narrative, as one does with Gadamer, is intriguing and the history of philosophy started to make sense for me in a way it never seemed to when seen as the doxographical gallery of heroes (and villains) presented in the analytic history of philosophy. The move from historiography to a more wilful concern for language was easy. The more Gadamer I read the more I came to see, especially when I struggled with the neglected last third of *Truth and Method*, how central linguisticality is in his work. This started me thinking about a possible comparison with Wittgenstein.

The suggestion of a comparison is not initially promising. Gadamer's 'Heideggerianism with a human face', to coin a phrase, reaches back into a philosophical and philological tradition quite alien to Wittgenstein's analytic and intuitive but deeply original approach to philosophical thought. And there is not only the difference in academic background and approach there is also the astonishing contrast in style. Gadamer's scholarly academic prose, studded with endless references to ancient and modern learning, is nothing like the snippets of ordinary language, the brief and frequently enigmatic and disjointed remarks of Wittgenstein's later writing. Yet there is much that brings them together – not to speak with one voice but to show, in their various ways, how everything participates in linguisticality.

This study started out life as a doctoral thesis for the National University of Ireland (University College, Dublin). Various people read bits of it at various times and their helpful assistance should not pass unrecorded. Richard Kearney was a constant source of support and encouragement. I also want to thank Andrew Bowie, Bruce Krajewski, Anthony Harrison-Barbet, John Hayes, Colin Dibben, Niall Keane, Mary Fox, and Tim Mooney for their critical but constructive comments on sections of this work. It goes without saying that whatever infelicities and misjudgements the book contains are entirely my own.

Special thanks are due to the patience of the staff at the Jesuit Library, Milltown Institute, Dublin, and the quiet efficiency of Phyllis Conran at the Mary Immaculate Library in Limerick.

This work would never have seen the light of day had it not been for the sustaining friendship and forbearance of Margaret Allen.

Parts of Chapters 5 and 7 appeared as articles in *Philosophy and Social Criticism* and *Philosophy and Literature*.

Chris Lawn, Desert Cross, Enniskeane, County Cork, Ireland
March 2004

Abbreviations

BBB   L. Wittgenstein, *Blue and Brown Books: Preliminary Studies for the 'Philosophical Investigations'* (Oxford: Basil Blackwell, 1972).

BT   M. Heidegger, *Being and Time*, trans. J. Stambaugh (Albany, NY: State University of New York Press, 1996).

CV   L. Wittgenstein, *Culture and Value* (Oxford: Basil Blackwell, 1980).

DD   D. P. Michelfelder and R. E. Palmer (eds), *Dialogue and Deconstruction: The Gadamer-Derrick Encounter* (Albany, NY: State University of New York Press, 1989).

LLGH   L. K. Schmidt (ed.), *Language and Linguisticality in Gadamer's Hermeneutics* (Lanham, MD: Lexington Books, 2000).

OC   L. Wittgenstein, *On Certainty*, trans. D. Paul and G. E. M. Anscombe (Oxford: Basil Blackwell, 1974).

PG   L. Wittgenstein, *Philosophical Grammar* (Oxford: Basil Blackwell, 1974).

PH   H-G. Gadamer, *Philosophical Hermeneutics* (Berkeley, CA: University of California Press, 1976).

PHGG   L. E. Hahn (ed.), *The Philosophy of Hans-Georg Gadamer*, The Library of Living Philosophers, vol. XXIV (La Salle, IL: Open Court, 1997).

PI   L. Wittgenstein, *Philosophical Investigations* (Oxford: Basil Blackwell, 1953).

PO   L. Wittgenstein, *Philosophical Occasions: 1912–1951* (Indianapolis, IN: Hackett, 1993).

TLP   L. Wittgenstein, *Tractatus Logico-Philosophicus*, trans. C. K. Ogden (London: Routledge & Kegan Paul, 1922).

TM   H-G. Gadamer, *Truth and Method* (revised second edition) trans. J. Weinsheimer and D. G. Marshall (London: Sheed and Ward, 1989).

TRB   H-G. Gadamer, *The Relevance of the Beautiful and Other Essays*, ed. R. Bernasconi (Cambridge: Cambridge University Press, 1986).

WR   A. Kenny (ed.), *The Wittgenstein Reader* (Oxford: Blackwell, 1994).

Z   L. Wittgenstein, *Zettel*, ed. G. E. M. Anscombe (Oxford: Blackwell, 1967).

Introduction

Words strain, crack and sometimes break, under the burden, under the
tension, slip, slide, perish, decay with imprecision, will not stay in place,
will not stay still

('Burnt Norton', *Four Quartets*, T. S. Eliot)

Throughout the twentieth century Western philosophy experienced a deep
rift dividing the discipline into two warring camps. For ease of use we tend
to speak these days of the division as 'Continental' or 'European' in opposition to 'analytic', or 'Anglo-American', or simply 'Anglophone' philosophy.
In recent years an increasing *rapprochement* between younger academics has
narrowed the gap but a basic tension, at times open hostility or mutual
incomprehension, more often a simmering distrust, persists with a regrettable
consequence, mutual ignorance. Against this general background it is hardly
surprising to discover that the pioneering work on language of Hans-Georg
Gadamer and Ludwig Wittgenstein from the opposing traditions has never
been put together as the object of detailed study.

A generally analytic perspective is frequently the norm for Wittgenstein
scholars. The *Tractatus Logico-Philosophicus* and *Philosophical Investigations*
are still canonical texts for those working in this area and links with non-analytical perspectives are infrequent and rare.[1] Gadamerians, on the other
hand, tend to align themselves with the modern Continental tradition and
study his work in so far as it develops out of Husserlian and Heideggerian
phenomenology and the rich post-Kantian philological and hermeneutical
inheritance this draws upon. Points of contact with work in the Anglo-American field are often ignored, consequently Wittgenstein, not normally associated with the European tradition,[2] does not get much of a mention from
Gadamer scholars. For cultural, historical, and institutional reasons related to
the mutual suspicion of the two traditions, a detailed study of the possible
continuities, not to mention inevitable conflicts, in the work of Gadamer and
Wittgenstein has yet to materialize.

The whole analytic/Continental division is deeply questionable and its sustaining mythologies and antagonisms are readily exposed by those willing to

work both sides of the street. Although the definitive narrative history of the Continental/analytic divide has yet to be written, Simon Critchley has made a modest beginning in this direction. His *Continental Philosophy: A Very Short Introduction*[3] is not, despite expectations, a catalogue of the lives and works of the great and the good in the tradition, but a penetrating insight into the origins of hostility and stereotyping. At the philosophical level it starts with the genesis of separation in radically different interpretations of Kant. From a cultural perspective alternative self-understandings and self-descriptions are shown to be chosen rather than imposed by philosophers in both camps. Without lining up on one side or another, preferring Critchley's strategy of even-handedness, the current study offers a sympathetic assessment of Gadamer as fellow traveller and critic of the Wittgensteinian approach to language. Philosophers, in both traditions, have pointed to the remarkable similarities between Gadamer and Wittgenstein but few have examined this beyond passing general comment on the centrality of *Spiel*, translated as 'play' and 'game', in the work of both thinkers and the emphasis upon language as a practical activity.[4]

The first chapter, 'The Nature of Language: Two Philosophical Traditions', is both historical and conceptual. The aim is to offer a broad context in which to locate Gadamer and Wittgenstein. Following Charles Taylor's account of language as designative and expressive the chapter draws up a historical map. Taylor's distinction is helpful as it assists in the contextualization of the approaches to language advanced by Gadamer and Wittgenstein. Tracing theories of meaning, and by extension theories of language, back to their origins in the history of philosophy is useful for the comparisons I intend to make. Expressivist accounts of language emerge from the Hamann–Herder–Humboldt German tradition; Gadamer's work can be clearly identified with this strand of thought. Wittgenstein's earlier work is unambiguously designative although the later writings move ever closer to expressivism. Taylor's classification, coming perilously close, perhaps, to a restatement of the analytic/Continental opposition, provides useful reference points for this study. I seek to show how Wittgenstein's later work is best seen as a slightly awkward candidate for expressivism, although an assessment of his achievement needs to go well beyond this classification.

Chapter 2, 'Gadamer and Wittgenstein: Contrasts and Commonalities', begins with an overview. This is followed by general comment upon the most significant contrasts and commonalities. Gadamer and Wittgenstein emphasize the inescapability of the linguistic as the starting point (and *terminus ad quem*) for all further philosophical investigations. This is best captured in Gadamer's phrase 'being that can be understood is language'. For both Gadamer and Wittgenstein our sense of a world is thoroughly linguistic and all of our activities and engagements, be they direct speech acts or the practical accompaniments to language-games, ultimately cash out as movements within the phenomenon of the word.

The consequences for philosophy are far-reaching as much anti-foundationalist thought since Nietzsche shows. The whole legacy of Cartesianism and, importantly, its effect upon modernist conceptions of language, needs to be re-examined and rewritten. In remarkably similar ways Gadamer and Wittgenstein question the authority of the Cartesian subject as the epicentre of meaning, and agree on the need to exorcise the subjectivist ghost from the modernist machine. Such a move brings to light a variety of disturbing consequences which shake the foundations of the dualistic worldview. An intersubjective dimension shows how ordinary language is sustained by consensus and publicly available agreements and not the inner reflections of the thinking subject. Gadamer and Wittgenstein work through the philosophical consequences of ditching Cartesianism, effectively threatening as it does the very enterprise of philosophy-as-metaphysics. This is a common theme in much contemporary anti- or post-foundationalist philosophies, whether of the analytical or the Continental variety.[5]

For all the anti-foundationalism, anti-psychologism, and anti-Cartesianism in Gadamer's position, his account of language and linguisticality wrapped as it is in a disguised teleological narrative may jar on analytic ears. For Anglo-American critics his work depends upon unacceptable metaphysical and ontological commitments. These are absent from Wittgenstein's putatively descriptive, that is non-theoretical and ontologically neutral, position.[6] On the other hand, Wittgenstein's focus in his later work upon interminable redescriptions of the language-games is equally questionable. Is it ever possible to move beyond description of the games we play with language? Gadamerians, from the perspective of hermeneutics, are willing, contra Wittgenstein, to speak of language's universal structural features and of linguisticality itself, insisting, as they do, upon seeing language within a historical perspective. Wittgensteinians fail to see the relevance of such a position. The chapter concludes with a few thoughts on the nature of philosophy as conceived by the two thinkers. What happens to the discipline once its concern is more for linguisticality, the way we talk about the world, than the substance of our talk is a pressing question. Does post-foundationalist philosophy give way to the more modest 'underlabourer' tasks of taxonomy, philology, or lexicography? The question of what supersedes philosophy brings Wittgenstein and Gadamer very close in some senses and yet at the same time divides them.

Chapter 3, 'Gadamer's Philosophical Hermeneutics and the Ontology of Language', fully thematizes language and linguisticality as the heart of his work. Since the publication in Germany in 1960 of his major work *Truth and Method* philosophical hermeneutics has attracted the attention of social scientists and literary theorists but little work, especially in the analytic tradition, has been done, as already noted, on the centrality of language for philosophical hermeneutics. 'It is a curious fact about recent Anglo-Saxon interest in Gadamer', remarks Martin Kusch, 'that Anglo-Saxon philosophers have not shown much interest in [Gadamer's] treatment of language and ontology.' He goes on tellingly to observe that 'of the two best-known expositions of Gadamer's views in the English-speaking world, neither Richard Rorty ... nor Richard J. Bernstein ... attempts a detailed analysis of this part of Gadamer's thought. This fact is all the more astonishing in the light of both authors' keen awareness of developments in the philosophy of language in general' (Kusch, 1989, p. 312). In *Philosophy and the Mirror of Nature* (1980) Rorty appropriates Gadamer's idea of philosophy as conversation, not in relation to an analysis of language *per se*, but to emphasize the post-philosophical move away from truth to 'edification'.

Starting from *Truth and Method*, especially the third part ('The ontological shift of hermeneutics guided by language') and focusing on the many subsequent short essays, Chapter 3 pieces together a general Gadamerian picture of language as it emerges from his philosophical hermeneutics.[7] This is supplemented by detailed discussion of the roots of philosophical hermeneutics' commitment to a particular ontological and historical account of language. What picture of language emerges from Gadamer? An idea taken indirectly from both Augustine and Heidegger is that the proposition is a distortion of living language, of discourse and conversation. In everyday discussion the rigidity of the proposition gives way to something more mysterious and flexible. For Gadamer, the language of the life world, and here he would include the elusive language of the poetic, is essentially non-propositional. It is dialogical and incompletable; a position unacceptable to the analytic tradition where emphasis is placed upon the timelessness and truth-functionality of the self-contained proposition. Wittgenstein was clearly, in his later work, constantly challenging the philosophical reverence for propositional truth although it is debatable as to whether he completely broke free from the fundamental dogmas of the *Tractatus*.

Chapter 4, entitled 'Wittgenstein and the Logics of Language', starts with a series of 'pictures' of language. Wittgenstein, in the Preface to the *Philosophical Investigations* speaks, with obvious frustration, of his work as being no more than a 'number of sketches of landscapes'.[8] Eschewing the possibility of offering a (metaphysical) theory of language – necessitating as it would for Wittgenstein a meta-language of language (outside language) – he settles for the more humble sequence of immanent pictures, snaps of the internal workings of our language-games. Accepting the prohibition of a clear view of language outside our everyday articulations we might say that, for all that, Wittgenstein still offers a coherent Galtonian picture of language.[9]

For all this, there is a general 'theory' of language on offer in his later work, centring on the language-game and the countless implications this has for the way we think about language and its relationship to the world. Wittgenstein's big idea that meaning is generated not by inner sensations or reference to a non-linguistic world (of thought or reflection) but by use, that is practical activity is both novel and emancipatory, freeing the language-user as it does from various ancient fables or mistaken pictures of a necessary relationship between word and world. Here Wittgenstein is very close to Gadamer.

Yet for all its originality Wittgenstein's position is not without its limitations and difficulties. Philosophical hermeneutics exposes some of the shortcomings of later Wittgenstein. A central and controversial claim here is that for all his innovation Wittgenstein is unable to jettison fully the idea of an underlying logic to language. The idea of a logic to language is, admittedly, the central demon in the *Tractatus Logico-Philosophicus* which he sought, in the later writings, to confront with notions of 'grammar' and 'language-games', but there is a sense in which he never fully lets go of some notion of a 'logic to language' (a recurring phrase even in the *Philosophical Investigations*). In hanging on to this idea various other implicit commitments within the putatively theory-neutral 'picture' of language become evident. To substantiate this argument I offer an unorthodox reading of the section on rule-following in the *Philosophical Investigations* (§§198–242). For many working in the analytical tradition this section is the heart of the *Philosophical Investigations*; it is where Wittgenstein is at his most penetrating and controversial.[10] In the light of Gadamer, we see how Wittgenstein's account of linguistic activity here fails to embrace novelty and change. The difficult question is this: How is it possible to follow rules and yet go beyond them? Rule-following in Wittgenstein seems to be little more than unreflective re-enactment. Gadamer confronts the same difficulty but via hermeneutics shows how this problem can be overcome.

Chapter 5, '"What has history to do with me?": Language and/as Historicality', as an excursus or extended aside, considers historicality as a principal feature of philosophical hermeneutics. Gadamer's account of language embraces central historicist ideas of 'fusion of horizons', 'effective historical consciousness', and tradition. Any interaction with language (and this means engagements with ourselves, others, and the world) necessarily involves a relationship with the historical. The focus then changes to Wittgenstein and his refusal to consider temporality and historicality. There is an unwillingness to embrace the historical, in the sense of viewing language through its past, a reluctance running through much modern analytic philosophy. This stems from an undynamic and undialectical position. Wittgenstein's inability to demonstrate the many ways the language-games of the past connect up with current language-games, and even the way language-games in one culture might link up to those of another, admittedly begs many questions about the exact nature of linguistic rules. Discussion of rules inevitably leads to consideration of temporality and change. Avoidance of such issues in Wittgenstein, I argue, leads dangerously close to linguistic and other forms of relativism, something Gadamer's historicist picture of language avoids.[11] Gadamer's amalgamation of philosophical hermeneutics and a variety of Hegelianism enables him to overcome the Wittgensteinian problems by highlighting the porous nature of language-games, showing their capacity to extend back into tradition and project forward to embrace linguistic novelty.

In Chapter 6, 'A Competition of Interpretations: Wittgenstein and Gadamer Read Augustine', emphasis is given to Augustine's proto-hermeneutics of the Trinity. Following the work of Jean Grondin (1995), the influential critic, the largely unacknowledged importance Saint Augustine has for Gadamer comes to light. This is set against the more familiar discussion of Augustine in the early stages of the *Philosophical Investigations*. Gadamer's Augustine is radically different to Wittgenstein's. The various contrasting approaches are investigated in so far as they throw light upon the opposing interpretations adopted by Wittgenstein and Gadamer of Augustine in particular and of the reading of ancient philosophical texts in general. Wittgenstein's sees in Augustine's autobiographical description of his own first encounters with language (in the *Confessions*) an example of a flawed but influential theory of language and reference, which has, since Wittgenstein, come to be known as the 'Augustinian picture of language'. Gadamer's less polemical and more scholarly and historical reading of Augustine highlights a radically different approach. In the early Christian reflections on language he identifies a move away from the Platonic downgrading of language to thought. The differing approaches adopted are instructive not only for Augustine interpretation but for what they tell us about Wittgenstein's and Gadamer's conceptions of language and for the differing ways they appropriate ancient texts in the history of philosophy.

In Chapter 7, 'Ordinary and Extraordinary Language: the Hermeneutics of the Poetic Word', the Wittgenstein critique is both extended and questioned. The criticism of Wittgenstein here does not concern the relationship between the language-user and the present or the past but the future. Language does not merely have a past it constantly projects into its own future in the form of linguistic novelty, neologism, and most significantly, the poetic. Much of Gadamer's recent work concentrates upon the relationship between ordinary everyday language and the poetic word, significantly the language of lyric poetry. For Gadamer, the poetic utterance is language at its most authentic and disclosive, revealing an intimacy between language and world.

Few of these motifs are explicit in the later work of Wittgenstein. There is very little in the later work on the theme of linguistic novelty or the language of poetry. In *Culture and Value* there are many intriguing comments and *aperçus* on particular (mainly minor Austrian) poets but very little relating poetry to philosophical thought. And yet he wrote in the early 1930s that 'Philosophy ought really to be written only as a *form of poetry*'.[12] How does this intriguing thought square with the absence of comment in Wittgenstein on the poetic and the figural? Using Goldmann's notion of the tragic and the ideas of Stanley Cavell the chapter concludes with the thought that Wittgenstein affirms the poetic in rather oblique and indirect ways. In this light Wittgenstein is not so far from the essentially Heideggerian position Gadamer adopts with respect to poetry.

NOTES

1. There are, of course, honourable exceptions and in recent years the position has started to look more encouraging. Pioneering works challenging this orthodoxy are Stephen Mulhall's *On Being in the World* (Mulhall, 1990) and Simon Glendinning's *On Being with Others* (Glendinning, 1998). Although they seek to show the proximity between Wittgenstein and modern Continental philosophy, notably Heidegger, they are both written from within the analytic idiom.

2. In a brilliant and to my mind, unjustly neglected work of the history of ideas Janik and Toulmin (1973) place Wittgenstein firmly within the milieu of mainstream European thought. Too frequently historians of philosophy neglect Wittgenstein's links with the German and Austrian traditions and, to distorting effect, place him intellectually somewhere between Bertrand Russell and G. E. Moore.

3. Critchley (2001). The first three chapters are particularly useful for understanding the philosophical and cultural roots of the basic tension within modern philosophy.

4. See, for example, in the Gadamer chapter in Dermot Moran's *Introduction to Phenomenology*, where he notes that 'both Gadamer and Wittgenstein see language as a rule-governed activity and hence one that is primarily intersubjective, shared and social' (Moran, 2000, p. 283). The comparison is merely noted rather than explored.

5. The collection of essays, *After Philosophy: End or Transformation?* (Baynes *et al.*, 1987) demonstrates how anti-foundationalism cuts through the analytical/Continental divide bringing together philosophers as diverse as Jean-François Lyotard and Michael Dummett.

6. Since the time of Habermas's review of *Truth and Method* (1986) and the subsequent debate, Gadamer has been criticized for an apparent 'linguistic idealism', a

thought Dermot Moran emphasizes in his discussion of Gadamer (Moran, 2000, pp. 284 and 286). Linguistic idealism 'elevates language above human beings' (Moran, 2000, p. 284). This is an unsustainable criticism of Gadamer but if we allow it to apply to Gadamer then it surely applies also to Wittgenstein for whom the language-game always takes precedence over the players and in one sense elevates language above its speakers. Why is this taken to be a demonstration of idealism? The totality of the game is always going to be more than the individual players. This does not hypostasize language; it merely demonstrates how words go beyond the control of individuals, an idea with which both Gadamer and Wittgenstein agree.

7. Part Three of *Truth and Method* is the least often discussed part of the work. Part One has had a marked influence on Continental (and, increasingly, analytic) aesthetics and Part Two is a frequent focus for social theorists on the central themes of the work (historicality, tradition, the relationship between the *Geisteswissenschaften* and the natural sciences), but the final part is often ignored. Georgina Warnke, for example, in her influential *Gadamer: Hermeneutics, Tradition and Reason* (1987) hardly touches on Part Three of *Truth and Method*.

8. *PI*, p. ix.

9. 'To make you see as clearly as possible what I take to be the subject matter ... I will put before you a number of more or less synonymous expressions each of which could be substituted for the above definition, and by enumerating them I want to produce the same sort of effect which Galton produced when he took a number of photos of different faces on the same photographic plate in order to get the picture of the typical features they all had in common' (Wittgenstein, 'A lecture on ethics', *PO*, p. 38).

10. The significance of this section has been highlighted by the work of Saul Kripke who links rule-following to the question of a private language. See Kripke (1982).

11. On the question of Gadamer and relativism see Bernstein (1983).

12. Quoted in Perloff (1996), p. 243. Perloff adapts the standard translation of *CV*, p. 24.

CHAPTER I

The Nature of Language: Two Philosophical Traditions

If I were as eloquent as Demosthenes I would yet have to do nothing more than repeat a single word three times: reason is language, *logos*. I gnaw at this marrow-bone and gnaw myself to death over it. There still remains a darkness, always, over this depth for me; I am still waiting for an apocalyptic angel with a key to this abyss.

(Hamann in a letter to Herder, 1784. Quoted in Heidegger, 1975, p. 191)

I. INTRODUCTION

Two diverging views about the nature of language dominate modern Western thought. One treats language as a cultural product and investigation into its nature is wider than strictly philosophical considerations incorporating anthropological, sociological, and historical perspectives. The object of study is language in its widest sense and speculation as to origins, as much debate in the eighteenth century demonstrates, is as significant as more restricted questions about the relationship and implications for philosophy between mind, word, and world. This tradition is marked by a linguistic holism and little significance is attached to the variety of discourses and the range of possible applications; for example, there is no crucial difference between what Wittgenstein calls 'the language of information'[1] and more figurative and literary uses of words.

This approach contrasts with another tradition which follows a narrower and more restrictive path of enquiry where wider cultural considerations are bracketed out in the name of a more 'scientific' perspective and the object of study is not so much language itself as the relationship between language and the world. The principal philosophical task in this tradition is to examine the various ways indicative sentences establish a truthful relationship between the minds of the speakers and language's referents. The question of reference is important here because it is one of the defining characteristics of the difference between the two traditions for the first position subscribes to a non-designative theory. Language is less to do with naming the world than the power of the word, as Herder realized, to bind a culture and a people. The second view, on the other hand, depends upon designation. Descriptive language, on this view, provided it is used with logical rigour, grants access to the mind of the user and gives an accurate picture of the world and its contents. Virtually a sub-discipline of philosophy of mind in the eyes of many contemporary practitioners, philosophy of language works on the assumption that attention to propositional truth is revealing from two different directions: a subjective (mind-dependent) route leads to disclosure of the nature of mind and cognitive 'processes', the other way offers an accurate representation of the 'external' world. Language communicates thought, which in turn is investigated via close attention to the way we come to describe it. Paradoxically, for all the concern for language in analytic philosophy, language, *per se*, seems to be of little intrinsic interest, being no more than a vehicle for the more philosophically significant ideas they grant access to; words are no more than tokens or ciphers for something intrinsically more valuable. The endless array of things we do with language, besides giving putative reports on states of mind or descriptions of the external world, are downgraded. The idea of language as meaningful through practical activity, as something to be actively used rather than taken as the passive receptor of cognition, has only relatively recently made its way upon the Anglophone philosophical stage.

Opposed to this, is and more in line with the Continental tradition, is the idea of language as constitutor of the world or as vehicle for celebration, solidarity, and community. The Kantian subordination of linguistic competence to the overarching structures of rational thought gave rise to an alternative position. This school of thought, running from Kant's foremost contemporary critic Johann Georg Hamann to Gadamer, includes the prominent luminaries in the history of modern German philosophy: Herder, Humboldt, Schleiermacher, Dilthey, and, centrally, Martin Heidegger. What unites them is not simply affiliation to a geographical region with a common cultural heritage but participation in an approach to language and a style of philosophizing generally at least at odds with that of its analytic counterpart. Here the expressive power of speech overshadows its communicative reach. The word rather than a token for thought is thought itself in all its imaginative and world-disclosing and world- (or at least linguistic community-) uniting potency. The point at the beginning of this chapter about the more diverse and culture-embracing approach to language in the Continental tradition seems to make itself manifest here. The expressive dimension of the word reaches well beyond its power to bridge mind and world. The power of speech is also the power to create a world, to forge solidarities, enact celebrations, and make possible the intricacies of social life.

The above represents a rather crude and over-general characterization of the dominant perspectives on language in the recent history of philosophy. But the fracture in modern Western approaches is worthy of note because it provides a useful background for locating Wittgenstein and Gadamer. Wittgenstein is more usually associated with the Anglophone analytic philosophy of language tradition but his work has many points of contact with the Continental tradition and this point is often overlooked.[2] Viewed from outside the narrow confines of the more orthodox stance, Wittgenstein begins to start to make more sense and his later work particularly looks strangely alienated from the more obvious positions with which he is associated. He begins to look in many ways like Gadamer. There are crucial stylistic and thematic differences but, as we shall see, there are many more similarities and a surprising degree of overlap in their treatment of language emerges. Wittgenstein needs to be unhinged from the conventional contexts of interpretation and placed within the co-ordinates of Continental thought.

The history of the rise of Anglophone philosophy of language constitutes an important narrative context within which to locate the work of Gadamer and Wittgenstein. Gadamer's hermeneutical and phenomenological insights into the actuality of everyday language significantly bypass the conventional wisdom of much of the analytic philosophy of language. Gadamer works in an alternative tradition, one emerging in German cultural life in the early eighteenth century and whose influence has been profound in Continental thought but only recently having an effect in the Anglophone philosophical world. As to where, or whether, Wittgenstein fits into this alternative tradition is problematical. He is, as ever, difficult to classify. Although tutored in the analytical style of Bertrand Russell, the whole thrust of his later work is to overthrow and subvert its fundamental ground revealing himself to be, in many ways, sympathetic to and moving towards the alternative tradition spoken of above. The extent to which Wittgenstein is successful in rejecting his early picture theory of language, the source and inspiration for much work in what came to be known as the analytical tradition, the extent to which he comes to adopt the expressivist position, form a large part of this work and will be outlined and expanded upon in subsequent chapters.

How do we properly characterize the treatment of language within analytic philosophy? The most important fact to note here is the modern epistemological tradition's allegiance to it. Analytical thought has been rather unreflective about its own self-understanding and generally ignored genetic and historically relevant questions; hence, until recent historical studies from Michael Dummett and others there is a paucity of material in this area. This said, I think the most reliable and illuminating work on this whole question is that of a thinker sympathetic to both positions, the Canadian philosopher Charles Taylor. Taylor does not offer a detailed history of the development of modern thinking about language but his basic classification is highly instructive.

II. CHARLES TAYLOR AND THE TWO THEORIES OF MEANING

A. Language as Designation

Taylor's analytical background allied to a basic sympathy for 'Continental' modes of thought, eminently entitles him to speculate upon the larger concerns in the Western tradition, as he has done frequently in his many essays on language. Through his encounters with the work of Hegel and historicism he tends to harness historical vision to his commitment to analytical insight. His seminal work 'Theories of meaning'[3] is a model of clarity and insight on the general nature of meaning in the Western philosophical tradition. This essay supplements his more specific historical explorations of theories of meaning and language in works such as 'The importance of Herder'[4] and 'Language and human nature'.[5]

Taylor's theories of meaning readily translate into theories of the fundamental nature of language; what language is and how the various traditions have conceived it. Taylor offers a basic distinction, much referred to and valuable as a taxonomic tool. He speaks of two accounts, we might say, rather than theories, of language: the 'designative' and the 'expressive' respectively. The former underpins and pervades what I have termed the analytic philosophy of language tradition. The mainstream Anglophone school largely neglects the other tradition, the expressive, which grew out of the post-Kantian Continental tradition of philosophy. Taylor also refers to this alternative tradition as the 'H–H–H' view of language; shorthand for a tendency that emerged out of German idealism, notably via the seminal works of Johann Georg Hamann (1730–88), Johann Gottfried von Herder (1744–1803), and Wilhelm von Humboldt (1767–1835). This alternative tradition inspired many non-analytical approaches to language (Taylor includes structuralist linguistics and the work of Habermas, Vygotsky, and Bahktin),[6] but most significant for our work is the inclusion of Heidegger's appropriation of hermeneutics; the foremost inspiration for Gadamer's work on language. To what extent does Wittgenstein's later picture of language, unwittingly perhaps, move in the direction of the H–H–H position without adopting all of its tenets? Before these exegetical questions can be answered we need to inspect both the representational and non-representational terrain more thoroughly.

One of the oldest views in the history of philosophy takes utterances and inscription to make sense and have meaning because at some fundamental level they represent, that is stand for, something in the world, or re-present (present once again) something to the mind. Representation names or describes objects and things; categories, things in the world, or mental events and phenomena. To say language represents is to say it points, refers, designates. Words are ciphers, tokens, signs for things and words are meaningful by virtue of their association with the things for which they stand proxy. 'Vocabula sunt notae rerum'[7] ('Words are signs of things') Cicero claimed, echoing a familiar position in Aristotle.

Communication is the essence of word-meaning on the representational account, and language is seen as nothing other than the motivating power of isolated words to 'stand for' the things they represent. The ability to describe states of affairs either to oneself or another is by means of a system of signs to which beliefs (either about oneself or the world) correspond. The signs or marks of language offer an accurate representation of the way things are or one might say, following the early Wittgenstein, a radical exponent of a version of this theory of meaning, they picture possible states of affairs, and the states of affairs are grasped by other similarly endowed language-users. Communication is impossible without a commonly accepted set of descriptions; the capacity to represent (re-present, to be able to present things to the mind again) makes this possible. Designation gives a foundation to the dominant analytic view of language in the Western tradition. It also spawns a multitude of related philosophical positions, notably epistemologically motivated ones as accurate designation rests upon belief states incorporating notions of knowledge and truth.

In relation to modernist theories of meaning Taylor takes as central the idea that the representational theories are invariably from 'the standpoint of the monological observer'.[8] Here meaning originates not from the tacit agreements in the public realm of language but the logical structures informing the inner world of the Cartesian consciousness. The implications of this view for philosophical and linguistic theory alike are of the greatest importance. Significantly, it makes the act of representing a solitary rather than a communal or social one.

Meaning is regulated and communication is possible because we do not directly represent the world through language; representation is second-hand, refracted through subjective ideas, that is, a secondary layer of representation. The master theoreticians of this position are the British empiricists Hobbes and Locke. 'Words in their primary signification', announces Locke, 'stand for nothing, but the Ideas in the Mind of him that uses them.'[9] This classical empiricist statement of meaning, a frequently uttered dictum, illustrates how simple object representation (words stand for things in the external world) can be reformulated. Here words do not directly represent objects in the world, things, rather words individually 'stand for' discrete ideas. The unit of sense is not a sentence but the mind-related depictive word and the isolated object for which it stands. Words are meaningful on Locke's account because language-users by way of subjective ideas validate the objects to which they correspond. Linguistic meaning, on this view, is stabilized because ideas, although subjective have some sort of commonality (individual meanings are derived from the naturalistic uniformity of mental representations). There is no way of confirming or denying this self-referential connection but the theory achieves its plausibility from its unverifiable assumption.

We need not dwell on the intricacies of Locke's account of meaning here but two things are worthy of comment. Obviously, with Locke we have an exemplary instance of Taylor's designative theory. Secondly, for Locke, the locus of meaning is not the public space of interpersonal communication but the privacy of individual consciousness; inner sensations give rise to the sense of an outer world of meaning. So, language is only indirectly a representation of the world since it is directly a representation of mind (and mind directly a representation of the world through the senses). Taylor's thought that designative theory is invariably from the 'the standpoint of the monological observer' starts to make sense. Locke's language-user is able to communicate with other language-users by virtue of the identical (or at least similar) ideas the words evoke. Language, implausibly, on this account, gives direct access not to the world but the mind of the speaker.

For Taylor the language-user appears as a detached observer since the speaker is somehow distant from language itself. The 'detached observer' is notionally able to generate full linguistic competence from the process of observing others perform and simple duplication. In the history of philosophy the *locus classicus* for such a theory, since Wittgenstein, is in the *Confessions* of Saint Augustine.[10] Augustine accounts for his own language acquisition by watching what happens in the adult world of speech and conversation. What draws the young Augustine into the realm of meaningful language is his realization that words stand for the objects they name. The central thought here is that Augustine, through introspection, was able, unaided, to make the connection between sounds uttered and word intended. But is this explanation of language acquisition not problematical? What inner resources does the wordless Augustine draw upon to give the sounds he hears meaning? To affirm introspection as the solution here is to beg the question.

There is another problem. Does not the process of uttering words, pointing at objects, and emitting sounds depend upon activities, processes, and practices that are intrinsically cultural and social and not instinctive, introspective, or natural (whatever these things might be without an intimate connection to the cultural and the social levels of explanation)? In the analytical tradition rejection of the detached-observer stance came on the philosophical scene relatively recently, pioneered by Wittgenstein's *Philosophical Investigations* with Augustine's account of language acquisition the initial catalyst for Wittgenstein's general attack on designation. Taylor locates the origins of the rejection of the detached-observer position in a much earlier debate. In France and Germany, and to a lesser extent in the Anglophone world, heated debate raged in the eighteenth century about the origins of language. Was society a precondition for language or language society? Did everything derive from God ('In the beginning was the word')? were some of the pressing questions of the age. To some extent a rerun of the Greek dispute about the origin of words in nature or convention, the debate, according to Taylor, witnessed an important rejection of the detached-observer idea. In an example not unlike the Augustinian one quoted above, the eighteenth-century French thinker Condillac, in his *Essay on the Origin of Human Knowledge*,[11] imagines the formation of language. Taylor summarizes the position as follows:

> (Condillac) offers a fable, a 'just so' story to illustrate how language might have arisen. It is a fable of two children in a desert. We assume certain cries and gestures as natural expressions of feeling. These are what Condillac calls 'natural signs'. By contrast, language uses 'instituted signs'. Condillac's story is meant to explain how the second emerged out of the first. He argues that each child, seeing the other, say, cry out in distress, would come to see the cry as a sign of something (e.g. what causes distress). He would then be able to take the step of using the sign to refer to the cause of distress. The first sign would have been instituted. The children would have their first word. Language would be born.[12]

Is this an implausible picture of the possible origins of language? Leaving aside the intelligibility of the historical question of origins here, Herder saw countless difficulties with this fable as an illustration of the workings of language. The children take for granted the causal connection between signs and say, distress, but this is precisely what needs to be explained. If the connection is innate then the instituted collapses into the natural and if it is not then how did the children make the connection in the first place? Even if the causal picture has some initial plausibility it needs a large social and cultural (that is, non-naturalistic) background to make it possible. Taylor cites Herder as the first critic of Condillac who saw the inadequacies of this fundamentally Lockean position.

Another founding father of the designative tradition in Anglophone philosophy is Thomas Hobbes. In *Leviathan*, language is a substitute (and often a poor surrogate) for ideas: 'The generall use of Speech, is to transferre our Mentall Discourse, into Verbal.'[13] At the heart of this version of representationalism, and it is evident in all early forms of classic empiricism, the assumption that language as a cipher, a representation, of thoughts and ideas further assumes that thought and ratiocination are somehow prior to language. This is the first of the many difficulties in Hobbes's position. If language is merely a mnemonic aid to thinking (language somehow makes complex thought more manageable according to Hobbes), what then is thought?

This question raises the whole vexed issue of wordless thought, one of the central issues dividing designative and expressive theories. For the empiricists, ideas are, in their original state, wordless until converted into sound or inscriptive tokens and then into mind-interpretable meanings. Is this a coherent idea? Why, contra this view, is it the case that cognitive development goes hand in hand with development of linguistic ability? Surely a child only acquires sophistication in its thinking as it becomes more adept in the use of language? The belief that ideas and thoughts precede language (logically and chronologically) is surely untenable, as we will see when we turn to non-designative accounts of language.

When theories of language concentrate upon the syntactical structure of sentences rather than focusing upon the representational relationship between words and objects or words and ideas, the next stage in the development of theories of language, the problems of representation are overcome. This is not the case. As Taylor shows, the Fregean move to sense (*Sinn*), that is to an emphasis upon the syntactical structure of sentences, there is an important shift in one sense but not in another. Frege locates sense within the context of reference and, thus, his account of language is still a representational, referring one. There is a move from the representation of ideas to the representation of sentences. Frege's discovery that meaning is not a feature of individual words but of rule-governed structured sentences is an advance but it is still wedded to the idea that language depicts a pre-existing, detached, and neutral world.

The representational picture of language, with its concentration upon the production of meaning it offers is, from the point of view of non-representative accounts of language, a distortion. From the mere fact of representation we get a portrayal of language as a clear medium through which ideas are transparently communicated: what Hobbes famously termed 'mental discourse'. Language is readily studied not as an end in itself – it is after all on this account no more than arbitrary ciphers – but as a way in to a scientific study of the individual's inner mental life. Philosophy of language is disguised philosophy of mind. The analytic philosopher's interest in language is not in language for its own sake but in its capacity to expose the various dimensions of mind. The countless textbooks in the analytic tradition entitled 'Philosophy of language' discuss propositional attitudes, theories of meaning, truth, and reference. Questions about the actuality of language are quickly overshadowed or forgotten. The diverse and extensive nature of language is overlooked and a limited concentration upon the dubious belief that language discloses states of mind neglects the phenomenon of language. The history of the changing face of language and the fact that it is socially rather than individually validated and produced is considered to be without philosophical significance; no doubt a suitable area of concern for literary theorists, psycho- and socio-linguisticians, philologists and so forth, but not 'real' philosophers. Even when theories of meaning and language advance from a focus upon ideas to the syntactical structure of sentences (with Frege and since) the representing relationship and the focus upon mind is still dominant.

B. Language as Expression

The focus now turns to the alternative tradition, peripheral and marginal to the analytic orthodoxy but a more fertile and, I shall argue, a more edifying disclosure of the ontology of everyday language. Whatever the virtues are of the representational position it clearly distorts and misrepresents the nature, the being, of everyday language as much by what it ignores and leaves out of account as by what it explicitly subscribes.

In the essay 'Theories of meaning' Taylor invites us to imagine a traveller climbing into an overheated railway carriage, presumably, on a scorching hot summer day, turning to the person in the next seat and interjecting 'Whew! It's hot!' (in an alternative example the traveller simply lets out a loud and ejaculatory 'Whew!'). A great deal can be made of this simple example, showing up the shortcomings of the designative position. The first point to make, and it is an obvious but important one, is that the phrases or sounds in question have meaning way beyond a capacity to describe or represent a particular state of mind (or body). The point of saying 'Whew! It's hot!' as Taylor explains, is not to describe or designate a feeling – overheated, hot and bothered, etc. – nor is it to point out a general description of the overheated state of the carriage. The resonance of meaning goes way beyond attempts to fix signification within the terms of the merely depictive and representational. For Taylor, and it takes us to the heart of the non-representational position, the real meaning conveyed here is not representational but cultural and social, explicitly pointing more to a form of solidarity and mutuality of discomfort than description. 'What the expression has done here is to create a rapport between us', Taylor claims, continuing, 'the kind of thing which comes about when we do what we call striking up a conversation.'[14] Interestingly enough the example concerns conversation, the life-blood of everyday speech and linguistic interaction, rather than the austerely formal focus of the proposition, the usual terrain of representation. Conversation, such a vital element of the everyday use of language has, *qua* conversation, no role to play in the formal analysis of language.

Conversations, which we 'fall into' or 'strike up' (the idioms are revealing and not easily analysed here), show aspects of language we tend to ignore and marginalize when we make the more formal aspects of language objects of study. Taylor, in his example, emphasizes the element of rapport, stated and unstated, existing in such social situations. In turning to a fellow passenger, wiping my brow, and interjecting 'Whew! It's hot!' I am not seeking direct communication: what I seek is something more subtle and extensive; the opportunity to share a mutual discomfort. One appropriate response, no doubt, is a nod of the head and a smile: 'Yes, I'm suffering too' the gesture's mimetic sub-text might suggest. The discomfort of the heat is mutual; we share a common response to the heat in a common language not of proposition but of sound or gesture.[15] The sense of commonality surrounding language is a dimension of what Taylor terms the move towards 'public space'. Public space is what is missing from the designative picture of language. Locke has language's 'signification' emerging from the depths of the inner self, the 'Ideas in the Mind of him that uses them'. Magically, inner sensations readily translate into outward communication. If anything, and the notion of public space endorses this, the sense of language tends to move from the outer to the inner rather than vice versa. Articulating the inner depths of the individual implies publicly available meanings. Without the fact of an already existing language, we might say, within the structures of public space, there can be no interiority – or at least none we can talk about.

Public space is an element of a sophisticated image of language having more to do with its inauguration and maintenance within a complex social network of agreements, consensuses, and 'rapports'. The point is that language is meaningful not because it depicts and refers in some precise one-to-one fashion but because it breeds forms of solidarity, the conditions of possibility of language, in the fertile ground of public space. What Taylor reminds us of, and it is all too easily forgotten when language is wrenched from life contexts and made the object of detached scientific investigation, is that language is a social product; more than this, language presupposes a kind of solidarity. 'Whew!' is more an invitation for a common social world to be shared than a description of the way one feels (although the meaning of what is said and done in the railway carriage needs to consider, amongst other factors, the context of intentionality and self-description).

There is a further element to Taylor's awareness of the intimacy between language and public space and it is the sense in which language discloses uniquely *human* concerns, something touched on with the shared discomfort in the railway carriage. Using the terms 'anger' and 'indignation' as examples Taylor suggests that although some animals may get angry as an impulsive (animal?) feeling, indignation is more complex, because linguistically mediated, and hence, uniquely human. To experience indignation is to be part of a moral world where notions of justice and injustice, dignity and indignity have currency within daily practices and the whole dimension of historical and cultural context, which need to be reflected upon. The creation of a moral, that is truly human, world is impossible without the possibility of expressing this linguistically. 'Man is a language animal', Taylor states,

> not just because he can formulate things and make representations, and thus think of matters and calculate, which animals cannot; but also because what we consider the essential human concerns are disclosed only in language, and can only be the concerns of a language animal.[16]

Public space and the singularity of language are essential ingredients of the human world highlighting features of language the representational position neglects.[17] Important in themselves, they are also a prelude to perhaps Taylor's most important critique of orthodox theories, namely, that language has what he terms 'expressive' and 'constitutive' dimensions. These are not added extras, optional bolt-ons, but crucial details in the whole nexus of linguistic meaning.

In the arena of public space, sentences, parts of sentences, interjections, are elements of conversations happening within what Wittgenstein calls 'form of life' and Gadamer tradition, where articulations and other activities – bodily, gestural – run together in socially circumscribed ways. The activities surrounding articulations are what Taylor terms, following Wittgenstein and the H–H–H tradition, the expressive power of language. Again use of Taylor's railway carriage example is instructive here. 'Whew! It's hot!' can be said in a variety of ways, in an assortment of possible contexts subtly altering the nuances of meaning, the forms of slippage, we might say, to which language is given. Tone of voice, body language including demeanour and deportment, physical level and manner of intimacy/distance, intended effect (serious, parodic, ironic, comic), manner of speaking, all contribute to meaning and overall effect. The whole wealth of contextual circumstances surrounding an utterance contributes to meaning and cannot, without massive misrepresentation, be omitted from the assessment of an utterance's meaning or effect.

Post-Fregean syntactical theories place a good deal of emphasis upon the importance of context, that is the contexts of words in sentences: sense and context have little to divide them. But the expressive position Taylor outlines here goes way beyond syntactical considerations. Context, like the notion of public space, embraces the social-historical world not to mention the embodied corporeal world of actual speech and speakers. Context of utterance is too bland a phrase to capture the full extent of *background* alluded to here in Taylor's formulation. To see language as no more than isolated units, propositions, and to analyse them as though they directly depicted states of affairs or states of mind presents a caricature of a natural language. A frictionless hypothetical language, say Esperanto or the purely formal language of logical propositions or the artificial languages of AI, have what Taylor calls 'depiction without expression'. Here the scientific ideal of artificial language (language as envisaged by the project of artificial intelligence) always fails to capture the richness, the ludic to and fro, the parry and thrust, of conversational, that is, expressive language. And there is a failure to grasp within its theoretical range the full inscrutability of context rather than reference, that is, the sphere of influence in which the nuances of conversation operate. The expressive power of language is made explicit when we become aware of the full range of activities accompanying articulations. The situation, intentions, unwitting meanings of speakers within the full range of possibilities (tone of voice, modulation, gesture, etc), in short context, expressively contribute to meaning. An aspect of the expressive is the 'constitutive'. Against the thought that language represents the world it is possible to refer to a constitutive role (language doesn't represent the world, it constitutes it as the site of a human world or environment). Here the thought is that in some way the world is linguistic or, put another way, without language there would not be what we know as a world. One major implication of the constitutive position is that there is not a unitary objective world 'out there', as it were, waiting to be discovered, there are as many worlds or 'world-views' (Humboldt) as there are languages.

Taylor refers to non-designative theories as expressivist. He also refers to them, already noted, as the H–H–H theory. Wilfully rejecting designation an alternative tradition starts with the work of Hamann. His position is taken up by Herder and Humboldt and becomes the inspiration for the hermeneutical work of the early Heidegger and, significantly, Gadamer.

Hamann's mysterious allusive prose, dismissive of orderly and systematic exposition, is seminal. In attacking the Kantian system and the very idea of 'pure' reason he hits on a central tenet of expressivist thinking, namely, that reflection and expression, thought and language are inseparable or at least dialectically rather than causally interrelated. A brief return to Hobbes and Locke highlights Hamann's objection to the concept of language utilized in the service of 'pure' thought. For the British empiricists, paradoxically an inspiration for Hamann, thought is antecedent to language; language merely serving to expedite the reflection upon and communication of complex thoughts. If this were in principle possible it gives rise to language-less thought. The power of reasoning, one assumes, springs into being fully fledged and prior to linguistic ability. It does not develop, it does not have a history, nor does it presuppose articulation or communication. This is not unique to empiricism; the same set of assumptions underwrites Platonism and Cartesian rationalism. 'Clear and distinct ideas' are the source of all knowledge for Descartes, and reason reflects upon itself without recourse to anything outside itself.[18]

Isaiah Berlin has championed the work of Hamann, opening it up to an Anglophone audience. He expresses Hamann's rejection of the Cartesian and Kantian legacy succinctly. According to Berlin, Hamann claims that

> The notion that there is a process called thought or reasoning that is an independent activity 'within' man ... which he can choose at will to articulate into a set of symbols that he invents for the purpose ... but which, alternatively, he can also conduct by means of unverbalised ideas in some non-empirical medium, free from images, sounds, visual data, is a meaningless illusion.[19]

Hamann rejects the accepted Kantian understanding of the pregiven structures of thought and rationality. Reason is logically structured. Without the aid of interpersonal communicative processes the unaided mind engages in self-directed concatenated thought. The mind is innately logical, that is, has the power to grasp logical principles, and is the authentic criterion of correctness. Kant's insights into the synthesis of rational and empirical thought make the massive assumption that the mind is regulated by autonomous reason. This is an important thought because much of Hamann's work is a direct criticism of the Kantian system and the impetus it provided for the rapidly developing rational thought of the Enlightenment, for which Hamann was a declared enemy. His prescient hostility to the very idea of enlightenment thinking does not make him an 'irrationalist' thinker, as Berlin suggests. Questioning the assumptions of rationalism does not make him irrational, merely suspicious of the grand claims made in the name of a transhistorical, commonly shared reason. That reason is localized and embedded in cultural practice rather than making claims to universal validity is a

position that finds favour with much contemporary thought especially that of
Gadamer and Wittgenstein.[20]

In the 1784 'Metacritique of the purism of reason'[21] Hamann satirizes
Kant, even mocking his terminology (as the title indicates). He identifies
three kinds of 'purification' of philosophy, clearly a reference to the Kantian
system but it is a criticism extended to most philosophy of the time. 'The
first', he comments,

> consisted ... in the partly unsuccessful attempt to make reason indepen-
> dent of all custom, tradition and belief in the latter.... The second is still
> more transcendental and aims at nothing less than an independence of
> experience and its everyday induction.[22]

Reason and experience are routinely abstracted from their life contexts and
subjected to a process of philosophical decontamination; an illusory and
denaturing purification, Hamann suggests. The final cleansing (the 'most
sublime') concerns language: 'the single, first and last *organon* and criterion
of reason, without any other credentials than *tradition* and *use*'.[23] In an
astounding reversal Hamann suggests that rationality is answerable to
language rather than the other way round. Reason is not a purified given
working its way into the capillaries of language; on the contrary, it is only
possible once language is a going concern. Language is not *causa sui* or kept
in place by autonomous reason; its only supports are the commonplace
'credentials' of tradition and use. We can link this detour through the work
of Hamann to Taylor's questioning of an account of language based around
designation. The depictive relationship on which such a theory depends is
plausible when autonomous reason makes the depicting connection between
word and object. But all credibility disappears when the suggestion of *a
priori* reason has been discounted. With Hamann's claim that instead of
a priori reason language is sustained by *tradition* and *use* (positions taken up
by Gadamer and Wittgenstein respectively) he is not resorting to magical
forms of explanation or naked 'irrationalism' as Berlin insinuates. Hamann
offers a different model of rationality, a more Hegelian one, placing reason
within the fabric of ordinary language where it forms part of the larger
structures of history and praxis.

GADAMER, WITTGENSTEIN, AND THE TWO TRADITIONS

This chapter focuses on designation and expression as tendencies in modern
Western thought about language. The terms are rather loose and approxi-

mate pointing in different opposing directions. They are not mutually exclusive but sit uneasily together. To recapitulate, I sought to show how work in the analytic tradition has depended upon foundational assumptions about the function of language as designative. The world, on this view, is constituted by ready-made objects and the task of philosophy of language is to identify and name them; this also works subjectively, within consciousness, as language identifies and labels preexisting states of mind. Designation presupposes an inert given world, one that predates the capacity to name it. Language is a collection of designative meanings mapped onto a detached preexisting world. The articulation of division and classification precedes the articulation of speech one might say. Ultimately language reflects the world. The consequences here are many and various. Meaningfulness is to be found among the assemblage of discrete individuated propositions and the claims to knowledge they make about the world. This permits the study to be scientific; epistemological rather than cultural or anthropological as designation gives an easy yardstick and suitable metric. Language need not be considered in its totality as historical product, hence the social, cultural, and political contexts within which linguistic exchange operates are philosophically irrelevant. The focus for study is quite narrow; analysis of propositions excludes rhetorical or figurative uses of language condemning much of the realm of literary endeavour to a philosophical limbo of vagueness and imprecision.

Expressivism starts out from an acknowledgement of the omnipresence of language; for Herder mankind is first and foremost comprised of 'language animals'. A wide gulf between mind and language is shown to be chimerical. Language gains its expressive potency, not from its power to represent, but from activity within a language-community, from which it develops and to which we all, one way or another, necessarily belong. The language-user is not a Cartesian subject in sovereign control of meanings; these are socially produced from the fabric of daily life within which various customs and practices are performatively enacted. The expressive subject matures as the capacity to engage with language develops but there is no point at which full control is achieved and full mastery is attained. Because the individual's relationship to language is so intimate, self and linguistically constituted self being synonymous, selfhood like language will always be in part opaque and uncontrollable. Much of the hostility to this position comes from the thought that language defies analysis and in some sense remains permanently mysterious and inexplicable. Whereas language is principally a vehicle for the articulation of thought on the designative model it is more the opportunity for self-discovery and self-expression for the expressivist. But if the self is linguistically constituted and hence meanings are constantly subject to redefinition it follows that the journey of self-discovery will be incompletable – always resisting attempts at final resolution in complete understanding. But this does not foreclose the urge for self-knowledge which the expressive tradition links to art and literary endeavour. The bond between art and language is important here. The expressivist abhors the idea that language is merely replication of rules of use. On the contrary speaking and writing are productive as opposed to repetitive acts. Linguistic exchanges like art unavoidably invoke creative procedures. Language is produced not reproduced.

Ultimately the purpose of language is self-expression and not, as it is for the more analytically inclined, a tool for investigating the scientific and detached nature of things: this for the simple reason that there is no detached nature of things. Science-led theories of language, in fact the whole scientific project itself, is placed in doubt from an expressivist point of view. As Taylor indicates, the AI dream of a language completely purged of expression in, say, sophisticated computer-generated languages or even Esperanto are only plausible when they are cut adrift from natural languages. What then do they represent? A terrible distortion of the thing they intend to replicate. What is missing or misrepresented? It is the expressive dimension to words including the manifold life-contexts ordinarily underpinning and supplementing living language.

Mention has been made of the tendency with designative theories to locate meanings within the compass of isolated words; this is particularly true of pre-Fregean theory in the philosophy of language. This is in stark contrast to the meaning holism so essential to expressive theories. Meanings are generated within an elaborate network of meanings. These are sustained not by one-to-one designation but tacit agreements, consensuses, and convention. These forms of mutuality and commonality have a history and the web of language extends both synchronically and diachronically within an ever-extending movement called tradition.

Little has been said of the many recent developments in both Continental and analytic philosophy of language which serve to undermine and blur the sometimes over-sharp distinctions on offer in this chapter. For example, much Anglophone philosophy in the latter half of the twentieth century and more recently has embraced and further refined many of the ideas from the expressive camp and distanced itself from some of the more unreconstructed versions of designation.

The stark contrast between the two positions provides a useful background for a comparison between Hans-Georg Gadamer and Ludwig Wittgenstein. Where do they fit into this schema? Gadamer's status as a key figure in the modern expressive camp is incontrovertible. The hermeneutical tradition within which he works is directly influenced by Schleiermacher who in turn owes much to the legacy of Hamann and Herder.

The case of Wittgenstein is much more problematical. Designation lies at the heart of his early work where the picture theory of meaning, that words picture possible states of affairs, occupies a central place in the *Tractatus Logico-Philosophicus*. Often referred to as a classic statement of this position it became a canonical text in the analytic tradition. It is well-known that Wittgenstein started to have doubts about the principal ideas in this work, especially thoughts about the nature of language, soon after the *Tractatus* was published.

What new position did he come to occupy in his later work, say in the period between 1929 and his death in 1951? Classifying it as 'linguistic analysis' or 'ordinary language philosophy', as commentators frequently do, fails to place the *Investigations* and the other post-*Tractatus* works within any identifiable school or tendency within the history of philosophy and fosters the canard that he was a one-off genius breaking all the moulds. Counter to this kind of squabble it is possible to utilize Taylor's basic distinction to locate Wittgenstein within larger debates about the nature of language. A move from designation to an increasingly expressive standpoint is evident in Wittgenstein's later work but the degree to which he is willing to completely break free from the strictures of the early analytic work is a difficult one to call. Subsequent chapters, notably Chapter 4, argue that Wittgenstein retains a vestigial commitment to earlier positions and fails to explore the full expressivist possibilities he open up. The fundamental vision of language-games sustaining the pragmatic dictum 'meaning is use'; the many rhetorical and argumentative strategies undermining the possibility of private languages (which are no more than affirmations of publicly grounded language); the idea of 'forms of life' as traditional practices, not to mention an increasingly aphoristic style ceaselessly undercutting analytical modes of thought, suggest an obvious proximity to central expressivist themes. Despite all this there is a clear distance between himself and Gadamer.

NOTES

1. *Z*, §160.
2. See A. Janik and S. Toulmin *Wittgenstein's Vienna* (Janik and Toulmin, 1973). Their work in intellectual history stressing Wittgenstein's deep roots in *fin de siècle* Vienna rather than the lecture halls of Cambridge is pioneering (and by and large neglected).
3. Taylor (1985), pp. 248–92.
4. Margalit (1991), pp. 40–63.

5. Taylor (1985), pp. 215–47.
6. See Taylor's essay 'The importance of Herder' in Margalit (1991), pp. 40–63.
7. *Topica* 8: 35.
8. Taylor (1985), p. 290.
9. Locke (1924), p. 225.
10. Gadamer disputes the representational reading of Augustine's account of language. See Chapter 4 of this work.
11. This work has been recently translated. See Aarsleff (2001).
12. Margalit (1991), p. 41.
13. Hobbes (1968), p. 101.
14. Taylor (1985), p. 259.
15. And it need not be a common language. To do this kind of thing in a remote part of the world is to share not a common language but a common humanity.
16. Taylor (1985), p. 263.
17. The work of J. L. Austin should not be neglected here. Like Wittgenstein, Austin's idea of 'performative' utterances shows that at least some aspects of language have illocutionary force and go beyond mere description and reference.
18. It is worth noting that in Descartes's radical doubt he never thinks to doubt the language in which the doubt itself is expressed. Wittgenstein, clearly siding with Hamann on the question of the impossibility of wordless thoughts, must surely have had Descartes's doubt in mind when he asks the following: 'Can I be making a mistake, for example, in thinking that the words of which this sentence is composed are English words whose meaning I know?' (*OC*, §158).
19. I. Berlin, *The Magus of the North*, p. 315. In Berlin (2000).
20. Andrew Bowie questions Isaiah Berlin's verdict that Hamann is an irrationalist. See Bowie (2003), pp. 43–5.
21. Griffith-Dickson (1995).
22. Griffith-Dickson (1995), p. 520.
23. Griffith-Dickson (1995), p. 520.

CHAPTER 2

Gadamer and Wittgenstein: Contrasts and Commonalities

He who speaks a private language understood by no one else does not speak at all.

(Gadamar, 1976a, p. 85)

It is not possible to obey a rule privately: otherwise thinking one was obeying a rule would be the same thing as obeying it.

(*PI*, §202)

I. GADAMER READS WITTGENSTEIN

Gadamer's philosophical hermeneutics slowly made its mark upon the Anglophone world and commentators noted parallels, often *en passant*, with Wittgenstein. David Linge, for example, in his penetrating Preface to the English translation of Gadamer's *Philosophical Hermeneutics*[1] shows how Wittgenstein's 'language-games' have much in common with 'Gadamer's own concept of prejudice structures'.[2] Robert E. Innis in his 'Translator's Introduction' to a work on Wittgenstein speaks of the 'the transformation of Heidegger by Gadamer' and suggests it 'ought to be considered alongside the Wittgensteinian project'. He continues:

> Gadamer's great problem is the 'linguistic constitution' of the world and the intrinsically language-constituted nature of human understanding of and comportment in the world.... Reading Gadamer along with Wittgenstein and reflecting upon the extensive historical and hermeneutical matrix of his work should enable one to see more clearly the scope and originality of Wittgenstein's own analyses and will perhaps help to forge another link between Wittgenstein and the continental tradition.[3]

Recently more detailed comparative studies have started to appear. P. Christopher Smith's *Hermeneutics and Human Finitude* (Smith, 1991) is largely a study of the ethical significance of hermeneutics but contains a useful comparison between Gadamer and analytic philosophy.[4] Ulrich Arnswald's essay 'On the certainty of uncertainty: language games and forms of life in Gadamer and Wittgenstein' is a case in point.[5]

Gadamer himself is clearly aware of the closeness of his work to Wittgenstein when he admits '[the] concept of "language-games" seemed quite natural to me when I came across it' (*TM*, p. xxxvi). And 'The way we [phenomenologists] trace the use of concepts back into their history in order to awaken their real, living, evocative meaning seems to me to converge with Wittgenstein's study of living language-games' (*PH*, p. 127).

In the 1962 essay 'The philosophical foundations of the twentieth century', Gadamer makes positive reference to the achievement of the later Wittgenstein, no doubt seeing in him elements of his own philosophical project:

> In his late work ... Wittgenstein showed that the ideal of an artificial language is self-contradictory, but not merely for the reason so often cited, namely, that the introduction of any artificial language requires that another language already be in use, thus entailing a natural language. Rather, the knowledge decisive for Wittgenstein's later insights is that language is always right, that is, it has its real function in the achievement of mutual understanding, and that the illusory problems of philosophy do not grow out of a defect in language, but of false, dogmatizing thought, an hypostasizing of operative words.[6]

The passage demonstrates Gadamer's acute knowledge of Wittgenstein and betrays an evident sympathy with the view that ordinary language is alright as it is and does not stand in need of reformation. In earlier works Gadamer sees much of his own hermeneutics in Wittgenstein and overlooks crucial differences, although in his later writings he adopts a critical edge. It was 'only after I had completed the path of thought that led to *Truth and Method*', Gadamer admits, 'did I have time to study the work of the later Wittgenstein' (Hahn, 1997, p. 19).

The present study does not depend upon direct familiarity of one another's work. If this were so the project would be flawed from the very beginning, as there is no evidence of Wittgenstein having met with or having read Gadamer. This is hardly surprising as the important work in hermeneutics was written long after the death of Wittgenstein, hence we cannot see Gadamer through the eyes of Wittgenstein. We should not ignore the point that many commentators have sought to demonstrate that Wittgenstein practises hermeneutics particularly in his later work. This position can be seen in the writings of early Wittgensteinians such as Peter Winch and Georg Henrik von Wright.[7]

In more recent years Gadamer's enthusiasm for Wittgenstein has been tempered and he speaks of weaknesses in the analytical project itself.

Logical rigor is not everything. Not that logic does not have its evident validity. But the thematisation in logic restrains the horizon of questioning in order to allow for verification, and in doing so blocks the kind of opening up of the world which takes place in our own experience of that world. This is a hermeneutical finding which I believe in the end converges with what we find in the later Wittgenstein. In his later writings he revised the nominalistic prejudices of his *Tractatus* in favour of leading all speaking back to the context of life-praxis. (Hahn, 1997, p. 39)

We have here a bold statement of what Gadamer shares with the later Wittgenstein notably a common emphasis upon 'leading all speaking back to the context of life-praxis'. But Gadamer takes Wittgenstein to task for failing to see that metaphysical questions do not all end in disengagement from the life-world but can, in *poetic* rather than *philosophical* discourse, reveal something about 'being-in-the-world', or put less abstractly, it can disclose something about what it is like to be human.

II. SPIEL:[8] WITTGENSTEIN'S 'LANGUAGE-GAMES' AND GADAMER'S 'PLAY'

Wittgenstein likens everyday language to a series of overlapping and inter-related games or 'language-games' in order to counteract and expose certain well established, but fundamentally misguided, conceptions of how language acquires meaning and how that meaning is sustained and disseminated. The comparison between language and game effectively undermines 'mentalist' accounts of meaning where the word achieves its effect through a direct connection to the inner workings of subjective consciousness. The totality of the game, that is the rules and social practices surrounding these, supplants the monadic isolation of the thinking 'I'.

Using the notion of play Gadamer initially challenges the Kantian subjectivization of aesthetics, the reduction of art to feeling, in Part One of *Truth and Method*.[9] Playfulness as a theme returns in the final section of this work when the idea of the universality of language makes hermeneutical play a dimension of linguistic understanding. Gadamer readily admits in the 'Reflections' essay that the importance of play to his work was not fully elaborated in earlier work and should have been given a more prominent, that is integrating, role in *Truth and Method*.[10]

What is a language-game? Although this is a key term in Wittgenstein's later work it is an elusive one and covers many possibilities. Wittgenstein steadfastly resists hard and fast definitions: the language-game militates against such Socratic closure. One of the reasons for likening language to a game is to highlight its imprecision and failure to divide into neatly circumscribed concepts. There can be no set of necessary and sufficient conditions to which language must conform. Instead he points to a loosely textured open-ended picture of language: an antidote to his own 'Tractarian'[11] rigid schematization of a unitary and strictly logical language. The very elusiveness of the language-game idea is illustrated by the constant changes in the way the term is written. What is the difference between 'language game' and 'language-game'? And what is the difference between '*language*-game' and 'language-*game*' and the many other possible permutations scattered throughout the *Investigations*?

Gadamer's overall project in *Truth and Method*, to reclaim and reinvigorate a lost pre-Enlightenment hermeneutic dimension to the *Geisteswissenschaften* (and ultimately all forms of understanding), initially shares little in common with Wittgenstein's more modest 'sketches of landscapes' (*PI*, Preface, p. ix), as he described his later work.

In order to bring to prominence the subjectivist dimension to the modernist account of the aesthetic and how this might be counteracted Gadamer looks to the notion of play for possible clues. Later in *Truth and Method*,[12] play becomes more than a limited response to the Kantian problematic; Gadamer turns it into a central metaphor for disclosing the ontological structure of language and it becomes a central feature of the dialogical fusion of horizons and historicity.

In Gadamer's initial discussion of play in *Truth and Method*, in Part One ('Play as the clue to ontological explanation'), a procedural closeness to Wittgenstein is evident. Seeking to tease out the meaning of play, Gadamer looks for clues within everyday usage, a strategy constantly at work in late Wittgenstein. Reference is made to 'the play of light, the play of the waves, the play of gears or parts of machines, the interplay of limbs, the play of forces, the play of gnats, even a play on words' (*TM*, p. 103). Curiously, he gives 'methodological priority ... to metaphorical usage' on the grounds that when 'a word is applied to a sphere to which it did not belong, the actual "meaning" emerges quite clearly' (*TM*, p. 103).

In the everyday exchange of language the 'to-and-fro movement that is not tied to any goal that would bring it to an end' (*TM*, p. 103) is witnessed. The striking feature of play is its dynamic for constant change, its to-and-fro-ness. In the play of games, 'ball games will be with us forever because the ball is freely mobile in every direction, appearing to do surprising things of its own accord' (*TM*, p. 106).

The to-and-fro is not so much a description of the movement of the participants within the game, although it is partly this, more pertinently it is the relation between the players and the game played. To understand the play of the game we need to focus not on the individual subjectivity of the players, but the dialectical open future, the dynamic oscillation between the players and the game. Play is pure activity. There is no game without players: 'all playing is a being-played' (*TM*, p. 106). Further, 'play is self-presentation' (*TM*, p. 108).

A description of its rules or a characterization of its point (to trap the King in chess or score a goal in football, for instance) does not fully explain the nature of a game; these aspects merely identify superficial features. The game is pointless, after all its rules are arbitrary and could easily be otherwise, and yet in play we are drawn into the game's own seriousness, by what is called the (indefinable) 'spirit' of the game. The game makes a claim upon its players and the players in turn come to see something of themselves in the game.

In the early stages of *Truth and Method* Gadamer offers the notion of play to intimate the relationship between the individual consciousness and the artwork claiming that understanding here is a dynamic interchange and not a subjective response. Gadamer widens the scope of discussion and play turns out to be a vital clue in highlighting a universal structure within language itself. Just as the aesthetic consciousness is subordinate to the artwork so the isolated language-speaker is dwarfed by the totality of language. The connection is made apparent when Gadamer observes:

> Play is not to be understood as something a person does. As far as language is concerned, the actual subject of play is obviously not the subjectivity of an individual who, among other activities, also plays but is instead the play itself. (*TM*, p. 104)

The to-and-fro-ness of play, the subordination of the player to the game, is a process and a structure ceaselessly at work in our daily encounters with language. Gadamer in the 'Reflections' essay makes the direct link between the play of art and the play language:

> Even the common language is never a fixed given. It resides in the play of language between speakers, who must enter into the game of language so that communication can begin, even where various viewpoints stand irreconcilably over against each other.[13]

For Gadamer and Wittgenstein, the analogy of the game is central. By pointing to its characteristics they bring to prominence the unworkability of the designative tradition in the philosophy of language. Central here, as we will see in subsequent chapters, is the attack upon isolated subjectivity, the idea that meaning is grounded in the solidity of the knowing subject.

Language is not anchored in representation but in the to-and-fro movement of the ludic practices within which it is played.

Sustaining language and making meanings possible across a variety of contexts is not the underwriting of the thinking 'I' of consciousness but elements of social life, the practical and the traditional. For Wittgenstein, language-games are stabilized by the context of customary 'forms of life' (*Lebensformen*) and the network of social practices they embody: 'To obey a rule, to make a report, to give an order, to play a game of chess, are customs (uses, institutions)' (*PI*, §199).

For Gadamer, the free flow of play at work in the dialogical interaction between the language-user and the weight of tradition, embedded in language, is language's only solid grounding. Wittgenstein and Gadamer share a thoroughgoing anti-foundationalism.

Language is praxis. Paraphrasing Wittgenstein, Brandt speaks of an 'institutionalised being-able-to' (Brandt, 1979, p. 56). 'The term language-game is meant to bring into prominence the fact that the speaking of language is part of an activity, or form of life' (*PI*, §23) Wittgenstein declares.

'The grammar of the word "knows" is evidently closely related to that of "can", "is able to"' (*PI*, §150). 'Grammar', that elusive almost figurative device in Wittgenstein, refers not to formal syntax but to the range of meaning possibilities available to the language user. The stress upon practical activity; the source of meaning is in the performance of the speaker rather than the structure and arrangement of words. Language is not a truth-functional grid grafted onto the inert 'external' world, as it was in the *Tractatus Logico-Philosophicus*. In the *Philosophical Investigations* there is a move away from the representational idea of language to a more pragmatic picture best described as a constant practical negotiation with an already existing human, social world.

Forcefully demonstrated in works like *On Certainty*, learning a language is a practical engagement rather than a process of rational reflection and introspection: 'Children do not learn that books exist, that armchairs exist, etc. etc., they learn to fetch books, sit in armchairs, etc., etc.' (*OC*, §476). Or, 'We teach a child "this is your hand", not "that is perhaps (or probably) your hand". That is how a child learns the innumerable language-games that are concerned with his hand' (*OC*, §374). These remarks also bring out the impossibility of calling into question certain features of the game, there is no getting behind the back of language, as it were, to authenticate its truth-affirming credentials. There can be no super- or supra-rationality we can appeal to, to test the veracity of a game. Wittgenstein warns: 'You must bear in mind that the language-game . . . is . . . unpredictable. . . . it is not based on grounds. It is not reasonable (or unreasonable). It is there – like life' (*OC*, § 559).

Gadamer's phenomenology of play as it re-emerges in *Truth and Method* in the section on 'The hermeneutic priority of the question' (*TM*, II, 3, c) is important here. Once Gadamer has rehabilitated notions of 'authority', 'prejudice', and 'tradition', occluded by the Enlightenment 'prejudice against prejudice', a remarkably 'Wittgensteinian' picture of language opens up. The play of the game, overshadowing the consciousness of the individual players, turns into the being of language itself.

If speech (rather than writing) in everyday contexts is the paradigm of ordinary language for Wittgenstein, then everyday conversation or dialogue is language at its most authentic in Gadamer. Authentic conversation, uncluttered by the refractions of modernity, reaches back to the openness of enquiry in Socratic dialogue. The characteristics of play (the to-and-fro movement, the seduction of play as it draws us into its own seriousness, the ontological priority of the game over its players) is at the heart of all dialogical encounters. But this is the chat and conversation of the building-site and the taxi cab, not the distorted communication of the philosophy seminar. For both Gadamer and Wittgenstein language gets into trouble ('goes on holiday') when it is pulled from its appropriate dialogical contexts. The notion of dialogue, as we will see in the following chapter, is central to Gadamer. In dialogue we seek both to understand and be understood. Dialogical 'play' is at the heart of all thinking, speaking, reading, in fact anything we may include under the rubric of a text in need of understanding. Richard Palmer expresses this well when he comments: 'Understanding, says Gadamer, is always an historical, dialectical, linguistic event – in the sciences, in the humanities, in the kitchen' (Palmer, 1969, p. 215).

In seeking to make sense of a text we are drawn into its horizon. For Gadamer, understanding is the fusing of the horizon of the interpreter and the horizon of the text. A text, initially alienated from the interpreter by historical or cultural distance and the inevitable strangeness of its idioms, is tamed and made comprehensible by the negotiating power of the fusion of horizons, a procedure whereby text and interpreter are drawn into the arena of the mutuality of dialogue.

Dialogue plays an important part in late Wittgenstein. He speaks of the need to 'do away with all explanation' so that 'description alone must take its place' (*PI*, §109). The theoretical standpoint, the one adopted in the *Tractatus* and the designative tradition generally, obscures the dialogical nature of everyday speech, blocking the way to pure description. Wittgenstein, it seems, attempts to capture the spirit of description in dialogue, in the fragments of conversations – which, on one level, is all the *Investigations* is. Critics speak of 'imaginary interlocutors' as though there is a formal argumentative dialectic running through the work. But this kind of closure would lead back to structures of explanation, precisely what Wittgenstein seeks to avoid. Questions relating to the structure and presentation of the *Investigations* will be returned to in Chapter 7.

III. CONTRASTS AND DIVISIONS: ON WHAT SEPARATES WITTGENSTEIN AND GADAMER

In the first part of this section of Chapter 2 I drew together Wittgenstein and Gadamer. But we need to appreciate the areas where there is a parting of the ways. The most prominent differences surround issues of historicity and creativity, and these, I maintain, have their origins in certain disagreements about the way language is conceived. Gadamer's account of language is able to comprehend its self-transforming character, he is able to show the various factors at work in the capacity of language to go beyond itself, to undergo subtle transformations and to overreach the domain of the conventional, of the already said. Through his overarching conception of *tradition* and the constantly changing narratives by which it is made manifest, Gadamer is able to link the conversations and dialogues ('language-games') of the past to the present: prima facie, such resources are unavailable to Wittgenstein.

Looking remarkably post-modern on some recent readings there is not a continuous narrative of historical continuity in Wittgenstein's picture of language but dislocation and fragmentation.[14] Current language-games are disjointed and fail to connect with the language-games of the past. To seek to step outside the present involves an illicit move in the game. For Wittgenstein, any theory-driven attempt to make meta-type statements about the nature of language would be, like philosophy-as-metaphysics, doomed to failure. The final line of the *Tractatus* is there as a constant reminder: 'Whereof one cannot speak thereof one must be silent' (*TLP*, 7). This whole subject of what we might call the 'old' and the 'new' in language, expressed alternatively as language's historicity and creativity, warrants special attention as it goes to the middle of what might be the gap between Gadamer and Wittgenstein. Localized agreements sustain individual language-games where the semantic field modifies as new practices come into existence. For Wittgenstein, the seeming fragmentation of linguistic practices is a surface appearance. Underlying agreements, made manifest in regular linguistic activity always guide the speaker into appropriate practice. However, at another level, as Lyotard suggests, there is a fragmentation between language-games.

When a language-game loses currency, as metaphors die and words invisibly slip into new uses, when the commensurate agreement passes away, does it follow that the superseded language-game loses both meaning and currency? Language here is, in essence, so parochial and relativized it can only sustain meanings in the present, and there can be no bridge across the chasm of historical distance. Present games become separated from those of the past with their incommensurable logics. Is this a fair reading of Wittgenstein? We need to deepen our investigation and examine more closely the relationship between language-games and temporality.

How, for Gadamer, does language advance and go beyond itself in ever new words and meanings? In learning the many uses of language, *one at the same time learns the condition of all possible usage* is the hermeneutical response. There is no internalizing of a set of rules for particular language-games, one is not merely socialized into the specifics of language but brought into linguisticality itself. In learning the initial language-games one at the same time develops the capacity to apply the games in new contexts and in relation to new games. Gadamer makes this point when he claims that

> the accumulation of vocabulary and the rules of its application establishes only the outline for that which in this way actually builds the structure of a language, namely, the continuing growth of expressions into new realms of application. (*PH*, p. 85)

All linguistic understanding takes place from within a specific horizon. In the first instance, the horizon is strictly regulated by convention and agreement ('the given'). Wittgenstein, from a Gadamerian position, never advances beyond this elementary stage of linguistic appropriation: the mature use of language is modelled upon early training and never takes into account the complex transformations undergone both by the speaker and language itself.

Gadamer's insight is into the ways language acquisition and use advance, how horizons extend, not by simple repetition of adult (socialized) language, but through the capacity for language to ceaselessly transcend the rules yet keep them in play through dialogue and conversation which extend (linguistic) horizons. Linge expresses this thought against Wittgenstein as follows:

> The hermeneutical dimension of language ... Wittgenstein ignores: with the learning of our native language we have at the same time learned how one learns languages in general. Thus, we can never again undergo training in the original sense. We already possess all other language games in principle, not by new socialization, but through mediation, translation. For Gadamer, to learn a new language involves using it, but we never learn the new language in a vacuum. Instead, we bring our native language along, so that learning is not a new socialization, but an expansion of the horizons with which we began.[15]

In the everydayness of articulation and dialogue horizons meet and interact. To accommodate another horizon, be it another language-user or a text, the speaker/reader ceaselessly interrogates and interprets what is being said. Ultimately, for Gadamer, all authentic uses of language involve *interpretation* as one both seeks to understand and be understood. Interpretations (and translation) are not reproductive acts; they are productive and hence creative. This is a cardinal dictum of hermeneutics.

Standing outside the historically given horizon is an impossibility. However, the horizon offers the conditions of possibility for understanding what another is seeking to say. This involves translating something initially 'foreign' (that is, outside the individual's horizon) into something familiar. The tacit rules grounding the horizon are modified unnoticed by the individual language-user as the range of linguistic application extends.

The necessity for interpretation is not always apparent as we frequently glide effortlessly on the surface of language, especially when the language-game is familiar and, as it were, without friction. This would be, for example, when we are on well-known territory (the simple procedure of naming and passing slabs, as occurs in the 'primitive' language-game of the *Philosophical Investigations*, would be a possible case in point). When language becomes problematical, when what the other is seeking to say initially defies sense making comprehension difficult, the usually invisible act of interpretation comes to the fore.[16]

The sort of example I have in mind here is when language is taken to the limit and used in a poetic or overtly metaphorical sense. Problematical in the dialogue between reader and poem is the new and unfamiliar, something disruptive of existing linguistic practice. The situation is invariably normalized when language finds a new but temporary resting-place in what Gadamer calls prejudice. Prejudice, the condition of judgement, limits the horizon and yet at the same time extends it. Unlike Wittgenstein's rules (of language-games), prejudices are extended and changed (but never foreclosed) in linguistic encounters, Gadamer claims.

Each horizon participating in the dialogue is transfigured. The initial prejudices, regulating what can be said are altered. A dialectical (or is it hermeneutical?) oscillation between the rules and their application is enacted. The range of applicability of words and sentences is regulated, but the applications themselves modify the rule. Wittgenstein sees only a logical relationship between rules and application; Gadamer sees the hermeneutic circle in operation.

Part of the dynamic of language is its inventiveness and interpretive possibilities, compelling it into ever-new formulations, expanding and shifting horizons. Another force at work is play or playfulness, as we have already noted. Following Heidegger, Gadamer speaks of language as essentially apophantic, disclosive. Opened up is the world itself and an arena of concerns, things that matter to those who operate within the disclosure (or the 'language-game'). Language is not transparent communication; this is a modernist fantasy, but reflexive dialogue in an already interpreted world. It may not be immediately obvious, when language is functioning as little more than a means of communication, but all language is indirectly a dialogue addressing our basic fears and concerns.

All concerns or matters at issue (*die Sache*), from the point of view of the horizon, motivate the linguistically mediated self, and its ceaselessly inconclusive quest for personal meaning. At another level, namely the totality of language, these concerns are the enduring questions endlessly posed and reformulated throughout the historical uncovering of language. Questions about the nature of justice and the good, for example, are perennially addressed in Western culture either formally in the history of philosophy or indirectly in our day-to-day concerns. Justice is a genuine matter of concern when actual rights are withdrawn from individuals, for example, more so than when the concept of justice is debated in the abstract.

Despite perennial questions there can be no definitive answers. At best there are contextualized moves within the 'logic of question and answer' as Gadamer terms it, drawing on the work of the English philosopher and historian R. G. Collingwood (*TM*, pp. 369–79). The current language-games offer no more than provisional possibilities; new ways of formulating time-honoured questions.

These Gadamerian thoughts may, perhaps, jar to Wittgensteinian ears. The idea of a perennial philosophy or endlessly recurring questions constituting the tradition and making up part of the fabric of language itself sounds like metaphysical pretension.

Historically conditioned concerns constitute another dynamic within language. Only from within the framework of inherited questions is language capable of change. Rules delimit concerns yet the concerns themselves reflect back, bringing about ever-new applications. The character of concerns is changed by the rule. The concerns reveal the limitations of the rules and further extend them.

Gadamer speaks of the 'fusion of horizons'. Horizons are fused in every linguistic encounter, in our day-to-day dialogical exchanges. Concerns draw the participants into dialogue and in the meeting both language and horizons are changed. A 'fusion of horizons' also takes place when one inevitably and unwittingly encounters the language-games of the past.

For Gadamer, past language-games are not inert repositories of redundant meanings. On the contrary, they sustain their effects in the present. Without

past meanings current meanings would be impossible. The dialogical structure of language in the present is preserved when there is an encounter with
the past. What makes the 'fusion of horizons' possible is the assumed
commonality of tradition. All possible horizons are captured in what is transmitted, the tradition. Whereas Gadamer is able to show the lines of communication between current and past language-games Wittgenstein is less than
illuminating on the connection. Is this a weakness in his philosophical
position? Does a thinker have an obligation to engage with the past or can
fresh insights be generated by wilfully ignoring the past?

There is no unbridgeable historical distance between the language-games
of past and present for Gadamer. Current language-games are part of an
ever-extending totality, the tradition. The actual web of meanings is never a
given starting point. It is itself the effect of former language-games. The past
continues to resonate in the present. Former language-games, enshrined in
the historical texts of the past, have their own horizons and they can be
productively encountered from the present. Ancient texts are not alien and
radically other, they have their own horizons, and they share common
concerns, and stand within an all-encompassing tradition. Interpretative
dialogue with the past is always possible; it is, in fact, unavoidable.

The continuity of language, its capacity to absorb and generate endless
novelty and change, brings everything within the ambit of tradition. Gadamer's vision of language as essentially historical and continuous runs against
the idea of the language-games as fragmented, discontinuous, and ceaselessly
ruptured.[17] Subsequent chapters seek to give more detailed accounts of the
importance for Gadamer of the temporal and the historical.

IV. AFTER THE LINGUISTIC TURN: GADAMER AND WITTGENSTEIN ON THE NATURE OF PHILOSOPHY

A. Gadamer on Philosophy: The Hermeneutical Truth of Remembrance

Gadamer and Wittgenstein are 'anti-foundationalists', that is, thinkers who
place in doubt the whole project of philosophy as traditionally conceived
since the seventeenth century. The history of modern philosophy as the
chimerical search for indubitable epistemological foundations to knowledge
and truth is well described in Richard Rorty's *Philosophy and the Mirror of
Nature* (Rorty, 1980, especially pp. 131–64). Significantly, Rorty puts
Gadamer and Wittgenstein (not to mention Dewey and Heidegger) together
as 'edifying' philosophers, that is, philosophers of a new breed who lead the
way in opening up a 'mirrorless' way of thinking.

In differing ways Gadamer and Wittgenstein, who embrace contemporary forms of anti-foundationalism, are ambivalent about the activity of philosophy itself in the light of the 'linguistic turn' but send it off in new, transformed directions. It would be wrong to regard both thinkers as harbingers and prophets of the 'end of philosophy' and more appropriate to look upon them as innovators searching for a newly defined set of tasks and aspirations for the subject formerly known as philosophy.

The subtitle of *Truth and Method* is (in translation) 'Elements of a philosophical hermeneutics'. Hermeneutics, traditionally conceived, was the art of interpreting 'difficult' texts, an *ars interpretandi*, where interpretation means rekindling forms of understanding lost in the mists of antiquity, for example. This raises an important question: in what sense then is Gadamer's hermeneutics a philosophical endeavour and why should we read *Truth and Method* as an important contribution to the subject, as it undoubtedly is? As if to address these questions directly Gadamer insists, 'My real concern (in writing *Truth and Method*) was and is philosophical: not what we do or what we ought to do, but what happens over and above our wanting and doing' (*TM*, Foreword to the second edition, p. xxviii).

Thus, we are *not* being offered 'a manual for guiding understanding ... in the human sciences' (*TM*, p. xxviii), nor reflection upon the nature of those sciences, but philosophical engagement with them. This begs a further question: what is uniquely philosophical about Gadamer's philosophical hermeneutics? If hermeneutics is, *inter alia*, a guide to the interpretation of texts surely it is a literary activity not a philosophical one?

In Gadamer the easy bifurcation between the literary and the philosophical is impossible. In his recent work, as we will see in Chapter 7, Gadamer, like Heidegger and others, subordinates the philosophical word to the poetic, witnessed in his various interpretive essays on the poetry of Rainer Maria Rilke and Paul Celan. A problem of modern foundationalist philosophy's self-understanding (reaching back to ancient taxonomy) is the marginalization of the aesthetic and the rhetorical, which it subordinates to the 'hard' sciences.[18] Philosophical hermeneutics reinstates these practices as part of the general task of understanding. Nowhere does Gadamer provide us with an easy and ready answer to the question about the relationship between hermeneutics and philosophy but this can be gleaned from various sources and ideas.

There is no escaping language, no fixed point outside our articulations from where we can view the world aright: this is one of the first principles of anti-foundationalist thought. Certain things seem to follow from this state of affairs. Our thinking itself is thoroughly linguistical and foundationalist philosophy, which presupposes something basic (and non- or pre-linguistic) like reason or introspective self-certainty, is impossible. Does this make philosophical enquiry redundant? Far from it. 'Being that can be understood is language', Gadamer tells us:[19] language is not an instrument of communication but communication itself. Hermeneutics as the quest for understanding has a universal dimension to it ('what happens over and above our wanting and doing'). The circular structure of understanding is common to all activities whether we call them textual interpretation, human sciences or cooking. This universality is the point at which Gadamer's hermeneutics becomes explicitly philosophical as Rüdiger Bubner explains:

> Hermeneutics has become more and more of a key word in philosophical discussions of the most varied kind. It seems as if hermeneutics creates cross-connexions between problems of different origin. In linguistics and sociology, in history and literary studies, in theology, jurisprudence and aesthetics, and finally in the general theory of science, hermeneutic perspectives have been successfully brought to bear. In this way, the traditional philosophical claim to universality is renewed under another name.[20]

The last sentence is particularly important; on this reading Gadamer is able to claim for hermeneutics a new task of philosophy.[21] This is not a case of reinstalling philosophy as the queen of the sciences or a matter of resurrecting the Cartesian-Kantian inspired inspector of the credentials of all other disciplines. It would be a matter of asserting the legitimacy of just one voice, albeit an important voice, in the more general conversation of the human sciences. Once again Richard Rorty seems to have picked up on this idea at the end of *Philosophy and the Mirror of Nature* where he talks of philosophy as 'edification' and conversation. It also informs his idea of a 'post-philosophical culture' in which literary, scientific, and 'philosophical' ideas and texts have parity of esteem and the human sciences are not relegated to a position subordinate to the natural sciences.[22] The modern philosopher 'however much he may be called to draw radical inferences from everything, the role of prophet, of Cassandra, of preacher, or of know-it-all does not suit him'.[23] Gadamer rejects the Promethean, heroic conception of philosophy but he does grant the thinker a special cultural status. 'The philosopher, of all people, must ... be aware of the tension between what he claims to achieve and the reality in which he finds himself.'[24] The awareness of the tension is, ironically, kept alive by the philosopher's appreciation of his/her limitations.

> (And) though the will of man is more than ever intensifying its criticism of what has gone before to the point of becoming a utopian and eschatological

consciousness, the hermeneutic consciousness seeks to confront that will with something of the truth of remembrance: with what is still and ever again real.[25]

Gadamer's philosopher does not capture, like Hegel's, the spirit of the age in thought, nor does he paint grey on grey (that is, only understand things after they have happened). His thinker, more like Walter Benjamin's storyteller,[26] preserves what we are by engaging with the tradition and reminding us of our too easily forgotten past. Incidentally, is not the whole history of philosophy an opportunity to rekindle lost perspectives and extend our involvement with our own past? Brice Wachterhauser sees in the 'Great texts of the *Geisteswissenschaften* ... the possibilities of self-understanding that everyday language lacks'.[27] Philosophy, for Gadamer, is very much a constant dialogue with its own past. Here there is an echo of the Hegelian dictum 'The study of the history of philosophy is the study of philosophy itself'.[28] But Hegel's identity of philosophy and the history of philosophy presuppose resolution when all oppositions and alienations in thought are overcome in the Absolute. Gadamer's vision of a close relationship between philosophy and the history of philosophy denies the possibility of resolution or completion. There can be no final conclusion to the questions of philosophy as our linguistically mediated relationship to being will always be mysterious. There is a problem here. In the 'logic of question and answer' and throughout Gadamer there is a commitment to openness; openness to texts, openness to the other. The questions of philosophy will always open up new ways of asking the question. However, Gadamer does not seem to be troubled by philosophical questions (in the way Heidegger and Wittgenstein are). He seems to want to defuse philosophical questions by showing that negotiation is always possible. This opens up all sorts of questions about alterity and difference. In Hegel's system there is no true alterity (his system amounts to the tautology A = A); is this the case with Gadamer, is everything to be solved and dissolved into the monological tradition?

Gadamer confronts questions about the task of philosophy once he admits to the omnipresence of linguisticality and the dissolution of philosophical problems into questions of textual interpretation. Again the question is asked, what happens to philosophy once it embraces hermeneutics? Gadamer's work is testimony to the universality and wide-ranging nature of hermeneutics. Everything becomes an object of study and investigation.

Since *Truth and Method* we have witnessed important studies on education and pedagogy,[29] and philosophically inclined works of literary criticism.[30] There is also the work on the hermeneutics of medical practice, *The Enigma of Health: The Art of Healing in a Scientific Age*.[31] This work is a model of 'applied philosophical hermeneutics', if such a term is not a tautology. It is a difficult work to classify being part philosophy, part history of ideas, and part ethics. It is also a powerful critique of the dangers of instrumental thinking when applied to health and healing. Gadamer sees in modern medicine's technologizing of the body a dangerous move away from the ancient art of healing. The dialogical relationship between doctor and patient was once a model of the hermeneutical transaction where the practitioner trod a fine line between intervention and the open domain of nature: the relationship becomes fractured as a consequence of medicine's rigorously scientific self-understanding.

Gadamer's writings on health, to be trusted from a man in his second century, show the extensive terrain philosophical hermeneutics can cover. They also show the critical edge of his analysis. The criticism of philosophical hermeneutics as an apology for the status quo, levelled by Habermas and others, is limited.[32]

B. Philosophy, The Fly and The Flybottle

What role is there for philosophy once language has been exposed as just so many rituals and ceremonies, so many different language-games? Must philosophy abjure its historic mission of revealing truth? Is it reduced to a far humbler activity; lexicography or a strictly empirical science, that of describing and laboriously recording the actual uses of everyday language?[33] But what is the point of endlessly recording the ways we talk about the world? What will it reveal?

Wittgenstein, like Gadamer, starts from the assumption that we ought to refrain from epistemologically driven metaphysics – the foundationalist philosophy we get in modernity, from Cartesianism to positivism – and stay close to the actual uses of language. Language is not anchored in self-certainty, accurately representative of the given world (Rorty's 'mirror of nature' idea); it is sustained by the contingencies of linguistic agreement and conventions.

Wittgenstein's personal dislike of academic philosophy and professional philosophers is well documented. There are endless jokes at the expense of philosophers in Wittgenstein's later work. 'I am sitting with a philosopher in the garden; he says again and again "I know that that's a tree", pointing to a tree that is near us. Someone else arrives and hears this, and I tell him: "This fellow isn't insane. We are only doing philosophy"' (OC, §467). And there are frequent biographical references to Wittgenstein deterring his students from graduate work in philosophy. His real criticism was not of the discipline per se but of philosophy as a vocation.[34] Facts of biography aside, the pretensions of philosophy are exposed in Wittgenstein's investigations: 'What we do is to bring words back from their metaphysical to their normal use in language' (*WR*, p. 265).

On this view philosophy is an aberrant parasitic discourse living off the authentic uses of words in ordinary everyday language situations. Failing to get a clear view of the way we talk about the world engenders the illusory sense of a philosophical problem.[35] There are no intractable puzzles about appearance and reality, say, only apparent conundrums to be dismantled or dissolved in the light of everyday linguistic practice ('The problems are, in the strict sense dissolved: like a piece of sugar in water' (*WR*, p. 272)).

The image of the trapped fly in the flybottle is a vivid and potent one. 'What is your aim in philosophy? – To show the fly the way out of the fly-bottle' (*PI*, §309). The philosopher, like the fly, is lured into a trap from which there is no escape; the flybottle is easy to get into but impossible to break away from. The trap is, of course, the seductions and enticements of language overreaching itself, enticing a certain kind of careless philosopher to go beyond the limits of what can be legitimately uttered, resulting in 'mental cramps' and nonsense. ('The question ... "What is meaning?" produces in us mental cramp' (*BBB*, p. 1).

In a wonderfully ambiguous pronouncement Wittgenstein declared philosophy to be 'a battle against the bewitchment of our intelligence by means of language' (*WR*, p. 282). The ambiguity turns on the 'by means of language'. Language is both the cause of problems and paradoxically the cure. It may engender mental cramps but at the same time it allows us to 'battle' as in fight and resist 'the bewitchment of our intelligence'. In the same way, language may lure us into the flybottle but being forewarned and forearmed provides the means of escape.

Philosophy is not simply destructive; it has a positive side. Occasionally (*PI*, §133), Wittgenstein likens linguistic philosophy to therapy.[36] The disease (dis-ease?), once again, can only be cured or at least confronted, once one admits to going astray by stepping outside the legitimate language-games. Wittgenstein's later descriptions of philosophy are frequently personal, autobiographical, and dramatically confessional in the manner of Rousseau and Augustine. The real point of doing philosophy, for Wittgenstein, is to enable him to stop doing it: philosophy is a kind of purgative: 'The real discovery is the one that makes me capable of stopping doing philosophy when I want to. – The one that gives philosophy peace so that it is no more tormented...' (*PI*, §133).

What Wittgenstein offers is not merely destructive (of traditional philosophical beliefs and practices), it can free the sufferer from philosophical pathology. In a series of brilliant examples, metaphors, and analogies, Witt-

genstein demonstrates how readily the philosopher's anguish can be defused
or neutralized, not by devising yet more dreary theory and '–isms' but by
something alarmingly simple and hence difficult to realize; hitting upon the
right expression or form of words. 'Sesame' is ludicrously simple but it
might take you a lifetime to hit upon it:

> There are some safes which can be opened by using a certain word or a
> certain number: before you hit on the right word, no amount of force can
> open the door, but once you do so any child can open it. Philosophical
> problems are like that. (*WR*, p. 269)

It is not just illicit uses of words and mistaken philosophical theories leading
us astray, language itself takes prisoners. 'A *picture* held us captive. And we
could not get outside it, for it lay in our language and language seemed to
repeat it to us inexorably.' The idea of the *Bild*, image or picture, as something both visual and linguistic, is very strong in the later Wittgenstein. It
has little in common with the earlier 'picture theory of meaning' in the
Tractatus.[37]   Reading the above quotation in tandem with the thoughts
expressed in later writings we see how, for Wittgenstein, when we take
possession of language we unwittingly, insidiously, inherit a picture of the
world.[38] For 'I did not get my picture of the world (*Weltbild*) by satisfying
myself of its correctness; nor do I have it because I am satisfied of its correctness. No: it is the inherited background against which I distinguish between
true and false' (*OC*, §94).

The picture is non-representational, if anything it is a condition of representation. Being neither true nor false it provides the background to what we
call true and false and it can be reimagined. Philosophy uncovers the
pictures by which we are held captive, and exposes them as just so many
snares to be avoided. In this sense the pictures within language act as something like ideology and some form of ideology-critique is possible.[39] For
Marx ideology can only be combated once the social conditions giving rise to
distorted views of the world are changed. I spoke earlier of philosophy as a
form of liberation for Wittgenstein. Liberation is not a turning over or
changing of the world; at best we can only change ourselves, adopt and
inhabit new pictures whilst never completely escaping the necessity for some
particular world picture, although Wittgenstein admits that only a
Nietzschean who kicks against the herd instinct will fully rebel against
linguistic conformity:

> Human beings are deeply mined in philosophical, i.e. grammatical confu-
> sions. And, to free them from these, would presuppose that they became
> disentangled from the enormously multitudinous network which holds

them captive. One would, so to speak, have to rearrange their entire language – But this language has … become like this because human beings had – and have – the inclination to think like this. Therefore only those can escape who live in accordance with an instinctive distrust of the language – not those whose whole instinct is to live with *that* herd which has created this language as its particular expression.[40]

Philosophy cannot be used as a way of reforming language or the world as various thinkers, Plato and Marx for instance, have dreamt of in the past. For Wittgenstein 'philosophy may in no way interfere with the actual use of language; it can in the end only describe it. For it cannot give it any foundation either. It leaves everything as it is' (*PI*, § 124).

These are only sketchy remarks but they demonstrate that for both Gadamer and Wittgenstein philosophy has a role to play in cultural life and the idea that it loses currency after the linguistic turn is thwarted.

In the beginning of this chapter the focus was on similarities and differences in the accounts of language offered by Gadamer and Wittgenstein. Whereas both start from a rejection of mentalist subjectivist theories of meaning, they differ quite radically in other ways. The differences can be best summarized as follows. Gadamer's philosophical hermeneutics is illuminating in its capacity to uncover the self-transformative character of language. He, unlike many theorists of language, reserves a special place for what we might term 'the poetic'. The poetic is language at its limits evoking a transgressive power to disrupt the ordinary and the everyday. But there is a price to be paid. Gadamer's insights into the creative dimension to language are, to many critics, only possible when bolted on to a grand Hegelian narrative of the unfolding of tradition. Such a narrative works within the structures of an unacceptable universalism (what Wittgenstein termed the philosopher's 'craving for generality').

Is Gadamer's hermeneutics dependent upon a re-enactment of Hegel? Gadamer constantly refers to Hegelian ideas for which he notes a 'tension-filled proximity'.[41] Yet he distances himself from the idealist dialectic and the idea of a historical *terminus ad quem*, an endpoint to the teleological unfolding of spirit. Gadamer rejects the formulaic dialectic of the Hegelian system with its optimistic movement towards self-understanding.[42] Gadamer judiciously absorbs the Hegelian notion of the speculative but offers a more open, searching tradition within which closure is never within sight. Self-understanding is always underway within language and never, as it is for Hegel, complete. Nevertheless, there is, despite his protestations, something of the system-builder in Gadamer and his proximity to Hegel may be closer than he is prepared to admit.

Wittgenstein testifies to the almost limitless specificity of language and steers well clear of overarching structures. Yet here there is another price to be paid when one stays with the confines of particularity. A lack of concern for the historicity of language coupled with a reduction of all poeticizing discourse to just another language-game makes Wittgenstein's position problematical. ('Something new (spontaneous, "specific") is always a language-game' (*PI*, p. 224)).[43]

NOTES

1. Gadamer (1976a), pp. xi–lviii.
2. Gadamer (1976a), p. xxxv.
3. Brandt (1979), pp. xii–xiii.
4. See Chapter Two, 'Language as the medium of understanding', in Smith (1991), especially pp. 105–30.
5. In Malpas *et al.* (2002), pp. 25–44.
6. *PH*, p. 126.
7. See 'Analytic hermeneutics', Howard (1982), pp. 35–85, and von Wright (1971).
8. *Spiel* is both 'play' and 'game'.
9. 'Play as the clue to ontological explanation', *TM*, p. 101.
10. See Hahn (1997), p. 41.
11. The adjective from *Tractatus Logico-Philosophicus* (*TLP*) and useful shorthand.
12. Part Three 'The ontological shift to hermeneutics guided by language'.
13. Hahn (1997), p. 29.
14. Jean-François Lyotard has taken up this Wittgensteinian idea of fragmented language-games and turned it into what he terms a general agonistics. We might call this an anarchic reading of late Wittgenstein. See Lyotard (1984), pp. 9–11.
15. *PH*, p. xxxviii.
16. In early hermeneutics interpretation was only felt necessary when the biblical text refused to offer up its meaning. Later hermeneutics worked on the principle that all understanding involved interpretation.
17. Discontinuity as a feature of 'discourses' was a key idea in structuralist approaches to language and history. See Foucault (1972), especially Parts 1 and 2.
18. Echoing C. P. Snow's Two Cultures idea or Richard Rorty's more humorous but instantly recognizable distinction between 'techies' and 'fuzzies' (see Rorty, 2000).
19. *TM*, p. xxxv. This is a formulation Gadamer constantly repeats echoing as it does Heidegger's 'language is the house of being'.
20. Bubner (1981), p. 45.
21. Wearing the hat of the 'applied' hermeneuticist Gadamer's recent enquiries have refreshingly moved well beyond the limitations of academic philosophy, ranging from literary criticism, to pedagogy, to unclassifiable discussions of medical practice and the 'enigma' of health.
22. Also see R. Rorty, 'Pragmatism and philosophy' in Baynes *et al.* (1987), pp. 26–66.

23. *TM*, p. xxxviii.
24. *TM*, p. xxxviii.
25. *TM*, p. xxxviii.
26. See 'The storyteller: reflections on the work of Nikolai Leskov' in Benjamin (1970), pp. 83–109.
27. B. R. Wachterhauser, 'Must we be what we say? Gadamer on truth in the human sciences', Wachterhauser (1986), p. 226.
28. T. M. Knox and A. V. Miller (1985).
29. For essays on education and the nature of the university, see Misgeld and Nicholson (1992).
30. For Gadamer's interpretations of the poetry of Paul Celan see Gadamer (1997a).
31. Gadamer (1996).
32. For the terms of the Gadamer-Habermas debate see D. Misgeld, 'Critical theory and hermeneutics: the debate between Habermas and Gadamer', in O'Neill (1976) and Mendelson (1979).
33. 'Philosophy may in no way interfere with the actual use of language; it can in the end only describe it' (*PI*, §124).
34. For biographical details of Wittgenstein's attitude to philosophy see Monk (1990). Edmonds and Eidinow (2001) give an interesting account of his relationship to another professional philosopher, Karl Popper.
35. 'A main source of our failure to understand is that we do not command a clear view of the use of our words. Our grammar is lacking in this sort of perspicuity' (*PI*, §122).
36. From a biographical point of view we can see Wittgenstein was clearly tortured by philosophical questions and it is easy to see why he saw it as disease or pathology. He confesses: 'The real discovery is the one that makes me capable of stopping doing philosophy when I want to' (*WR*, p. 276). In passing we should note that Gadamer regards hermeneutics as a kind of therapeutic talking cure. See his 'Hermeneutics and psychiatry' in Gadamer (1996), pp. 163–73.
37. For details of the way the notion of the picture works in later Wittgenstein see Genova (1995) and W. J. Earle, 'Ducks and rabbits: visuality in Wittgenstein' in Levin (1997).
38. Frequently in *On Certainty* there are references to *Weltbild* or 'world picture' (*OC*, §§93, 94, 162, 167, 233, 262).
39. They also call to mind Heidegger's 'world picture'. See M. Heidegger, 'The Age of the World picture' in Heidegger (1977).
40. From the 'Big Typescript' (quoted in 'Wittgenstein in relation to his times', von Wright (1982), p. 209).
41. 'Gadamer is powerfully drawn to Hegel's thought as a source of insight he cannot do without. At the same time he sees it as a seductive force that he must use every energy at his disposal to resist, lest it lead him to forsake his own deepest insights. Still it would not be helpful to call him ambivalent ... it is just because he knows who he is and where he stands that he finds it necessary to say both yes and no to Hegel' (M. Westphal, 'Hegel and Gadamer', in Wachterhauser (1986), pp. 65–6).
42. Against Hegelian optimism Gadamer cites Aeschylus who learnt through suffering 'not this or that particular thing, but insight into the limitations of

humanity, into the absoluteness of the barrier that separates man from the divine' (*TM*, pp. 356–7).

43. Does this mean poetry is, for all its seeming innovation, never truly transgressive, since it can always be shown to be already part of an actually existing language-game?

CHAPTER 3

Gadamer's Philosophical Hermeneutics and the Ontology of Language

Being that can be understood is language

(TM)

I. INTRODUCTION TO TRUTH AND METHOD

Truth and Method is a vast, sprawling, dauntingly erudite text ranging in scope from interpretations of classical thought to engagements with many post-Kantian Continental thinkers. With so much going on in the work it is difficult to isolate a key theme as he covers, in a desultory way, much ground, thematically and chronologically.[1] Without doubt a major motif in the work is a defence of the truth claims of the humanities. Emphasis in the modern age upon *method* and the need to establish infallible procedures for revealing *truth* sheds light on the short title of this long work: 'Truth or Method' may be a more accurate title as Gadamer highlights a basic tension or disjunction. Scientific method rather than establishing and advancing truth overshadows it and is in danger of silencing deeper truths. Reflections on our basic condition, insights into the brevity and fragility of human life, glimmerings of understanding about the nature of our existence in the world which art and humane learning offer, are overshadowed by the assumed methodological precision of scientific knowledge. To reclaim the voice of liberal learning Gadamer casts doubt upon the legitimacy of method. Language has a crucial role to play here. Adopting the expressivist position he reveals all forms of understanding to be inescapably linguistic.[2]

Hans-Georg Gadamer's reputation since the 1960s rests largely upon the part he played in the revival of hermeneutics. Initially, the art of interpreting texts, biblical and latterly legal and aesthetic, hermeneutics is transformed by Gadamer into a new kind of enterprise; no longer a regional but a universally applicable activity, philosophical hermeneutics. 'Interpretation is necessary', he says, 'where the meaning of a text cannot be immediately understood. It is necessary wherever one is not prepared to trust what a phenomenon immediately presents to us' (*TM*, p. 336).

The connection between interpreting intransigent texts and the enterprise of philosophy is to be found in the broad notion of understanding (*Verstehen*). Striving for understanding is a fair description of all our engagements in the world.

Understanding, a key concept in early historical and social theory, more than knowledge or truth, the concepts usually associated with modern philosophy, defines our relationship to the world and it is from here the relationship is analysed. Gadamer's project, in the first instance, is to enquire into the phenomenon of understanding; in *Truth and Method* he stresses what he terms its 'hermeneutical' dimension.

As a prerequisite it is necessary to clear away many of the implicit distorting structures of philosophical modernism. Hints of this strategy, as already observed, are revealed in the very title of his work where 'truth' and 'method' pull in opposite directions; the modernist dependence upon method obscures unsystematized truth. Philosophical modernism, the prioritizing of scientific method as the self-grounding matrix of knowledge, works in the opposite direction seeing only the emergence of truth of its own making, via the kind of procedures and method advocated by Descartes in his *Discourse on Method*, a canonical text for methodologists.

To rethink, that is, to think differently, the modernist narrative, Gadamer needs a dramatic move away from the hegemony of scientific rationalism and the illusion that a carefully thought through method will offer up certain knowledge. What is required is a dramatically altered account of the history of the present connecting 'modes of experience outside science ... with the experiences of philosophy, of art, and of history itself' (*TM*, p. xxii). The project of a philosophical hermeneutics has, in the first instance, a negative dimension, namely, a radical questioning of those foundationalist elements of the modern philosophical tradition that depend upon the construction of method. The legacy of Cartesian philosophy amounts to: a dependence upon the subject-object divide; reliance upon natural science as a more reliable form of truth than the human sciences; a dependence upon the individual consciousness as a source of meaning; and finally, related to this last point, a reliance upon epistemological procedures and method. Hermeneutics avoids many of the pitfalls and shortcomings of philosophical modernism. When understanding is modelled on the practice of interpreting texts – rather than setting up a mirroring relationship between object by subject – another perspective on the human and the natural world is disclosed.

Although Gadamer plots the course of the history of modern hermeneutics in meticulous detail,[3] partly because his own story depends upon a narrative about the occlusion of hermeneutical thought when, in the post-enlighten-ment era, it searches for a credible scientific matrix; the idea of the herme-neutical circle has an important place in his work. Intolerable to those philosophers on the look out for formal fallacies but 'The hermeneutic circle is not "vicious" because it is not a logical circle which posits formal axioms from which further propositions are deductively derived, but rather the intrinsically circular structure of a temporal existence whose future projects are necessarily determined and guided by past preoccupations'.[4]

Acknowledged by the founding fathers of modern hermeneutics and brought into prominence in early Heidegger, the hermeneutical circle describes a central conundrum, identifiable in the practice of interpreting texts and possessing wider philosophical and, for Heidegger, ontological significance.

Hermeneutical interpretation is always an incomplete movement between whole and part. Making sense of a text is a complex process. As one reads part of a sentence one is at the same time projecting a totality of meaning upon the whole. What are the philosophical implications of this account of textual interpretation? For Gadamer, the movement of the hermeneutical circle is not merely a description of the reader's encounter with a text but a model of all understanding.[5] All our engagements, reflective and otherwise, presuppose the kind of circularity textual interpretation takes for granted. This is the sense in which Gadamer universalizes hermeneutics and brings it within the domain of the philosophical.

II. PHILOSOPHICAL HERMENEUTICS AND THE QUESTION OF LANGUAGE

Gadamer entitles his major work *Truth and Method* but there is little in the work directed to the question of truth. Bernstein observes the following:

> Although the concept of truth is basic to Gadamer's entire project of philo-sophical hermeneutics, it turns out to be one of the most elusive concepts in his work.... It might seem curious ... that in a work entitled *Truth and Method*, the topic of truth never becomes fully thematic and is discussed only briefly toward the end of the book.... (I)f we closely examine the way in which Gadamer appeals to 'truth', we see that he is employing a concept of truth that he never makes explicit.[6]

Uncharitable critics have suggested that the very notion of truth becomes redundant in his work. Why so? Part of the purpose of the hermeneutical circle is to demonstrate the implausibility and vulnerability of adequation, the designative linking of language or reason to the external world. *Adequatio* has a venerable philosophical history reaching back to Plato's dialogues and forward to Aquinas and scholasticism. And it is central to what Gadamer terms 'reflective' philosophy. Epistemologically grounded philosophy presupposes a rigid division between knower and known, knowing subject and known object.

The search for an indubitable method in modernity attempts to ground this division scientifically. If the correct method is carefully followed it should be possible to use the knowledge of the knowing subject as an accurate guide to the nature of the external world. This does not simply depend upon the acquisition of an indubitable method, like Descartes's geometric rules in the *Discourse on Method*; it also depends upon the principle of adequation, that the thing known is adequate to the knowing subject.

Gadamer's hermeneutics, in the wake of groundbreaking insights regarding the self-referentiality of the subject–object divide in Husserlian phenomenology, questions the very foundations of epistemology. The neat division between knower and known or, as we might view it from an alternative description, the division between subject and object, cannot be sustained. The philosophy of the modern period is, from the hermeneutical perspective, unable to close the chasm between knower and known, subject and object. This inability is implicit in the very structure of the hermeneutical circle. Just as part and whole are mutually dependent so, for hermeneutics, knower and known are equally symbiotic.

Gadamer calls into question the division between subjects and objects in modern epistemology. Its many assumptions; that the right method secures truth and certainty, that knowledge can be built on indubitable foundations, that truth is static and atemporal, that logical procedures will guarantee certainty, are problematical.

Understanding is not a matter of turning thought in upon itself to recognize its scope, limits, and necessary underpinnings. True understanding (*philo-sophia*, wisdom) is a realization of the impossibility of such a task. In hermeneutical understanding there is no absolute grounding for thought. The justifications for this take us back to the hermeneutical circle. If part and the whole are inseparable, surely in the epistemological quest for absolute grounding the knower and the known are likewise mutually implicated?

The so-called 'circle of epistemology', used by many critics to fault Descartes, demonstrates this. Descartes grounds thinking in 'clear and distinct ideas' and yet he makes the grounding also a substantial claim about the nature of knowledge, consequently arguing in a circle.[7] Whereas the 'epistemological circle' is self-stultifying, the 'hermeneutical circle' is 'productive' as Heidegger described it. The hermeneutical circle militates against the idea of finding some absolute grounding for thought. As is well known the important move for Gadamer is away from the metaphysics of foundationalism to the revival of a key hermeneutical term, tradition.

A. Tradition

There is little concentrated discussion of 'tradition'[8] in *Truth and Method* yet it occupies a very important place in the overall structure of Gadamer's work. Part of the critique of the rigid subject–object dichotomy recognizes a failure to engage with the historical and the temporal. Interpretive understandings of the world (or texts) have no absolute grounding but they operate within the temporal unfolding of linguistic change. All claims to understanding take place not as self-conscious moments of reflection for a thinking subject but as (experienced) events within the happening of a common tradition.

The knowing subject of reflective (and classical empiricist) philosophy, the thinking 'I', for example, in Descartes, is an isolated self-reflecting consciousness. Dimensions of temporality and the social do not impinge upon consciousness; hence Descartes is able to exclude them from his *cogito* argument. For Gadamer, such a move is impossible. The thinking consciousness is not isolated; the conditions of possibility for thinking itself are dependent upon linguistic patterns unavailable to reflective awareness.

Drawing attention to the incompleteness of Cartesian scepticism hits upon the impossibility of isolating the reflective subject from the objects of thought. The claim here, and it is central in Gadamer, is that we cannot readily, as Descartes mistakenly assumes, sideline our social and historical engagements. Descartes implicitly acknowledges this. He evokes a 'provisional moral code' to sustain himself in the period of radical doubt. The code turns out to be no different from the values he ordinarily subscribes to. This says something about the impossibility of subjecting ethical being to the scrutiny of impartial reason. The social and the historical are principal features of the linguistic, we might say that we cannot sideline our engagement within language. At another level of generality, we might say that the linguistic, the social, and the historical are all constituents of an even greater whole, which Gadamer calls collectively 'tradition'.

The post-Cartesian world, in its search for an unassailable method for sure and certain knowledge ignores tradition. In some sense method is no more than a device for bypassing tradition. Once Gadamer demonstrates the indispensability of tradition and can show how it is not readily removed from our thinking he can start to put back into place other features of our knowing and understanding relationship to the world demonized by the Enlightenment and subsequent trends in modern thought. Jürgen Habermas, Terry Eagleton, and others have taken Gadamer to task on the idea of a homogeneous tradition. Habermas emphasizes alternative traditions of resistance to orthodoxy, i.e. traditions of dissent and critique. Gadamer's overarching 'tradition' is, they argue, too abstract and lacks the resources for a critique of the tradition itself. The Enlightenment project can only be defended if tradition can be made an object of rational enquiry.[9]

B. The Rehabilitation of 'Prejudice'

Tradition works hand in hand with prejudice. And prejudice, like tradition, was squeezed from the philosophical lexicon with the dominance of new science and the emerging Enlightenment. For Gadamer, all our understanding necessarily happens via prejudice. Prejudice is not irrational thought, as it came to be understood. There is an older meaning of prejudice; prejudgement, that which makes judgement itself possible. Without prejudice there can be no judgement. All reflection in this sense is thus prejudicial:

> The history of ideas shows that not until the Enlightenment does *the concept of prejudice* acquire the negative connotation familiar today. Actually 'prejudice' means a judgment that is rendered before all the elements that determine a situation have been finally examined.... Prejudice certainly does not necessarily mean a false judgment. (*TM*, p. 270)

There is nothing necessarily sinister about this proclamation. The point made here is that thinking always takes place against a background of preexisting commitments. The thought of disembodied, timeless subjectivities gazing into the world of given objects (Nagel's 'view from nowhere') is a modernist fantasy already noted. The structures of prejudice illustrate engagement with the world before any measure of reflection is possible.

There is no radical separation in the event of understanding (between knower and known) because everything happens within the context of the common denominator, tradition. The interpreter is an integral part of tradition; complete with his or her prejudices. The object of understanding is itself something within tradition's purview. The act of understanding is not a subject appropriating an object but what Gadamer terms a dialogue; a dialogue with and within tradition. Why, for Gadamer, is all understanding historical? Is this not just one point of view, perhaps the legacy of Hegel or some other brand of outdated historicism? All understanding is necessarily historical because all understanding is, in some sense, a dialogue with tradition's past.

Traditional reflective philosophy operates on the assumption that knowledge is acquired when the subject accurately represents, is acquainted with, the object (thing or idea). Built into this is the idea that from this act of representation human thought can generate a series of timeless truths about the nature of the world. Truths are timeless because they embody universality, that is, they are true irrespective of time, place, circumstance, or context. For reflective philosophy context is largely irrelevant as regards truth or meaning. 'Snow is white' is meaningful (and true) whatever the circumstances it is often argued. Much of Gadamer's work seeks to undermine this position via an alternative account of language. For hermeneutics context is everything. Whatever is to be understood is always to be understood against a specific background; as was evident in the hermeneutical circle part cannot be understood without whole nor whole without parts. We have two ideas running together here: that understanding is essentially historical and that it is contextual. These are both contained within the assertion that understanding is always an understanding within a tradition – be that tradition written (and heard and spoken), thought, or enacted within a linguistic context.

Reminiscent of Humboldt's conception of language as a worldview, Gadamer talks of the sense in which the speaker inhabits a 'horizon', a horizon of understanding: the horizon as the way we picture the world (and our individual sense of a place within that world), including ideas, and states of affairs. The horizon replaces the introspective thinking consciousness of traditional (reflective) philosophy. It is conditioned by prejudices and this simply means that interpretations of the world and the perceptions of meaning, human and natural, always emanate from a particular historical and social location. The speaker always has a history and a rooted perspective bearing upon the horizon (most obviously every horizon will be unique as every historical situation is unique). Running against the grain of much contemporary Anglophone philosophy, there is a certain relativistic plausibility about this position. But Gadamer is no unreconstructed Nietzschean-style perspectivist.

The horizon may be unique to each individual but the horizon cannot exist without other horizons; like the structure of Hegel's argument for self-consciousness through consciousness of the other, other horizons are the condition of my own horizon, and I only have a horizon because I acknowledge, in some fundamental sense, the horizons of others.

Acts of understanding necessitate what Gadamer famously calls the 'fusion of horizons'. This is, in effect, one possible description of what happens in any attempt to understand a text, a point of view, or a historical event. This might be alternatively described as dialogue. In seeking to understand one attempts to engage the other in dialogue. Our understanding of the world is not assertive or propositional, it is not a question of assembling putatively truthful statements about the world; in essence understanding is dialogical.

Prejudice, horizons, and ultimately, tradition, the category beneath which all others are subsumed, are not dimensions of mind but aspects of our linguisticality.

The fusion of horizons is the encounter not of individual consciousnesses but elements of the totality of language engaged in conversation, questioning, and dialogue. Fusion happens down and across time. It might happen across cultures where speakers of relatively isolated communities make contact and negotiate common meanings. Alternatively it might be a fusion of historically separate horizons in the activity of interpreting an ancient text.

From the point of view of the analytical tradition Gadamer's claims look either fanciful or misguided metaphysics, or both. He rejects the approach of semantic analysis and starts out from the basic claims of philosophical hermeneutics, claims that draw upon the expressivist philosophical tradition.

There are two aspects of the proposition we need to attend to as they demonstrate a marked difference between the language of the proposition and the language of the everyday world. Before we speak of these aspects we should say that the very fact that the language of the proposition fails somehow to capture the language of the everyday world limits it *ab initio*.

For Gadamer, language is thoroughly non-instrumental. The instrumental theory of language sees words as tools for revealing the contents of the speaker's mind; language allegedly reveals states of consciousness. Such a view of language is, as Gadamer, following Heidegger, shows so convincingly, a distortion. The performative dimension to language highlights its non-instrumental character:

> The meaning of a word cannot be detached from the event of proclamation. *Quite the contrary, being an event is a characteristic belonging to meaning itself*. It is like a curse, which obviously cannot be separated from the act of uttering it. What we understand from it is not an abstractable logical sense like that of a statement, but the actual curse that occurs in it. (*TM*, p. 427)

Emphasis upon subjectivity neglects the social fabric necessary for language; it also starts out from an impossible position. Language does not so much reflect a given world as permit us to enter into an already interpreted world, that is, a world we share by means of the language we hold in common. As well as contesting the idea of language being dependent upon human subjectivity Gadamer shows how language is implicated in temporality. We need to return to the proposition for a moment. The propositions of analytic philosophy of language assume timeless truths, truths independent of time and history.

Language is thoroughly historical in that language is part of a continuously transforming tradition where the meanings of the past bear upon and 'fuse' with the present. The proposition, assuming a view of language as stasis and completeness, ignores historicity.

Central to Gadamer's position, and it ties in with the issue of language's history, is dialogue. Language (as enshrined in propositions) is singular and self-contained. It is, by virtue of its being self-contained, essentially whole and complete, independent of extraneous factors for the production of meaning. Language perceived as dialogue is incomplete. It is also incompletable, for meaning is essentially unstable through the vicissitudes of historical development and the incessant movement of the dialogue.

Language is dialogue because words retain meaning not by virtue of isolated monadic acts of consciousness but through the unstable 'givenness' of language. To speak of givenness here is not to lapse into the passivity of empiricism. In using language we enter into codes and conventions whose existence precedes individual acts of consciousness. A relationship with language is always a two-way street: we bring ourselves to language as much as we find ourselves within it. Language is speculative, a speculum, a mirror in which we play and at the same time are played. Because language is incomplete and constantly changing its identity it is thoroughly historical. The language of the proposition, on the other hand, is a timeless zone. The dialogical and speculative aspects of language will be developed later in this chapter.

An ability to talk meaningfully about the world is not, at bottom, the ability to generate truth-functional propositions, as indicative statements are themselves dependent upon context and a subtle interplay between speakers and the rituals of social life. The very possibility of constructing assertions demonstrates a more intimate engagement with language before the proposition itself is articulated. Language speaks us before we speak it. This idea, owing much to Heidegger's hermeneutics in *Being and Time*, is central to the construction of Gadamer's position. Incidentally, it is also a dominant idea in Wittgenstein's *On Certainty* where the apprentice language user takes the whole of an actually existing language on trust before creative engagement begins, demonstrating a point common to Heidegger and Gadamer that the language we speak can never be fully transparent and an object of detached enquiry.

Gadamer's analysis of Heidegger relies heavily upon his interpretation of §32 of *Being and Time* entitled 'Understanding and interpretation'. Here we meet with Heidegger's ontologized version of the hermeneutic circle which is not to be reduced to the level of a vicious circle, or even of a circle, which is merely tolerated. In the circle is hidden a positive possibility of the most primordial kind of knowing, and we genuinely grasp this possibility only when we have understood that our first, last, and constant task in interpreting is never to allow our *fore-having*, *fore-sight*, and *fore-conception* to be presented to us by fancies and popular conceptions, but rather to make the scientific theme secure by working out the fore-structures in terms of the things themselves. (*BT*, p. 153) (My italics – CL)[10]

As Gadamer says, 'the point of Heidegger's hermeneutical reflection is not so much to prove that there is a circle as to show that ... [it] possesses an onto-logical significance' (*TM*, p. 266). Dasein, as human existence, has its own being as the object of inquiry. 'An entity for which, as Being-in-the-world, its Being is itself an issue', Heidegger observes, 'has, ontologically, a circular structure' (*BT*, p. 195).

The fore-structure of understanding points to that which we understand prereflectively but makes possible more reflective noetic forms: under-standing is quite literally under where we stand. The point Heidegger makes is that understanding is only comprehensible, in outline, if we assume a threefold fore-structure. There is no raw given of pure intuition.

Any object of understanding already exists within a comprehending pre-structure. Thus, even before we interpret and move towards understanding we already *have*, *see* and *conceive* in some rudimentary (prereflective) sense. It is for this reason that assertion is a derivative mode of interpretation.

All interpretation is grounded on understanding. That which has been articulated as such in interpretation and sketched out beforehand in the understanding in general as something articulable, is the meaning. In so far as assertion is grounded on understanding and presents us with a deri-vative form on which an interpretation has been carried out, it too 'has' a meaning. (*BT*, p. 195)

Assertions, statements about the world, are dependent, as interpretations, upon a background understanding we might say, although Heidegger does not use such an idiom. The nature of this understanding is something we share as language-users and it arises out of our practical engagements with the world. The true nature of the assertion for Heidegger, spelt out in §33 of *Being and Time*, 'Assertion as a derivative mode of interpretation', is ontolo-gical and the traditional account of understanding as a part of a more general epistemological enquiry is misguided.[11] Understanding is not the grasping of a given object by a subject; hence it is not an act of consciousness. Under-standing is not representational but hermeneutical. Understanding is a practical background orientation to the world and presupposes something communal and ultimately social, at any rate something shared.

A more primordial sense of assertion, Heidegger claims,

> [M]eans 'communication' (*Mitteilung*), speaking forth. As communication, it is directly related to 'assertion'.... It is letting someone see with us what we have pointed out.... Letting someone see with us shares with the Other that entity which has been pointed out in its definite character. (*BT*, p. 197)

Language as the disclosure of a shared world is something Gadamer takes over from Heidegger and, as we will see in subsequent chapters, this idea, albeit in a radically altered guise and context, reappears in the later work of Wittgenstein.

Heidegger's threefold fore-structure of understanding becomes for Gadamer simply 'prejudice' (*Vorurteil*). 'The fundamental prejudice of the Enlightenment', Gadamer observes, 'is the prejudice against prejudice itself' (*TM*, p. 270).

Speaking against the priority of consciousness over historical being we are offered the following thoughts:

> The self-awareness of the individual is only a flickering in the closed circuits of historical life. That is why the prejudices of the individual, far more than his judgments, constitute the historical reality of his being. (*TM*, p. 281)

In yet another reversal prejudice takes pride of place over the self-reflective judgement. Our engagements in the world are invariably guided not by intro-spection but the forms of habituation constituting our shared world. If these prejudices 'constitute the historical reality of our being' in what sense can they guide reflection and action? *Ex hypothesi* they seem to be closed off to reflection.

Describing the process of interpreting a text, Gadamer speaks of 'the experience of being pulled up short by the text' (*TM*, p. 268). Prejudices reveal themselves as an experience of thwarted expectation when the familiar encounters the unfamiliar. Prejudices reveal themselves not reflectively but through the effect they have. Understanding is always a prejudicial anticipation of meaning frequently surprised by the unexpected and unanticipated.

The surprise is short lived. Alertness to new meanings and their effect unwittingly becomes part of the newly negotiated prejudicial structure of understanding. Heidegger's ontologizing of the hermeneutic circle allows Gadamer to rehabilitate prejudice in such a way. Prejudice is only a moment in a larger configuration, tradition.

In one of the fullest statements of what Gadamer understands by the term tradition, a notoriously slippery term to define, we are offered these thoughts:

> The [hermeneutic] circle ... is not formal in nature. It is neither subjective nor objective, but describes understanding as the interplay of the movement of tradition and the movement of the interpreter. The anticipation of meaning that governs our understanding of a text is not an act of subjectivity, but proceeds from the commonality that binds us to the tradition. But this commonality is constantly being formed in our relation to tradition. Tradition is not simply a permanent precondition; rather, we produce it ourselves inasmuch as we understand, participate in the evolution of tradition and hence determine it ourselves. (*TM*, p. 293)

Prejudice, fore-understanding, is grounded in commonality and agreement is rooted in tradition. But tradition is not a fixed entity, it is not a discarded trace left by the forward march of spirit or history, it is sustained by constant redefinition as the prereflective structures of understanding come into contact ('interplay') with the rest of tradition.

The temporality of understanding relates to the interpreter's situation. In seeking to understand a phenomenon the interpreter projects into the future (the 'anticipation of meaning') as the prejudices of the fore-understanding encounter something new (something yet to be interpreted). At the same time understanding is always simultaneously an encounter with the past ('the commonality that binds us to tradition'). Prejudices are silently and unreflectively inherited. Appreciation of Gadamer's notion of tradition is best achieved when considering the problems associated with understanding the past. When approaching, say, a document from the past the difficulty, for the interpreter, is to find a neutral position for interpretation. It is clearly inappropriate to impose present meanings upon the past and yet it seems a conceptual impossibility to dissolve the present and understand purely in terms of past meanings. In general terms, what is missing is some common denominator, some means whereby the bridge of historical distance can be crossed and present meanings brought into line with those of the past. On this matter Gadamer offers the following thought:

> Temporal distance is not something that must be overcome ... the important thing is to recognize temporal distance as a positive and productive condition enabling understanding. It is not a yawning abyss but is filled with the continuity of custom and tradition, in the light of which everything handed down presents itself to us. (*TM*, p. 297)

The very fact that both past and present (and future) are part of a larger configuration, tradition, is the key to overcoming the problem of historical distance. Past meanings and present meanings are not radically separate but fragments or moments within a relatively homogeneous tradition.

An interpreter stands within the ambit of a horizon and in interpreting an ancient text, for example, or seeking an understanding of cultures in the past (or even alien to that of the interpreter), he or she does not swap horizons around but 'fuses' them; he or she enters productively into the other horizon *without losing sight* of the initial horizon. In seeking to understand a text of the past the interpreter extends the horizon of the present to embrace and make contact with the horizon of the past. Every interpretation of the past amounts to a reinterpretation; not merely a reproduction but a creative production. Interpretations are not fixed but move as tradition itself moves.

III. DIALOGUE AND THE 'LOGIC OF QUESTION AND ANSWER'

Language's true existence is essentially mysterious and never revealed by the formal proposition or the statement. The proposition is taken to be static, timelessly true (or false), impervious to the accidents of history and circumstance, analysable irrespective of context, and immutably meaningful without reference to the motives and intentions of the utterer. This description of language is one Gadamer's hermeneutics places under sustained attack. The proposition militates against an ontological understanding of language. It suppresses its dynamic and historical qualities.

In a key section of *Truth and Method* ('The hermeneutic priority of the question', *TM*, pp. 362–79) and in many of the later essays, Gadamer speaks of dialogue as the real key to making sense of language. We can now see why non-formalizable dialogue and conversation will help break the spell of the logic of the proposition. Gadamer initially discusses the idea of dialogue in relation to the hermeneutical structure of understanding. The image of the dialogue not only reveals the constitution of language but also becomes a perfect metaphor for it. To appreciate this Gadamer offers a reappraisal of Socratic dialogue in the section in *Truth and Method* entitled 'The model of Platonic dialectic' (*TM*, pp. 362–9).

There is a long-standing tendency, in introducing beginners to the discipline of philosophy, to present the dialogues of Plato as elementary exercises in the art of straight, and often crooked, thinking. The device of *elenchus* and the procedures of formal logic, exemplified in Socrates's engagements with sophistry and rhetorical trickery, are seen as models of rational thought and argumentation. Gadamer's interest in Socratic argument concentrates on a neglected interpretation of dialectic as dialogue. On this reading the emphasis is not so much on the adversarial and combative winning of argument but a collective search for the truth of a matter at issue, where the various possible points of view are refined and examined.

In the early dialogues Socrates's description of himself as the midwife, present at the birth of truth, is telling. Against more formalistic interpretations of dialogue as procedural dialectic, Gadamer emphasizes a key element missing from the more formal accounts, 'openness'. Phenomenological description looks to the 'logical structure of openness' (*TM*, p. 362). Here 'logical' means openness to the *logos*. The reference is to *logos* as 'language', 'matter at issue', or 'concern' (*die Sache*). The idea of a systematic science of valid reasoning (what logic ultimately became) could not be further from what Gadamer, or, he infers, Socrates, has in mind. After all what would a systematic science of openness look like? Authentic dialogue, nothing more elevated than the quotidian to and fro of conversations in the agora (the Socratic dialogues were after all presented as spontaneous and unrehearsed conversations), has the structure of openness in the following senses: there is no prearranged agenda; the conversationalists just 'slip into' dialogue as we say, and, as we know from the early Socratic dialogues, reach no unanimous conclusions. The idea of openness, like the other key Gadamerian term 'play', indicates a refusal of closure, a resistance to attempts to systematize and limit the conversation with method or an imposed formal structure.

What are the limits of openness? 'The openness of a question is not boundless', answers Gadamer, 'It is limited by the horizon of the question. A question that lacks this horizon is, so to speak, floating' (*TM*, p. 363). The question limits and guides the conversation and holds the participants in thrall. Authentic dialogue is a constant deference to the conversation itself and invariably defers to the 'priority of the question' (*TM*, p. 363). Hostility to Socrates, where he is portrayed as the arch manipulator setting traps and Aunt Sally arguments for his interlocutors, engaging in endless logical and rhetorical battle to trick or trump sophistry, in a slavish attempt to win the argument, is not the only possible interpretation. On a more benign reading, the midwife is merely providing the conditions for the openness to be put in place: 'The Socratic dialectic – which leads, through its art of confusing the interlocutor, to ... knowledge – creates conditions for the question' (*TM*, p. 365).

Socrates's other self-description as the 'stingray' (in the *Meno*) is unrelated to an ability to silence interlocutors with deadly logic but to confounding those who foreclose truth, dogmatically resorting to answers and hence giving up on the question. The theme of openness is related to the question of the question: to ask a question is to bring something out into the open. As Gadamer states:

To ask a question means to bring it into the open. The openness of what is in question consists in the fact that the answer is not settled. It must still be undetermined, awaiting a decisive answer the significance of questioning consists in revealing the questionability of what is questioned. (*TM*, p. 363)

In one sense the conversation is pointless, being interminable and resisting resolution; in another it is fundamental to what we are as language-animals. Dialogue is not a progressive dialectic moving incrementally towards the truth, this is Hegelian distortion. Conversation has no *telos*, no point of resolution where divisions and conflicts are resolved. Dialogue is not a contribution to an expanding body of knowledge. The truth we seek is ultimately self-understanding. The revealed truths of the eternal dialogue accompany the written and spoken exchanges in tradition.

Hegel attempts to capture 'the totality of the determinants of thought' (*TM*, p. 369) as they are made manifest in the 'continuum of meaning' (*TM*, p. 369) in dialogue. By implication this will not work alongside the Hegelian commitment to a methodized structure of the dialectic where dialogue is reduced to monologue and seeks to 'carry out in advance what matures little by little in every genuine dialogue' (*TM*, p. 369). Of course the question remains, does Gadamer put enough critical distance between himself and Hegel? When it comes down to it, is Gadamer really a closet Hegelian?

Dialogue reaches far down into our being bringing to mind Hölderlin's 'we are a conversation.'[12] Dialogue extends beyond the character of language, touching ethical and political life. Gadamer implies an ethics of dialogue by suggesting that in our daily conversations we learn how to relate to each other. If dialogue is openness to the voice of the other there must be a preparedness to let the other speak. Notions of respect and obligation surround genuine dialogue. The ethics of duty, obligation, respect and discretion are all integral to the free flow of genuine dialogue and conversation.

There is also a suggestion of the need for courage to accept what may not be in one's own interests but favours others, and the existential burden of responsibility choice carries with it. Gadamer writes: 'Openness to the other ... involves recognizing that I must myself accept some things that are against me, even though no one forces me to do so' (*TM*, p. 361). There is an obligation to seek out the kernel of truth in what the other says, however crazy, misguided, unacceptable, or unpalatable it may first appear, for 'dialectic consists not in trying to discover the weakness of what is said, but in bringing out its real strength' (*TM*, p. 367). This defending the weak against the strong, learning the values of tolerance and respect for the other, hints at a possible hermeneutical ethics which Gadamer declines to develop but emerges in latent form in this section of *Truth and Method*.[13] In passing it is worth noting that liberalism is the political context best suited to a dialogical picture of language and social life. Everything John Stuart Mill champions in the realm of mature political debate: tolerance; respect for the other; diversity of points of view; the free exchange of ideas; and the fallible nature of truth are all of a piece with what Gadamer claims for authentic dialogue.

How does language-as-dialogue undermine language-as-proposition? Gadamer supplements the idea of dialogue with what the English philosopher and historian R. G. Collingwood calls the 'logic of question and answer'. Using Collingwood's original conception,[14] Gadamer turns it to his own advantage. Collingwood seeks to supplant the logic of the proposition; hence, it is curious that he chose to refer to the 'logic' of question and answer. J. P. Hogan, in his essay 'Hermeneutics and the logic of question and answer'[15] concludes that 'the logic of question and answer is a misnomer in that it goes far beyond the investigation of the logical form of the proposition'.[16] And Hogan, quoting Mink the historian, says '[the logic of question and answer] is not a theory of logic at all ... nor is it a theory of semantics, it is a hermeneutic'.[17]

For Collingwood every utterance, every statement about the world, even every proposition is, despite having the form of an assertion, an answer to a, in many cases, forgotten question. The 'logic of question and answer', outlined in his *An Autobiography*,[18] was originally devised as a stratagem for making sense of the events and artefacts of the past by reviving, as far as possible, the historical context of the original question. A professional interest in Roman archaeology inspired the procedure which proved useful in solving practical problems about the nature of the past. It first occurred to him when observing the Albert Memorial, which he initially found aesthetically repellent and readily dismissed. Overcoming his initial response he sought to make sense of the artefact by enquiring into the circumstance of its production rather than giving in to an initial unquestioning emotional response. He mused as follows:

> What relation was there ... between what he (the architect) had done and what he had tried to do? Had he tried to produce a beautiful thing; a thing, I meant, which we should have thought beautiful? ... Was I looking in it for things it did not possess, and either ignoring or despising those it did? (Collingwood, 1939, pp. 29–30)

This mode of enquiry readily extends to the interpretation of texts. He derided the absurdity of his 'realist' (that is, analytical) contemporaries[19] who treated ancient philosophical tracts as though they were repositories of timeless argument. Against this he favoured the more historically sensitive procedure of treating a work as a totality of meaning, whose sense could only be disclosed when the text is treated as an answer to a question: a question formulated by the author or, in the case of historical events, the reconstructed enquiry into the activities of the key players.

The same sort of procedure is applied to the interpretation of texts in the history of philosophy. With Descartes's *Discours de la Méthode* for example, the historian of philosophy would be better placed if he or she sought the broad brushwork of the questions that provoked Descartes into writing, as opposed to getting lost in abstract argumentative detail, fruitlessly logic-chopping a way through the text.[20] For Collingwood, and it is a dictum Gadamer endorses, truth is revealed when the text is awoken, opening up novel lines of enquiry and drawing the reader into dialogue. Without the interplay of question and answer the philosophical work remains inert, a seemingly lifeless repository of argumentative positions dislocated from historical context. Strict analysis of philosophical texts has only limited value if the significance of a past work is to be fully explored. Gadamer notes the following:

> If one analyses with logical methods the arguments in a Platonic dialogue, [one] shows inconsistencies, fills in gaps, unmasks false deductions, and so on, one can achieve a certain gain in clarity. But does one learn to read Plato by proceeding in this way? Does one make his questions one's own? Does one succeed in learning from Plato instead of just confirming one's own superiority? What applies to Plato in this case applies by extension to all philosophy. (*PHGG*, pp. 38–9)

The 'logic of question and answer' describes the dialogical movement between interpreter and text and the search for the wider meaning and significance carried by the text.

For all his admiration of the critique of realism and the rejection of the logic of the proposition, Gadamer finds fault with Collingwood's logic for 'unfortunately he never elaborated it systematically' (*TM*, p. 370). Gadamer sees in the new logic not just a procedure for interpreting texts and assessing historical events but a hermeneutical 'logic' at work in every act of understanding. Gadamer is critical of Collingwood for other reasons. Attention to the historical easily slips into a dubious historicism. There is also the suggestion that Collingwood still thought in terms of a rather traditional historical truth. Hogan explains:

> Gadamer argues that Collingwood fell into the historicist trap and limited his questioning process to the possibility of reconstructing the author's or

agent's original intention. The claim of *Truth and Method* is that the sense of the text goes beyond the original intention of the author or agent.[21]

Collingwood confined his analysis to recovering intentionality. The meaning of an event, like the meaning of a text, goes well beyond the purposive control of the agent or author.

What is the meaning and historical significance of the Battle of Trafalgar (one of Collingwood's examples discussed by Gadamer)?[22] The logic of question and answer might suggest a search for the agents' intentions. 'What was Nelson's battle plan?' is a useful place to start when investigating the historical event we now know as the Battle of Trafalgar. Collingwood is right to make this kind of reconstructive connection but the hermeneutical problem arises here: Nelson's battle plan is more than the sum total of historical documents recording the event. Reclaiming intentions as the key to unlocking historical problems is a dangerous activity. It assumes the agent's complete control over the meanings they recorded and excludes the hermeneutical dimension. Take all the documents you will, the element of interpretation is still required. Did Nelson know Nelson's battle plan? Why assume a neat battle plan? What is the test of authenticity? What if Nelson played everything by ear, that is, had no battle plan?

Answering historical questions by contextualizing records of events is a reasonable way of proceeding but intentions are not some historical given. Even when taken for granted, unless you presuppose crude behaviourism, they prove notoriously difficult to establish. If the agent's self-description is a guide to intentions, how are Nelson's intentions reconstructed? This raises all sorts of questions about subjectivity. Gadamer moves beyond subjectivity. The individual's relationship to history, like his or her relationship to language, moves well beyond intentionality. 'History does not belong to us', Gadamer claims, 'we belong to it. Long before we understand ourselves through the process of self-examination, we understand ourselves in a self-evident way in the family, society, and state in which we live' (*TM*, p. 276).

If Collingwood sees historical reconstruction as little more than the establishment of intentions and mental states then he fails to do justice to the historical, and, further, will distort the hermeneutical.[23] The logic of question and answer is not just a procedure for unravelling historical events: in treating the history of philosophy as an unending dialogue between its *dramatis personae*, it describes a vital feature of human understanding.

Truth and Method gestures towards a way of writing the history of philosophy as the enactment of the logic of question and answer; here Gadamer and Collingwood are in complete agreement. Plato, Aristotle, Augustine, Hegel, Schleiermacher, Dilthey, Collingwood, and Heidegger are all participants in the dialogical unfolding of the Western tradition. The suggestion of an identity between philosophy and its history brings to mind Hegel's 'The history of philosophy is philosophy and philosophy is the history of philosophy'. Gadamer draws upon the strengths of this position without capitulating to the sense of an impending closure of the Hegelian system. The dialogue within the logic of question and answer is interminable.

IV. THE SPECULATIVE STRUCTURE OF LANGUAGE

Truth and Method concludes with the thought that language is, by its very nature, speculative. What Gadamer means by this is by no means obvious. It makes most sense when considered in relation to the dialectical logic of question and answer. The main discussion of the speculative is in the Part Three of *Truth and Method* ('The ontological shift of hermeneutics guided by language') and it suffers, like much of the rest of the section, from being less coherent than the earlier parts of the work. When quizzed by Grondin about the evident vagueness in Part Three Gadamer answered completely sincerely that this third part even appeared to himself as linguistically indistinct. He goes on to explain that 'he had run out of breath at the end of the work on so long a text, so that the third part was composed more hastily, whereby the precision of the formulations was given less attention'.[24] The 'linguistic indistinctness' demonstrates, no doubt, the truth of the hermeneutical belief that the author is not in supreme control of the meanings a text generates.

Plato is important for Gadamer's account of language in two important respects. The logic of question and answer is fundamentally Platonic emerging as it does from the conversational narrative of Socratic dialogues. The dialogues not only offer conversation as the model of philosophical procedure but they incorporate the structure of the dialectic itself. The process of questioning is really, despite appearances to the contrary, an unsystematic, and playful, unfolding of the various dimensions to truth. A playful element to the dialogues is not merely a contribution to the dramatic effect, it is a comment upon our relationship to truth.

Truth is not established by examining the relative strength of arguments or procedures of verification but by clearing 'the path on which the subject matter led' (*TM*, p. 464) by way of public debate. Platonic dialectic is guided not by the thoughts and ideas of the interlocutors but the subject matter that holds all participants under its spell. Further, 'dialectic is nothing but the art of conducting a conversation and especially of revealing the mistakes in one's opinions through the process of questioning and yet further questioning'

(*TM*, p. 464). Despite modern temptations to reduce dialectic to a formal procedure (thesis-antithesis-synthesis or affirmation-negation-negation of negation in the Fichtean and Hegelian versions) Gadamer reminds us of the original Platonic formulation where the contrived logic of procedure is over-shadowed by the free play of open-ended dialogue. Dialectic is not limited by a logical structure any more than language is.

Plato's dialectic is found wanting. Although Plato speaks of the soul *in dialogue* with itself, hinting at a conception of mind modelled on the linguistic, he ultimately downgrades the word making it, like the objects of the sensible world, just a simulacrum of something more real. Plato's self-dialoguing soul is only attained when the visible realm of the uttered and the audible is transcended, when the intelligible sphere of the supremely rational is reached, as the analogy of the 'divided line' in the *Republic* makes plain. So the dialogue of the soul with itself is only a dialogue in the most extended and metaphorical sense, trapped as the soul is within the mysteriously speechless world of the *eidos* or forms, far removed from the domain of living dialogue and conversation.

As the *Republic* and the *Cratylus* suggest, ordinary language is capable of no more than representation (*mimesis*) and the validity of the word is only to be guaranteed once transcended by the move from the realm of opinion or *doxa* to the non-linguistic heights beyond. Plato's dialectic flourishes in the intelligible realm of reason once the reliance upon the linguistic has been superseded. It is difficult to establish precisely Gadamer's relationship to Plato, a figure in the history of philosophy to whom he constantly returns, starting from the time of his first book (1931), translated as *Plato's Dialectical Ethics*.[25] In 1993 when told that his hermeneutics was 'an instance of the anti-Platonism of our age' Gadamer declared, teasingly, to the contrary, 'I am a Platonist' (quoted in Wachterhauser, 1999, p. xi). On other occasions he is at pains to distance himself from Platonic positions. His hermeneutical readings of Plato[26] flow against the tide of much modern classical scholar-ship, especially work in the analytic tradition,[27] observing as it does the hermeneutical principle that one understands forwards as it were; Plato in the light of Hegel and early Plato in the light of the later work.[28]

The elements of dialectic appropriate to language never fully blossom in Plato as dialectic is seen as a realm exclusive to languageless reason. On Gadamer's rejection of the Platonic dialectic Weinsheimer observes how 'dialectic takes place not in the wordless realm of the logos but instead in spoken language, not in the opposition of statement and counterstatement but in the exchanges of conversation and dialogue, in question and answer rather than assertion' (Weinsheimer, 1985, p. 250).

Plato's dialectic leads onward and upward to the infinite truth of a mind fully present to itself. Gadamer's informal dialectic moves from projection to retraction, affirmation to disconfirmation, triumph to despair. It does not offer a royal road to self-authenticating truth – this is a modern philosophical myth. A more detailed comparison between Gadamer and the modern Platonist, Hegel, shows how the hermeneutical dialectic lacks an all-knowing teleological character. Language ceaselessly shadows the unpredictable but non-arbitrary dialectic.

The to and fro of understanding, the oscillation between reader and text, the play of everyday conversation, and the movement between linguistic rules and their application is dialectical. This is not a dialectic of reason, where rationality suffers reversals and affirmations; it is a dialectic at work within the self-unfolding of language, constituting, under another description, the dynamic of tradition. The idea of a 'self-unfolding' process may, to analytically trained ears, sound like an idealist process; as if the juggernaut of Language fails to engage fully with language-users and rides independently over the thoughts, intentions, and desires of its speakers. This extreme form of 'linguistic idealism'[29] is not what Gadamer has in mind although it has been used as a stick to beat him by his critics. Alternatively, 'self-unfolding' suggests that language is always more than the sum total of those thoughts, wishes, and desires to which language gives rise and cannot be reducible to a mentalist story. Language is socially produced and its rules and conventions emerge from the intricacies of collective historical life. This idea Gadamer readily agrees to but this does not commit him to the view that language, on this description, is reducible to its constitutive rules and conventions, nor is language detached from the undergrowth of everyday articulations. Language is always greater than its users just as the game is always greater than its individual players. The question of the autonomy of language will be considered again in relation to Wittgenstein.

Language is both dialectical and speculative according to Gadamer. To reclaim a forgotten dimension to 'speculation' we are reminded of one of its original senses. The word 'refers to the mirror relation' (*TM*, p. 465) and recalls *speculum*, the Latin word for mirror. Gadamer continues:

Being reflected involves a constant substitution of one thing for another. When something is reflected in something else, say, the castle in the lake, it means that the lake throws back the image of the castle. The mirror image is essentially connected with the actual sight of the thing through the medium of the observed. It has no being of its own; it is like an 'appearance' that is not itself and yet allows the thing to appear by means of a mirror image. The real mystery of a reflection is the intangibility of the image, the sheer reproduction hovering before the mind's eye. (*TM*, p. 466)

The mirror relation, by analogy, points to something at the heart of language. Just as the reflection owes its existence to the object so language reflects being. Establishing the vital link between language and being is the culmination of a good deal of the exposition in *Truth and Method*. But we must be careful with this idea of reflection. Reflection is not mere representation; we have not moved full circle and returned to the designative idea of representation discussed in Chapter 1. The castle reflected in the lake owes its existence to the castle but the reflection, for all its ontological dependence upon the object, is not reducible to it, hence Gadamer's idea of the 'mystery' and 'intangibility' of the image which always goes beyond its immediate aetiology. The image is speculative in the sense that it cannot be dogmatically, that is, non-speculatively, reduced to an identical copy of itself. The move is to another sense of speculative, namely that which is not foreclosed by identity or reproduction: language is more associated with the contraries non-identity and production.

Gadamer's criticism of Hegel in *Truth and Method*[30] centres on the idea of the speculative; the *locus classicus* for Hegel's exposition of this is in the Preface to the *Phenomenology of Spirit*.[31] Hegel uncovers the element of the speculative as 'an instinctive prefiguring of logical reflection' (*TM*, p. 469). The speculative operates in the realm of the philosophical. There is something unique about philosophical propositions in that the relationship between subject and predicate in a philosophical statement moves not just dialectically but speculatively. This is Gadamer's example:

> The philosophical proposition does not pass over from the subject-concept to another concept that is placed in relation to it; it states the truth of the subject in the form of the predicate. 'God is one' does not mean that it is a property of God's to be one, but that it is God's nature to be a unity. (*TM*, p. 466)

Gadamer does not fully explain and explore this difficult exegesis of Hegel but what he has in mind is something like the following. 'God is one' is a speculative proposition in that God's oneness succeeds to the idea of his unity, an idea that is not contained in either the subject or the predicate of the statement. We might liken this to the castle and the reflection of the castle since the reflection, like God's unity, supersedes its origin. 'God is one' is not a statement about a state of affairs, in this sense it is speculative, 'it presents the unity of the concept' (*TM*, p. 467). Gadamer suggests that the idea of the speculative is appropriate to a description of all language, but Hegel stopped short of acknowledging this. The limitation in Hegel, according to Joel Weinsheimer, is that he eventually 'dissolves the speculative in the dialectical'. Of the difference he observes:

The distinction is not preserved because as heir of the Greek logos philosophy, Hegel confines his attention to propositions. He therefore subordinates language to statement and thereby subordinates speculative relation (which retains the difference between a reflection and what it reflects) to dialectical identity, unmediated by language. (Weinsheimer, 1985, p. 252)

Weinsheimer captures the heart of the Gadamerian critique of Hegel when he speaks of the subordination of language to statement. Witnessed throughout this chapter is Gadamer's portrait of dialogical language of the 'lifeworld' subverting the proposition as a complete, discrete unit of linguistic meaning truthfully corresponding to a particular state of affairs. So although Hegel got to the point of identifying the speculative he failed to see it as a dimension of language and located it within the self-unfolding of the concept. For this reason he failed to see the speculative as a characteristic of language, instead he identifies it as a formal property of spirit.

NOTES

1. The most authoritative work on the history of the writing of this book is Jean Grondin's, 'On the composition of *Truth and Method*', Schmidt (1995), pp. 23–38.
2. *TM*, pp. 474–5.
3. Not that carefully according to Manfred Frank and Andrew Bowie who charge Gadamer with misrepresenting Schleiermacher's hermeneutics on the question of divination and the alleged psychological approach to hermeneutics. See Bowie's Introduction to Schleiermacher's *'Hermeneutics and Criticism' and Other Writings* (1998).
4. T. Kiesel, 'The happening of tradition: the hermeneutics of Gadamer and Heidegger', in Hollinger (1985), p. 7.
5. See *TM*, pp. 265–71.
6. Bernstein (1983), pp. 151–2.
7. An example of this kind of thinking can be found in Norman (1976), 'The dilemma of epistemology', pp. 9–28.
8. Discussion of tradition in *Truth and Method* is principally pp. 357–61, 389–91, and 537–8.
9. The Habermas–Gadamer debate centres round the notion of tradition; once again see O'Neill (1976). Eagleton's outburst against Gadamer's treatment of tradition is in Eagleton (1983), pp. 72–4.
10. Quoted in *TM*, p. 266.
11. Gadamer's use of the hermeneutical circle highlights the structure of incompleteness in interpretation. Does this mean Gadamer is not interested in the Heideggerian project of fundamental ontology? This is an important question. I suspect the frequently repeated 'Being that can be understood is language' means the being question is always an issue for Gadamer. For details of the relationship to Heidegger see the essays in Gadamer (1994a).

12. Michael Hamburger translates as follows: 'Much have men learnt. Have called by
    their names many of those in Heaven since we have been a discourse and able to
    hear each other' (from F. Hölderlin, 'Conciliator, you that no longer believed
    in...', *Friedrich Hölderlin: Poems and Fragments*, London: Anvil Press Poetry,
    1994, pp. 445–53).

13. P. Christopher Smith has sought to develop a Gadamerian ethics based on the
    ideas of tradition and custom. See Smith (1991).

14. According to Gadamer Collingwood took the logic of question and answer from
    Croce. See *TM*, pp. 370ff.

15. Hogan (1987), p. 265.

16. Hogan (1987), p. 265.

17. Hogan (1987), p. 265.

18. Published in German, at Gadamer's instigation, as *Denken*. For details of this and
    the English original see *TM*, pp. 370ff.

19. He was seen as a singular voice. He was one of the last of the British Hegelians
    and his attack upon scientific realism, which is after all what the logic of question
    and answer opposes, fell on deaf ears at Oxford.

20. The logic of question and answer is potentially a fruitful procedure in
    constructing a coherent narrative of the history of philosophy and unmasking the
    ahistorical pretensions of what passes for this discipline in the analytical tradition.
    (Collingwood was acutely aware of this when he castigated his Oxford 'realist'
    colleagues in the 1930s for a failure to see what was happening in Germany at the
    time. On this matter, see Collingwood (1939), especially the final chapter.)

21. Hogan (1987), p. 273.

22. *TM*, p. 371.

23. Hogan thinks Gadamer unfair to Collingwood on this point since there is allow-
    ance for some measure of mediation and, albeit fitfully, Collingwood is
    'committed to the radical historicity of the interpreter'. He admits that Colling-
    wood 'puts more emphasis upon context and original intention' and puts this
    down to Collingwood's (principal) instinct as a historian. See Hogan (1987), pp.
    274 and 280.

24. J. Grondin, 'On the composition of *Truth and Method*', in Schmidt (1995), p. 37.

25. Gadamer (1991).

26. Collected in *Dialogue and Dialectic: Eight Hermeneutical Studies on Plato*,
    Gadamer (1980a).

27. This is vividly demonstrated in an exchange between Gadamer and Nicholas P.
    White. See Griswold (1988), pp. 247–66.

28. See 'Gadamer's dialectical Platonism' in Wachterhauser (1999).

29. A term that comes out of analytic philosophy, originally with reference to certain
    ways of reading Wittgenstein. It is taken up by scholars in relation to Gadamer.
    See, for example, Moran (2000), p. 282.

30. *TM*, pp. 464–74. Gadamer defines his relationship to Hegel as a 'tension-filled
    proximity'. Detailed accounts of Gadamer's relationship to Hegel can be found in
    Hegel's Dialectic (Gadamer, 1976a) and the two essays on Hegel ('Hegel's philo-
    sophy and its after effects until today' and 'The heritage of Hegel') in *Reason in
    the Age of Science* (Gadamer, 1981).

31. Hegel (1977), Preface, pp. 1–45.

CHAPTER 4

Wittgenstein and the Logics of Language

Everything descriptive of a language-game is part of logic

(*OC*, §56)

I. TWO WITTGENSTEINS?

A. The Tractatus Logico-Philosophicus

The *Tractatus Logico-Philosophicus*, the only significant work published in Wittgenstein's lifetime, is a distillation of his thought in the 'early' period. Philosophical logic is a key thread in the work, as the title suggests, but it is underpinned by a designative theory of language. 'The totality of propositions is language' (*TLP*, 4.001), he asserts, and 'a proposition is a picture of reality' (*TLP*, 4.021), making genuine language propositional and genuine propositions pictorial. Designation is the power to represent possible states of affairs. The ambiguities and imprecisions of 'colloquial' language (*TLP*, 4.002) hide from view the strict one-to-one logical relation between propositions and the world. Everyday language lacks unitary form making it 'humanly impossible to gather immediately the *logic of language*' (*TLP*, 4.002). Meaning is rigidly circumscribed and conforms to a strict logical structure. The complete arrangement (in 'logical space') of possible propositions gives a total picture of the world in so far as can legitimately be represented. All that can be said about the world is all that we can say about the world paraphrases Wittgenstein's tautological conclusion. This is expressed more rhetorically in the oracular, 'Whereof we cannot speak thereof we must keep silent' (*TLP*, 7). Absent in the *Tractatus* is any attempt to give relevance to the workings of ordinary language; the social contexts of history and culture are philosophically insignificant. Also missing is an appreciation of dialogical interplay so central in the hermeneutical tradition. These points are highlighted for two reasons. First, because they offer such a contrast to the later work on language, where the tables are turned and the specifics of ordinary language (conversations, imaginary dialogues) are examined in obsessive detail, replacing the Tractarian emphasis upon logic form. Second, because they highlight the distance from Gadamer in the early work and the apparent convergence in Wittgenstein's later work.

B. The Picture of Language in the Later Wittgenstein

Some years after the publication of the *Tractatus*,[1] in the late 1920s, Wittgenstein returned to the life of professional philosophy after an extended period of absence from academic life. The 'later' work, as it has come to be known, the extensive writings between 1945 and his death in 1951, is characterized by a period of radical questioning, followed by an outright repudiation, of the *Tractatus*. The process is more or less complete when, in 1945, he recognizes the 'grave mistakes' (*PI*, p. x) in his 'old way of thinking' (*PI*, p. x). The *Philosophical Investigations*, the collection of posthumously published writings Wittgenstein was preparing for publication, is a detailed record of his struggle to break with the past and develop a new way of thinking, one capturing the expressive richness and diversity of linguistic forms (so evidently lacking in the *Tractatus*).

Correspondence and biographies confirm dissatisfaction with the *Tractatus* which is progressively undermined by what eventually superseded the 'old way of thinking'. Its displacement matured over a considerable number of years although there were occasional key moments, flashes of insight.[2] One such epiphany occurred during a chance conversation with his colleague and friend from Cambridge, the Italian Marxist economist, Pierro Sraffa. The tale is recounted in Norman Malcolm's memoir and it is worth quoting in full:

> One day (they were riding, I think, on a train) when Wittgenstein was insisting that a proposition and that which it describes must have the same 'logical form', the same 'logical multiplicity', Sraffa made a gesture, familiar to Neapolitans as meaning something like disgust or contempt, of brushing the underneath of his chin with an outward sweep of the finger tips of one hand. And he asked: 'What is the logical form of *that*?' Sraffa's example produced in Wittgenstein the feeling that there was an absurdity in the insistence that a proposition and what it describes must have the same 'form'. This broke the hold on him of the conception that a proposition must be literally a 'picture' of the reality it describes. (Malcolm, 1984, pp. 57–8)[3]

The anecdote is important because it obviously crystallizes Wittgenstein's nagging doubts about the *Tractatus*. The gesture's meaning does not derive from a connection with a particular feeling of disgust or a capacity to name or describe a state of affairs: meanings overreach the one-to-one naming relationship, even extending into the realm of non-verbal communication. Meaning here is strongly expressive, being part of the fabric of a certain way of life ('form of life', as Wittgenstein was to describe it later). The gesture's specificity, its application within a limited geographical region, is an affirmation of its cultural origins. The fact that the brushing of the chin is done in a certain way, within a specific context, must also have had significance for Wittgenstein when set against his earlier position. Key elements in the later 'language-game'; the intrusion of gesture, embodiment, and the practical dimensions of context generally, constitute irreducible aspects of the game. The example of the Neapolitan gesture is a vivid illustration of the limitations of the *Tractatus* and offers an alternative picture of language, one clearly moving in a more *expressivist* direction.

Another aspect of living language Wittgenstein draws upon in the formation of the later position, contributing in no small part to the move away from the *Tractatus*, is reflection upon the process of its acquisition. In the 1920s,[4] in the wilderness years away from philosophy, he worked as a primary schoolteacher in remote locations in rural Austria. During this time he published, at his own expense, a short *Dictionary for Elementary Schools*.[5] This signifies, perhaps, a move away from the lofty heights of the grand abstraction of the *Tractatus* to a consideration of the more practical aspects of language acquisition, particularly orthography. The organic process of learning highlights developmental aspects; language is a going concern long before individuals become skilful within it. Language as a process of skill acquisition takes Wittgenstein ever further from the *Tractatus* and becomes a central motif in the later work. The reference to Saint Augustine's *Confessions* focuses on language learning and the *Investigations* is full of constant reminders, when inquiring into the meaning of a word, to think back to the conditions of its initial acquisition ('Always ask yourself: How did we *learn* the meaning of this word?' (*PI*, §77)).

From 1929 onwards the working model for language shifts. The hierarchy, with elementary propositions at the apex and the philosophically uninteresting loose talk of everyday language at the bottom, is replaced by a more egalitarian vision. Wittgenstein aims to jettison the idea of a logic to which all language conforms. The *Philosophical Investigations* wilfully sets out to challenge this very notion.

How successful is Wittgenstein? Although the later work moves away from the earlier logic of the *Tractatus*, it stays within its domain albeit more parochially defined; the ghost of the 'logics of language' infiltrates the later work. The new emphasis is upon the multiplicity and variety of language-games and the ways they are woven into the fabric of the rituals and practices of everyday life. This said there is a strong sense that escape from a *Tractatus* model of the calculus is never finally complete.

II. LANGUAGE-GAMES

The idea of the language-game has great therapeutic power, a cure for that malignant philosophical condition, a 'craving for generality' (*BBB*, p. 17),[6] It is an illusory need, an addiction to abstraction, professional philosophers particularly could well do without. When language is likened to a game it creates an awareness of the sheer, almost endless, diversity of types and instances of words, of speech, of linguistic forms, a remedy for that dangerous fixation on the universal and the essential. To picture language as a game is to see not essence and unity, as in the *Tractatus*, but diversity, endless variety.

There is no universally agreed definition of the 'game', no one game of which all localized games are mere shadows; to search for this is to fall under the spell of that most ancient 'craving for generality', the hunt for Platonic essences. Wittgenstein's later work makes way for overlapping variegated logics, but is it the informal logics of hermeneutical expression or the original Tractarian logic of the calculus?

There is a wide variety of textual references to actual and possible language-games in the later writings but Wittgenstein acknowledges three main types. These are referred to as *primitive language-games* (*PI*, §2), and *language-games as objects of comparison* 'which are meant to throw light on the facts of our language by way not only of similarities, but also of dissimilarities' (*PI*, §130). There is also what one might call the *totality of language-games*.

Primitive language-games are either the unsophisticated language of a 'primitive' (preindustrial? preliterate?) people, or more frequently 'primitive forms of language' (*BBB*, p. 17), the elementary uses of language, as in the rudimentary speech of children. The 'primitive forms of language' are 'simpler than those we use ... [in] our highly complicated everyday language' (*BBB*, p. 17) but the difference is merely one of scale. Wittgenstein has in mind the language-games of language-acquisition, particularly those enacted by adults and children through 'ostensive definition'; the socially regulated practice of indicating the meanings of words by pointing to an associated object. This is paradigmatic of a primitive language-game.[7] Ostensive definition does not in itself conjure up a world of meaning. On the contrary, naming through pointing is more of a ceremony or ritual than mediation between word and world, presupposing a background of acculturation, a learnt nexus of social activities. The practice of pointing and naming is built into many of the 'teaching-children-elementary-uses-of-words' language-games. Trouble occurs when this is taken as a model for language acquisition itself, when the whole of language is reduced to an idealized form. Ostension is actually just one of the many ways names are learnt.

In likening the acquisition of a language to a game Wittgenstein is emphasizing both the absence of a necessary relationship between words and things, undermining designative theories and bringing out an arbitrary dimension to meaning, and the fact that language acquires its signification through social practice. Occasionally, Wittgenstein speaks of 'forms of life' (*Lebensformen*) (*PI*, §§19, 23, 241); these are the larger practical contexts in which the living language-games flourish: '"So you are saying that human agreement decides what is true and what is false?" – It is what human beings say that is true and false; and they agree in the *language* they use. That is not agreement in opinions but in form of life' (*PI*, §241). In isolating language from its practical contexts, a not uncommon practice of philosophers, 'language goes on holiday'.

Paring down a natural language for a more perspicacious view of its operations, is to depict a primitive language game. There is the suggestion that this does violence to the actuality of language-games which are not so readily teased apart. The description of builders, fetching and carrying slabs in the early stages of the *Investigations*, is an illustration of a possible primitive language game (*PI*, §2). Here Wittgenstein's builders play the 'game' of issuing orders and fetching and carrying slabs on a building site. This is just one relatively trivial game but it shows how an isolated 'language game ... brings into prominence the fact that the *speaking* of language is part of an activity' (*WR*, p. 47). Activities accompany forms of address in specific ways; the meaning of the command 'Slab!' is defined by the context.

A language-game is invariably accompanied by regulated human activity, providing the necessary context for meaning.

Wittgenstein speaks of language-games in the second sense:

> Our clear and simple language-games are not preparatory studies for a future regularization of language – as it were first approximations, ignoring friction and air-resistance. The language-games are rather set up as objects of comparison which are meant to throw light on the facts of our language by way not only of similarities, but also dissimilarities. (*PI*, §130)

Simplified language-games are devised in contrast to the more complex everyday games as a way of highlighting neglected or hidden aspects: 'Our method is not merely to enumerate actual usages of words, but rather deliberately to invent new ones, some of them because of their absurd appearance'

(*BBB*, p. 28). A similar idea is conveyed when he says, 'Nothing is more important for teaching us to understand the concepts we have than constructing fictitious one' (*CV*, p. 74).

The philosopher's 'craving for generality' permeates a general theory of language. Wittgenstein, throughout the *Investigations*, struggles with the temptation to find that illusive Archimedean point from which to '*command a clear view* of the use of words' (*PI*, §122). He is quick to draw back in the realization that such commanding heights are unavailable ('I don't know my way about' (*PI*, §123) is a more realistic description of our involvement in language). Resorting to cliché, there is no escaping the 'web of words', no meta-game outside the clutter and imprecision of regular language-games to give that 'clear view' so infuriatingly out of sight. To gain partial clarity and insight invented language-games fulfil a useful purpose serving as a guide to the actually existing ones. This is possibly what Wittgenstein has in mind when he speaks of the 'importance of finding and inventing *intermediate cases*' (*PI*, §122). The *Investigations* is full of whimsical games (reminiscent of the croquet match in Lewis Carroll's *Alice in Wonderland*).[8] For example, try playing the game of getting the left hand to give the right hand a gift (*PI*, §268). The impossibility here draws our attention to what is required for the ceremony of the gift – and what is missing here. It also casts light on the nature of language:

> Why can't my right hand give my left hand money? – My right hand can put it into my left hand. My right hand can write a deed of gift and my left hand a receipt. – But the further practical consequences would not be those of a gift. When the left hand has taken the money from the right etc., we shall ask: 'Well and what of it?' And the same could be asked if a person had given himself a private definition of a word; I mean, if he has said the word to himself and at the same time has directed his attention to himself and at the same time has directed his attention to a sensation. (*PI*, §268)

To combat the belief that the word 'pain' is only to be understood through a direct first-hand experience of pain, for example, Wittgenstein invites us to play a beetle-in-a-box game. The rules of the game are alarmingly simple: 'Suppose everyone had a box with something in it: we call it a "beetle". No one can look into anyone else's box, and everyone says he knows what a beetle is only by looking at his beetle' (*PI*, §293). If the word 'beetle' has a place in the language of those playing the game then, Wittgenstein adds, 'The thing in the box has no place in the language-game at all; not even as a something (for) the box might even be empty' (*PI*, §293).

The unplayable beetle-in-a-box language-game exposes the redundancy of a subjective image to account for the word 'beetle'. The mental image of a first-hand experience of pain has no part to play in our everyday uses of the word 'pain'. 'Pain', like every other word, is meaningful as part of an actually existing language-game. The procedure of comparing past impressions with current ones is philosophically dubious and runs counter to everyday linguistic experience and practice.

The 'disease' of mentalism, the misguided process of seeking to authenticate words via an inner mental act, is an 'idle ceremony', a stultifying self-reference not unlike the person who says, 'I know how tall I am' and puts his hand on his head to prove it (*PI*, §279). The life-blood of language is the tacit agreements, conventions, and consensus, unreflectively, silently disseminated through the manifold language-games.

The view that language requires individual acts of authentication to make meaning possible is a subjectivist dream. The 'already there' of language is the simple fact that we always operate within a vast network of variegated, overlapping, preexisting language-games, picked up and utilized by the apprentice language-user. To learn a language(-game) is to 'master a technique' (*PI*, §§150, 199, 692). Such dominance assumes institutionalized preformed agreements, the practical ability to enter into the activity of the game.

In the posthumous writings published after the *Philosophical Investigations*, Wittgenstein slips readily into speaking of *the* rather than *a* language-game: this is the position I called 'the totality of language-games'. A tendency to move away from the particularity and individuality of the various games is most evident in *On Certainty*. For example, in disputes involving a clash of cultures Wittgenstein asks whether we might be 'using our language-game as a base from which to *combat* [another]' (*OC*, §609). Here language-game is synonymous with natural language. The shift from 'language-games' to 'language' is not an indication of a return to a universal form, ignoring the variety and specificity of the games, it is an acknowledgement that language is no more than the manifold games of which it is constituted. The slogan 'There is nothing outside the language-games' summarizes Wittgenstein's stance here, echoing Jacques Derrida's 'There is nothing outside the text'.

III. RULES AND RULE-FOLLOWING

In likening language to games Wittgenstein draws attention to their practical dimension. Game playing is more than the formal manipulation of rules. Play is rule-governed no doubt but it is, first and foremost, a practical activity. In like fashion linguistic activity is made up of criss-crossing, variegated patterns of usage, underwritten not by a strict logical schema or merely formal procedure but by the habituated regularities of social praxis.

In team games there is more to the activity than mere regulated play. Team spirit, the style and flair of the players defining the character of the game, the playful, ludic element ('playing the game'); these factors are not peripheral but at the heart of what the game is. There is a certain indefinable element we may call the 'spirit' of the game that cannot be encapsulated in a description of the rules. Rules themselves have an imprecise, indeterminate quality and are in constant need of reinterpretation.

It is here that a chasm opens up between Wittgenstein and Gadamer. Wittgenstein plays down the interpretive element necessary for the application of linguistic rules; it is specifically on this point that I want to claim Wittgenstein is unable to move from the brittle calculus model of language to the more open domain of hermeneutics. Wittgenstein is committed to the idea that the linguistic rules of the customary are uninterpretable (*PI*, §§199, 200). Conceivably the failure to make a 'hermeneutical' turn and see in language the necessity for interpretation gives rise to the many problems associated with Wittgenstein's position.

A good deal of controversy surrounds §§198–242 of the *Investigations*, often known as the section on 'rules and rule-following'. For many it is the cornerstone of Wittgenstein's later position. As with so much of the later work the various voices in the text advance a variety of opposing perspectives and it is difficult to find amongst them an authoritative voice, if such a voice exists.[9]

Wittgenstein's deliberations on rules emerge from a cluster of questions relating to meaning, understanding, and interpretation. The rules under discussion start out (*PI*, §§197, 200) as the rules of games such as chess but gradually rules in general are considered. Wittgenstein considers any rule-governed activity going beyond the playing of games to activities as varied as the use of language ('language-games') and the ability to perform calculations and internalize theorems in mathematics.

The initial catalyst for the rules discussion in the *Investigations* is a pedagogical debate[10] about what it is to *learn* and demonstrate an ability to *follow* and obey a rule correctly. Immediately he discounts recourse to intuition, insight, decision, that is, strictly cognitive activities (*PI*, §186). Mentalist accounts are excluded for the aim is to show how rule following is learnt and taught, emerging, as it does, from a network of social agreements rather than a causal story about self-generated rational principles. And rule-following is *praxis*, ability, a 'knowing how-to' rather than a 'knowing that'.

The section on rule-following is a foil to mentalist accounts resorting to introspection to explain the capacity to 'know' what a rule entails and have the capacity to apply it. Mentalism gives rise to the problem of self-reference.

The monadic rule-follower is like the mythical 'private language'-user who lacks a standard other than fallible memory to generate regularity. In the absence of publicly checkable criteria, appearance and reality converge: 'to *think* one is obeying a rule is not to obey a rule ... it is not possible to obey a rule "privately": otherwise thinking one was obeying a rule would be the same thing as obeying it' (*PI*, §202).

What overrides the insecure solipsism of self-reference is the public realm of actually existing regularities, external criteria acting as checks and balances upon inappropriate application: 'The word "agreement" and the word "rule" are *related* to one another ...' (*PI*, §224). Following a rule does not depend upon a body of knowledge, it is simply the *ability* to follow publicly arranged and verifiable 'agreements'. Of the agreements that make language possible he says they are based upon 'judgements' (*PI* §242). I take this to mean that at bottom agreement can only get off the ground on the assumption that we, as a species, are structured in similar ways, biologically and physiologically. This raises the question of Wittgenstein's naturalism which is discussed in Chapter 6.

Where do the agreements, by which rules are possible, originate? Such a question is unanswerable. The agreements, which form the basis of rules, have no rational or empirical justification; they are simply part of the fabric of our inherited past. At best all we can say is: 'If I have exhausted the justifications, I have reached bedrock, and my spade is turned. Then I am inclined to say: "This is simply what I do"' (*PI*, §217). Language, like much else we do in the social world, is unreflective. Learning a language is much more like picking up habits from the tradition than learning its rules by rote. Rule-following is also an ability, a practice (*PI* §§206, 208). As we will see presently this fact is very important for Gadamer, depending as it does upon a 'hermeneutical' reading of *phronesis*.

Not unlike Aristotle's outline of the process of becoming morally expert in the *Nicomachean Ethics*, rule-following is a practical not a theoretical matter. In the first instance it depends upon the prereflective process of habituation (*hexis*). The simple *ability* to continue a series and carry out instructions is all one needs to follow a rule. To view rule-following as a process of reflection, internalization of precepts, or understanding rational principles, simply gives rise to scepticism and confusion. Precepts and principles insinuate justification and it is part of Wittgenstein's purpose to demonstrate the futility of relying upon first-person accounts where, at this level of explanation, none are forthcoming. In following a rule we just, as it were, carry out orders: 'When I obey a rule, I do not choose. I obey the rule *blindly*' (*PI*, §219). 'Blindly' because the rule-follower cannot give reasons for doing as they do.

Rules are based upon agreements but the agreements are, in one sense, arbitrary, that is they are not grounded in reason, they lack reflective justification. So there is no sense in asking 'Why should I carry out a rule in this way rather than another?' When asked to justify the use of a word or the reasons for a practice the response in many circumstances might properly be: 'This is simply what I do' (*PI*, §217). This relativistic line of thought is continued with greater emphasis and focus in *On Certainty*.

Bringing together the many strands of thought on rules and rule-following in the *Investigations* the following pronouncement, possibly summarizing Wittgenstein's position *in nuce*, will come as no surprise: 'To obey a rule, to give an order, to play a game of chess, are *customs* (uses, institutions)' (*PI*, §199). One could even liken rules to traditions. Customs, echoing David Hume's device to eclipse metaphysical reasoning with an evocation of the 'habits and customs of the mind', are habitual. Customs are intrinsically social and 'other-regarding', emerging from the structures of social life. Further, they have a historical dimension linking the user to a collective past. The temporal and historical dimension to the notion of the customary Wittgenstein fails to consider.[11] Significantly, it is precisely these features that play such a prominent role in Gadamer's appropriation of the idea of tradition.

IV. WITTGENSTEIN AGAINST INTERPRETATION

In various places in the *Investigations* the idea of interpretation as an aspect of rule-following is entertained briefly – only to be rejected. His position can be best summed up in the dictum: 'Interpretations by themselves do not determine meaning' (*PI*, §198). On another occasion we get a similar comment: 'There is a way of grasping a rule which is *not* an *interpretation*' (*PI*, §201).

Wittgenstein comes to this conclusion as the resolution to the paradox outlined in *PI*, §201:

> No course of action could be determined by a rule, because every course of action can be made out to accord with the rule. The answer was: if everything can be made out to accord with the rule, then it can also be made out to conflict with it. And so there would be neither accord nor conflict here.

This passage is much discussed by analytic philosophers in the light of the work of Saul Kripke[12] who sees here a sceptical paradox and what he terms an equally (sceptical) conclusion. Kripke's assessment fails to engage with the real importance of the rule-following section.

Wittgenstein here draws attention to a problem about rules in that the extreme positions are irreconcilable and unsustainable in themselves. To say nothing conforms to a rule (because the rule can always be vindicated on some interpretation) makes nonsense of the idea of a rule's commanding authority. On the other hand to say everything conforms to the rule ignores the fact that we can 'go against it' (*PI*, §201) by misapplying the rule or making a mistake: at some level it means getting it wrong.

Wittgenstein rightly rejects the 'anything is possible' attitude that says one can always find another rule to account for the limitations of the first rule, and so on *ad infinitum*.[13] However, this does not mean he is left with only one alternative: that rules must be completely inflexible rigid codes.

If rule-following presupposes subjective interpretation 'where every course of action can be made out to accord with the rule' then the idea of following and breaking rules seems to make no sense at all. 'What this shows', we are told, 'is that there is a way of grasping a rule which is *not* an *interpretation*' (*PI*, §201). This thought is further captured when Wittgenstein imagines the possibility that rules are 'rails laid to infinity ... infinitely long rails correspond[-ing] to the unlimited application of a rule' (*PI*, §218).

We cannot logically conceive of language as guided by interpretation because such elucidation presupposes self-reference which in turn negates the idea of regularity (already established as a prerequisite for language itself) or gives, in the case of the 'rules as rails' an unacceptable infinite regress. We should note here that for Gadamer, interpretation does not collapse into self-reference. All language conforms, at some level, to rule-governed social consensus, yet at the same time he imagines it as constantly open to various interpretative possibilities for reasons to be explained presently.

Wittgenstein plays down the element of interpretation in rule-following and by extension language usage, no doubt in the belief that its 'subjective' dimension is a threat to the publicly verifiable agreements. Rules and interpretations, on this account, are mutually exclusive.

Wittgenstein claims, at one point, that rules are followed 'blindly' (*PI*, §219). On the face of it this seems extraordinarily counterintuitive thought given the conventional wisdom that judgement and reflection are necessary for intelligent communication. On this account linguistic rules are not formally stated imperatives the initiate internalizes before proceeding, as with geometry, for example (the 'rules as rails' idea). On the contrary, they are agreements: 'the word 'agreement' and the word 'rule' are related to one another, they are cousins. If I teach anyone the use of the one word, he learns the use of the other with it' (*PI*, §224). Regularities are disseminated through the language-games with the cohesion of shared agreements sustaining them. Consensus is ultimately a practical affair: agreements are made manifest not through procedural formalities but human activities ('It is what human beings say that is true and false; and they agree in the language they use. This is not agreement in opinions but in a form of life (*Lebensform*)' (*PI*, §241)). Language acquisition is essentially a social affair. In following a rule I am habituated to do as others in the linguistic community, that is the language tradition, do. Wittgenstein's judgement about the blindness of rule-following runs in parallel with the associated assertion: 'Interpretations by themselves do not determine meaning' (*PI*, §198). The same thought applies here. If language is regulated by fundamental agreements and linguistic rules fix meanings, meanings are not interpretations, where an interpretation is taken as a subjective act of choosing from a range of possible significations. At the beginning of *PI*, §198 Wittgenstein considers the possibility that every application of a rule is an interpretation – only to reject it:

> 'But how can a rule show me what I have to do at this point? Whatever I do, is on some interpretation, in accord with the rule' – That is not what we ought to say, but rather: any interpretation still hangs in the air along with what it interprets, and cannot give it any support.

The image of 'hanging in the air' suggests a need for something more grounded and fundamental, that is, a rule, which is not itself open to the imprecision of interpretation.

Rule-following excludes interpretation, according to Wittgenstein, if it is taken to mean flexibility within the rule such that a set of alternative meanings are possible ('substitution of one expression of the rule for another'). Whatever we do on this account is, invariably, in conformity to pregiven procedures. Linguistic rules are little more than given agreements, unreflectively ('blindly') followed, like the rules of chess, for example. Rules make no demands upon the individual's interpretive resources or forms of judgement. All the language-user requires for the purposes of understanding is an ability to conform to the actually existing linguistic codes and conventions, the embedded complex structures of social life. Understanding here is no more than social praxis.[14]

Towards the end of the *Investigations*, in the section on 'aspect blindness', Wittgenstein reinforces the idea that rules and interpretations are to be kept separate. On page 212 he says, 'To interpret is to think; to do something'. And in the next sentence is the following comment: 'It is easy to recognize cases in which we are *interpreting*. When we interpret we form hypotheses, which may prove false.'

These comments are made within the context of the phenomenology of seeing and perceiving and readily apply to linguistic interpretation. Discussion of 'aspect dawning' and 'aspect blindness', and the whole question of 'seeing as' in relation to the 'duck-rabbit' appears, prima facie, to be a shift in Wittgenstein's position to more a hermeneutical solution to the problem of interpretation. This notion is dispelled on further reflection. The idea that interpretations are (reflective) 'hypotheses' sits uncomfortably with the other Wittgensteinian premise that rules are unreflective and passed on through customary channels.

Although Wittgenstein departs radically from the abstract atomism of the *Tractatus*, developing much less structured, more informal, variegated, pluralistic, and socially produced logics of meaning, the Tractarian semantics is never entirely shaken off. The turn in the later work to a pragmatics of ordinary language, with its rich texture of vocabularies and practices, makes manifest a configuration with a logic immanent within each language-game. This is where Wittgenstein meets with difficulties. The agreements enshrined in language, ignoring all the surface variation, are assumed to be essentially autonomous. Rationality at the core of each of the many language-games may be specific to the game, hence language's almost limitless semantic possibilities, but the isolated relationship between the rules and their circumscribed applications is never seriously challenged. The Tractarian calculus never fully gives way to the loose texture of the game.

By shifting the point of production of meaning from private consciousness to the social realm of publicly scrutinized rules and agreements, a strategy constantly at play in the later work, Wittgenstein effectively outflanks epistemologically based theories. The strength of the attacks upon mentalism and privacy cannot be underestimated. But altering the site of meaning to social production gives rise to all those problems associated with the later work of Wittgenstein: the vanishing of subjectivity, experience, and consciousness, in fact the disappearance of anything tainted by the inner world of subjective consciousness: 'What is hidden ... is of no interest to us' (*PI*, §126).

Further difficulties arise. If language-users are imprisoned within a plurality of isolated language-games, what common ground makes it possible to reach out to the past, that is, the textually enshrined language-games remote from the present? What sense of commonality is available to link present and past? What kind of bridge connects current language-games to those of the (?) same culture but from a redundant 'form of life'? More problematical is the question of translation (an issue raised by Habermas in his critique of Wittgenstein).[15] Accurate translation (whatever this may be since the very notion of translation is at issue) across cultures and radically different natural languages is impossible.

About past language-games and the possibility of translating them into present idioms Wittgenstein says very little. 'Language-game[s] change with time' (*OC*, §256) he admits rather unhelpfully. He is unwilling to speculate about cultural and historical factors effecting social, hence, linguistic changes and is silent on the whole problematic of the relationship between current language-games and those of the past.

The processes, if there are such processes, which advance and modify language, are, for Wittgenstein, like Hume's causes, 'totally shut up from human curiosity and enquiry'. To seek to homogenize language-games with an overarching or synthesizing theory a meta-game is erected outside the limits of ordinary language, moving into the dangerous terrain of (philosophical) non-sense. Perhaps this is the essentially Humean thought behind the rhetorical question in *Culture and Value*: 'Who knows the laws according to which society develops?' (*CV*, p. 158)

Given that utterances are always within language, the construction of meta-positions about the movement, connection, and development of language-games appears as a conceptual impossibility, on Wittgenstein's account. He is suspicious of any approach to language incorporating historical theory, specifically developmental, historicist speculations about organic unfolding. A sceptical silence about the alleged grand narratives of history is quite a different issue from the question of the historicality of language. Wittgenstein offers a stark and illusory choice; either stay within the bounds of ordinary language or lose oneself in the entrapments of metaphysics.

The choice is artificial because there are legitimate ways to inquire about the temporal constraints upon language, about how and why language-games acquire legitimacy and why they eventually decline and become superseded. Expressivist theory, in ways closed off to Wittgenstein, shows how, despite the fact that language-games inevitably change, meaning is always in principle possible and is thus, in some sense, continuous. Without some story about the preservation of meaning within the unsettling historical diversity of language, chaotic fragmentation is apparent.

The conventions sustaining language do not change gradually, on Wittgenstein's model, for there is no structural device for them to do so. Change must occur not through organic historical development but via sudden paradigm shifts. Language is a vast network of interconnected games, however, they are hermetically sealed off from one another, and change unaccountably over time. 'When language-games change', he says, 'there is a change in concepts, and with the concepts the meanings of words change' (*OC*, §65).

Diversity rather than unity characterizes everyday language. In §24 of the *Investigations*, Wittgenstein reviews the different games and concludes with the following reflection:

It is interesting to compare the multiplicity of the tools in language and of the ways they are used, the multiplicity of kinds of words and sentence, with what logicians have said about the structure of language (including the author of the *Tractatus Logico-Philosophicus*).

In his earlier work, Wittgenstein sought to represent language as anchored in something more fundamental than itself, namely, a hidden logical structure. For the early Wittgenstein the possibility of meaning depends on anchoring language in something outside itself. It is not the structure of the world that makes meaning possible but a logical concordance between language and world. Wittgenstein, in his later work, attacks the whole idea of grounding.

In the *Investigations* and *On Certainty* foundationalist theories of meaning are the object of concentrated attack. Not only is his own Tractarian position under fire but so too is Augustine and the whole philosophical tradition he inaugurates. There is no secret key to unlock the door of language: this was Wittgenstein's mistaken assumption in the *Tractatus*. Augustine makes a similar mistake by reducing meaning to representation. Rationalists and empiricists alike assume that the knowing subject generates meaning from the inner recesses of private sensation. The idea that meaning is generated within the privacy of consciousness is a typical one in epistemologically inspired accounts of meaning. Linguistic meaning here is grounded in the knowing subject, the 'I' of 'I think.'

Linguistic meaning, Wittgenstein concludes, as the result of his many and varied descriptions of the use of language, cannot be grounded in logical structures or subjectivity. Meaning is hidden within the multiplicity and variety of the language-games.

I want to consider ideas Hilary Putnam advances in a short essay entitled 'Was Wittgenstein a pragmatist?'[16] Putnam, attributing the view to Richard Rorty, rejects a reading of Wittgenstein. According to Putnam, Rorty takes Wittgenstein's rules to be like a 'program' and 'a program is one which leads to *identical* behavior in all the members of a speech community'.[17]

According to Putnam, Wittgenstein is quite clear in pointing out that language is not simply a matter of following rules (like calculating rules). To think this way is to read the text 'carelessly',[18] says Putnam, pointing to a neglected section of the *Investigations* for a completely different way of understanding rule-following. In the following excerpt from the *Investigations*, quoted in the Putnam essay, Wittgenstein imagines a disagreement about 'whether someone is pretending to have a feeling that he doesn't have':[19]

'You don't understand a thing' – so one says when someone doubts what we recognize as clearly genuine, – but we can't prove anything.

'Is there such a thing as 'expert judgment' about the genuineness of expressions of feeling? – Even here there are those whose judgment is 'better' and those whose judgment is 'worse'.

Correcter prognoses will generally issue from the judgments of those who understand people better.

Can one learn this knowledge? Yes; some can. Not, however, by taking a course in it, but through 'experience'. – Can another be one's teacher in this? Certainly. From time to time he gives him the right *tip*. This is what 'learning' and 'teaching' are like here. – What one acquires is not a technique; one learns correct judgments. There are also rules, but they do not form a system, and only experienced people can apply them right. Unlike calculating rules.' (*PI*, p. 227, quoted in Putnam, 1995, p. 36)

The sentiments expressed here run counter to the line of thought I seek to defend.[20] Putnam (via Wittgenstein) insinuates that performance in language-games is not calculative, that is, mere reproduction or slavish adherence to a body of preestablished precepts and conventions. The fact that there is an element of judgement in effecting rules (some *judge* well and others badly), demonstrates Wittgenstein's conception of linguistic rules is not reducible to mere calculation (given the inclusion of a subjective and evaluative element).

Putnam offers an arguable riposte to Rorty but an intractable question still remains: how can he square this alternative reading with the unambiguous references in the *Investigations* to rules as imperatives?[21] The Wittgenstein quotation shows him pulling in two opposing directions. How can the inclusion of the element of judgement sit comfortably with the idea of blind obedience to rules? When Putnam suggests that judgements cannot fully be codified, he (and Wittgenstein) nods in the direction of hermeneutics. Anyone reading the quotation above will be readily reminded of Aristotle; many of the principal themes in the *Ethics* are unwittingly alluded to here.[22] This could be a description of the acquisition of moral virtue. Aristotle's idea that moral virtue cannot be taught but comes through habituation looks remarkably like Wittgenstein's idea of picking up 'the right *tip*'. The distinction between 'judgment' and 'technique' is also thoroughly Aristotelian.

V. GADAMER AND LINGUISTIC RULES: A HERMENEUTIC QUESTION

A Gadamerian reading of Aristotle, based on the section of *Truth and Method* entitled 'The hermeneutic relevance of Aristotle' (*TM*, pp. 312–24), implicitly confronts the difficulties encountered in the 'rules as imperatives' reading of Wittgenstein Putnam seeks to challenge. Whereas Wittgenstein sets up an opposition between rules and judgements for Gadamer's hermeneutics, judging is in principle no different from rule-following, both are questions of application. For hermeneutics application is always a question of 'concretising something universal and applying it to oneself' (*TM*, p. 332). Rules as much as judgements involve the coming together of the universal and the particular in the interpretive act of application. With this in mind, it is as if Wittgenstein, when discussing rules and judgements in the *Investigations*, frequently sees only the universality of the rule and the particularity of the judgement. He misses the essential hermeneutical dimension, thus only partially making the link with judgement.

Techne with regard to production and *phronesis* with regard to action are part of Aristotle's taxonomy of practical states of mind. *Techne*, although a 'state by virtue of which the soul possesses truth' (1139b15), is clearly not the state of knowing appropriate for action because the end of *techne* is production unlike other states of knowing where the object is an activity. Technical knowledge presupposes the application of rules and techniques with the object of creating something, a clear conception of which is grasped beforehand. Preceding the act of production the agent possesses both knowledge of what is to be made and a firm grasp of the guiding principles and rules to which the object conforms. Success in production is determined by conformity of the procedures to the object.

Concerning the sphere of moral action there are neither hard nor fast principles to be drawn upon nor an object to which prior knowledge is directed. The good person knows he or she has to act or refrain from acting in a certain way but never reflects in advance upon the appropriate response. Technical knowledge is always for the sake of something else: not so with action. The quality possessed by the good person is *phronesis* (usually translated as prudence or practical wisdom), a 'reasoned state or capacity' (Aristotle, *Nicomachean Ethics*, 1339b15), or an intuition, about the appropriate action to perform (in the light of more general understanding about the constituents of a good life). The knowledge required for action is intrinsically related to the self-conceptions of the agent and cannot be codified or formulated in terms of principles, nor reduced to a reliable method and taught. The good person is one disposed to act out of habituation.

Becoming good is a relatively unreflective matter. Habits of character are picked up by following the example of those already in possession of virtue. We are drawn into the moral tradition of desirable actions, generous acts, truthful acts, and so forth, but the accumulated habits will not offer guidance as to whether in this particular situation one must choose X or Y. Each situation is utterly unique, its strangeness exposing the inadequacy of general rules. Rules by their very nature can never be programmatically applied to specific cases.

The hermeneutical dimension to *phronesis* is now explicit in the problem of application. In performing an action knowledge acquired in the past is applied to the present. *Phronesis* reveals the real structure of understanding; not as a knowing subject grasping an object but as an experience through which the prejudices or habits, passed on in the tradition, encounter the strange and the new: every moral action is the application of general principle to the particular (and unique) situation now encountered. The novelty is not tamed by being classified according to some organizing principle; on the contrary, it is disruptively experienced as it pulls the agent up short. For example, in deciding what to do, either X or Y, there is no way of knowing whether X or Y are genuinely classifiable as instances of general rules. Everyday morality informs me that I must not lie but there is always an interruptive problem in practice. Is the particular action I now contemplate, for example, lying or something else? And what I am doing *now* is not identical to anything I have ever done before, however similar. This is the sense in which every situation is experienced as both novel and unique. But for all these problems the person of *phronesis* will be able to proceed since customs and habits by their nature are both flexible and adaptable to the situation. On the other hand, explicit rules do not allow for any measure of interpretive negotiation; they are intrinsically brittle and rigid.

For Gadamer, rule-following, like ethical performance, is not a process of confirmation through repetition; rather it is disconfirmation, a hermeneutical experience, an encounter with the new. The novelty of all situations and social encounters unhinge our fragile self-conceptions. The person of *phronesis* is morally wise with respect to the good life. For such wisdom, he or she does not accumulate knowledge over time but gains a greater or more intense openness to experience. Wisdom is not the possession of universal knowledge about some abstract conception of the good, as it is with Plato; it is fundamentally self-knowledge, knowledge for the self. Such knowledge is intrinsically practical; it exists only in performance, only in specific contexts of application. Gadamer is not commending mere conformity to habit nor is he falling back on some instinctive notion of self-preservation.

An oscillation between the universal and the particular is a structural characteristic of all understanding and provides one of the many versions of the hermeneutical circle. Using Gadamer's essay 'Semantics and hermeneutics',[23] there is the suggestion that this opposition may be helpful in drawing attention to some of the weaknesses in Wittgenstein. In the essay Gadamer covers some of the same ground as Wittgenstein although his purpose is to emphasize the distinction between a formal semantic approach to language and his own hermeneutics. Gadamer's criticisms are directed at semantically based analyses of language and it is safe to assume that the criticism applies to Wittgenstein. 'Semantics appears to describe the range of linguistic facts externally, as it were.' But mere description is inadequate as hermeneutics demonstrates:

> Hermeneutics, in contrast, focuses upon the internal side of our use of this world of signs, or better said, on the internal process of speaking, which if viewed from the outside, appears as our use of the world of signs. (*PH*, pp. 82–3)

I take this to suggest that rule-following in language needs to be understood not simply from the point of view of the speaker's observable commitment to the rules but in relation to the speaker's self-understanding of those rules as well. Gadamer is not here capitulating to the idea of the privacy of meaning. The 'subjective' element is actually a 'forgetfulness of oneself ... in self-surrender to the subject matter made present in the medium of language' (*PH*, p. 87).[24] This dimension is neglected by pragmatic, Wittgensteinian semantics and brought to the fore in hermeneutics.

Gadamer acknowledges the unavoidable rule-governed dimension to language when he says, 'the fact that one can never depart too far from linguistic conventions is clearly basic to the life of language'. Ironically, perhaps, his justification for this thought is pure Wittgenstein for, he continues, 'he who speaks a private language understood by no one else, does not speak at all' (*PH*, p. 85). The 'private language argument', adverted to by both Gadamer and Wittgenstein, demonstrates the public, intersubjective nature of language-based conventions. At the other extreme, what we might call the completely public language argument, which Gadamer mentions in the next sentence, is also a non-starter:

> On the other hand, he who only speaks a language in which conventionality has become total in the choice of words, in syntax, and in style forfeits the power of address and evocation that comes solely with the individualization of a language's vocabulary and of its means of communication. (*PH*, pp. 85–6)

He makes a similar point elsewhere, observing that 'No language is just the system of rules that the language teacher has in mind or that the grammarian abstracts. Every language is continually underway to change itself.'[25]

On this analysis speaking a language involves a coming together of the conventional and the individual. For hermeneutics the two do not exist as separate entities. An undynamic opposition between individual and convention is possibly what prevents Wittgenstein from being more obviously hermeneutical in his approach. By implication, semantics, and we could include Wittgenstein here, only works at the level of the conventional. Further, for Gadamer, the two levels are never in harmony: 'One will find conflict between the continuing tendency towards individualization in language and that tendency which is just as essential to language, namely, to establish meanings by convention' (*PH*, p. 85).

The friction between the already said of linguistic rules and the individualization of what is currently being thought or uttered is another version of the hermeneutical circle. Wittgenstein sees only the consensual conventions of language and misses out the (historically) dynamic by which new meanings are forged. Crucial in Gadamer is the thought that there is always a surplus of meaning. New meanings, nuances, and interpretations are made possible by the tradition when tradition is understood as the (historical) movement of novelty and conventionality. This movement is unobtrusively at work in the to and fro of everyday conversational exchanges. It bursts forth and is most conspicuous in the poetic: this is a theme to which we shall return in Chapter 7.

If language's viability is dependent upon conventional rules and these lack epistemological foundations, as the Wittgensteinian position suggests, what grounding has language and what then is the relationship between word and world? In the *Tractatus* language depicts the world in unambiguous ways but in the later work this one-to-one association disappears. Effectively language has a life of its own, defying reduction to fundamental facts about subjects and the irreducible nature of the world. When Wittgenstein struggled to escape the *Tractatus* position and move cautiously towards the later view he reflected on the differences between the rules of language and other types of rule-governed activity. He confronted the possibility that grammatical rules might be no more than arbitrary conventions:

> Why don't I call cookery rules arbitrary, and why am I tempted to call the rules of grammar arbitrary? Because 'cooking' is defined by its end, whereas 'speaking' is not. That is why the use of language is in a certain sense autonomous, as cooking and washing are not. (*Zettel*, §320)

The rules of cookery are, on this account, non-arbitrary because structured by the nature of the activity. On the other hand language is, according to Wittgenstein, 'in a certain sense autonomous'[26] because it is not instrumentality defined; it does not have a *telos*. Nor is language 'subject to external authority', Hubert Schwyzer tells us, for 'it is not beholden to the world, or to the mind, or to rules'.[27]

Language-games are not beholden to the world because meaning derives not from its mysterious power to refer to the world but through use: 'the meaning of a word is its use in the language' (*PI*, §43).

The world is touched not by the ostensive power of words to stand for or name objects but by grammar reaffirming language's autonomy:

> The connection between 'language' and 'reality' is made by definitions of words, and these belong to grammar, so that language remains self-contained and autonomous. (*PG*, p. 97)

Nor is meaning derived from the mind of the user, hence Wittgenstein's powerfully directed criticisms at mentalism and subjectively based semantics. And rules lack the coercive power of an external authority because they are, as we saw in the *Zettel* quotation above, arbitrary.

This is all familiar territory. Wittgenstein is right to distance himself from naive theories of reference, emphasizing as he does a conventionalist basis for words, but there are a few unanswered questions in all of this. How does language relate to the world (even if naive reference theories are inadequate)? And is language autonomous? Put differently, is it no more than self-referential?

In *Zettel* Wittgenstein radically challenges conventional wisdom when he says, 'Do not believe that you have the concept of colour within you because you looked at coloured objects – however you look. (Any more than you possess the concept of a negative number by having debts)' (*Z*, §332).

By the same token a blind person lacks the necessary hardware for sight, the appropriate cones and rods. They also lack the ability to associate words with the world but this on no account debars them, on the Wittgensteinian picture, from the linguistic community. The ability to use language depends upon socialization, training, instruction and the ability to follow rules, as we have seen, not the capacity to check words and concepts against an independent reality (a capacity denied even the sighted person).

Wittgenstein is surely right to contest referential theories of meaning by showing how the language-games are sustained by agreements, but the conventions cannot be completely arbitrary. Language does not describe an already existing world but neither is it a completely contingent network of self-referential games. The danger of collapse into complete linguistic autonomy and arbitrariness is an omnipresent one in late Wittgenstein.

Ulrich Arnswald, in a recent essay,[28] pursues a different line of argument. Instead of taking linguistic rules as the issue around which Gadamer and Wittgenstein are clearly divided, he seeks to show, on the contrary, that it is precisely on this matter their views of language converge. Forms of life are human ways of acting and it makes no sense, says Wittgenstein, to ask why we act as we do. To ask this question is no more than to ask why we are human in one way rather than another. We just act as we do within a form of life and this is readily likened to a tradition. Different forms of life are not a bar to understanding. According to Arnswald's reading of Wittgenstein, language-games (and forms of life) are 'open to movements between various articulations that allow for reaching an understanding with the other' (Malpas *et al.*, 2002, p. 31). Is this comparable to Gadamer's thought that in the hermeneutical situation of acquiring language one at the same time acquires the resources for 'reaching an understanding' (albeit one that is incomplete, hence, tentative and provisional)? I suggest not. On my reading, Wittgenstein so relativizes the language-games that the appropriate mutuality and intercourse within and across games is missing. Arnswald finds a space for flexibility to make negotiation possible. He argues against the kind of rigidity my reading of Wittgenstein assumes. No doubt because Wittgenstein emphasizes practical activity, Arnswald assumes that language ability includes, 'a kind of linguistic core competence peculiar to human beings, and it is this competence that allows us to make transitions between two language games' (Malpas *et al.*, 2002, p. 31). Quoting Rudolf Haller, Arnswald sees language games as 'variable, mutable and transitory. More precisely, one ought to say that human societies and communities invent, maintain and even forget language games' (ibid., p. 31). Change is empirically evident but transformation does not in itself show rules (and their applications) to be capable of organic growth, the kind of mutability Haller and Arnswald see in Wittgenstein. Arnswald claims to find the resources for the possibility of change in Wittgenstein, concluding that background customs and traditions (which he refers to as *'natural history'*, seemingly confusing the natural and the social) are their precondition. In comparing Wittgenstein to Gadamer, Arnswald uncovers an 'astonishing accordance' (ibid., p. 40). Building on assertions about Wittgenstein's alleged capacity to bring together the plurality and diversity of language-games and an awareness of the constant change to which language games are subjected, he likens this to Gadamer's hermeneutics.

In the next chapter reservations about the capacity for language-games to change are extended to a consideration of language's relationship to its own past. On this topic Gadamer has much to say whilst Wittgenstein is deafeningly silent.

NOTES

1. First published in English in 1922.
2. For all the emphasis in the early work on an austerely logical approach to philoso-

phical problems Wittgenstein sets great store by momentary flashes of insight. The 'picture theory of meaning' in the *Tractatus* suddenly came to Wittgenstein when he read a newspaper report on an accident. The report reenacted the incident with a diagram suggesting 'the nature of propositions – namely, to *picture* reality' (Malcolm, 1984, p. 57). And the problems with the *Tractatus* (and their solution) seem to have occurred to Wittgenstein when puzzled by the Neapolitan gesture (discussed below). All of this has hermeneutical significance demonstrating the essentially creative dimension to thought.

3. Malcolm adds as a footnote to this anecdote: 'Professor G. H. von Wright informs me that Wittgenstein related this incident to him somewhat differently: the question at issue, according to Wittgenstein, was whether every proposition must have a 'grammar', and Sraffa asked Wittgenstein what the 'grammar' of that gesture was. In describing the incident to von Wright, Wittgenstein did not mention the phrases 'logical form' or 'logical multiplicity' (Malcolm, 1984, footnote 3).

4. 1920–6.

5. In Wittgenstein (1993).

6. 'The philosopher's treatment of a question is like the treatment of an illness' (*PI*, §255).

7. Augustine's error, manifest in the celebrated Chapter 8 of his *Confessions*, where he reminisces about his earliest encounters with language, assumes all words acquire meaning through ostensively defined origins. Wittgenstein's ambiguous use of this section from the *Confessions* as a prelude to the *Philosophical Investigations* indicates the importance he attaches to the Augustinian account of meaning, as we will witness in a later chapter. For Wittgenstein, there is something profoundly instructive about Augustine's appreciation of the social context in which he acquired language (*Philosophical Investigations*, §1). Yet the assumption that all words derive meaning because they name objects is misleading. The ritualized practice of bringing children into language by pointing to objects and 'naming' them is just one of a vast repertoire of (primitive) language-activities (games) we, and earlier cultures, enact.

8. Lewis Carroll in *Through the Looking Glass* satirizes, like Wittgenstein, the view that language is meaningful because of the utterer's intentions. 'When *I* use a word,' Humpty Dumpty said, in a rather scornful tone, 'it means just what I choose it to mean – neither more nor less.' See P. Gardiner (ed.), *The Annotated Alice* (Harmondsworth: Penguin, 1965).

9. This again raises the question of dialectic. Are the various narrative voices in the *Philosophical Investigations* different unresolved aspects of the author, Wittgenstein, or are they different sides of an argument, or even a simple argumentative device (like the fictional doubter in Descartes's *Meditations* who never really doubts)?

10. The nature of teaching and learning are constant preoccupations of Wittgenstein in the *Philosophical Investigations*. Perhaps trainee teachers should be encouraged to read this work.

11. This may be too harsh a judgement. Wittgenstein is, from time to time, alert to the sense in which the customary is intimately connected to the past. Take the following (Gadamerian) reflection: 'Tradition is not something a man can learn;

not a thread he can pick up when he feels like it; any more than a man can choose his own ancestors' (*CV*, p. 76).

12. Chapter 2, 'The Wittgensteinian paradox', pp. 7–54, in Kripke (1982).

13. The 'rules to explain rules' idea is indirectly satirized in the Marx Brothers' *A Day at the Races*. An enterprising Chico sells a gullible punter, Groucho, a form book subsequently explaining that the first book cannot be understood without another form book and so on. After parting with a small fortune Groucho ends up with a pile of form books and is seemingly none the wiser.

14. 'To understand a language means to be master of a technique' (*PI*, §199).

15. Discussed in J. Habermas' 'Review of (Gadamer's) Truth and Method' in Wachterhauser (1986), pp. 243–76.

16. Putnam (1995), pp. 27–56.

17. Putnam (1995), p. 37.

18. Putnam (1995), p. 36.

19. Putnam (1995), p. 36.

20. Wittgenstein's ambivalent relationship to deconstruction is much discussed in recent literature. Worthy of note is Henry Staten's use of deconstructive strategies to rebut the interpretation of rules and rule-following I attribute to Wittgenstein. See particularly 'Wittgenstein deconstructs' in Staten (1984), pp. 64–108.

21. 'When I obey a rule, I do not choose. I obey the rule *blindly*' (*PI*, §219), or 'Following a rule is analogous to obeying an order. We are trained to do so; we react to an order in a particular way' (*PI*, §206).

22. Wittgenstein claimed never to have read any Aristotle. 'Drury: Did you ever read anything of Aristotle's? Wittgenstein: Here I am, a one-time professor of philosophy who has never read a word of Aristotle!' Quoted in M. O'C. Drury's 'Conversations with Wittgenstein', in Rhees (1984), p. 158.

23. Gadamer (1976a), pp. 82–94.

24. The need for self-understanding and appreciation of the 'matter at issue' to which the rules are directed is not exclusively a hermeneutical insight. Rush Rhees also makes these observations in his posthumous writings (Rhees, 1998). It is remarkable how close to Gadamer Rhees gets in his critique of the language-games idea stressing as he does language's unitary and dialogical character. I thank Stephen Mulhall for pointing out this connection to me.

25. H-G. Gadamer, 'Boundaries of language' (*LLGH*, p. 15).

26. Without wishing to sound like an analytical philosopher I wonder whether there can be degrees of autonomy? In the endless debates with Althusserians about the Marxist relationship between 'base' and 'superstructure' the term 'relative autonomy' was coined to overcome deterministic readings of ideology. In this context and the current one nothing is gained by the move towards relativity.

27. H. Schwyzer, 'Autonomy', in H-J. Glock (2001), p. 289.

28. U. Arnswald, 'On the certainty of uncertainty: language games and forms of life in Gadamer and Wittgenstein', in Malpas *et al.* (2002), pp. 25–44.

CHAPTER 5

'What has history to do with me?':[1] Language and/ as Historicality

You must say something new yet it must all be old. In fact you must confine yourself to saying old things – and *all the same* it must be something new

(*CV*, p. 40)

There is nothing more stupid than the chatter about cause and effect in history books; nothing is more wrong-headed, more half-baked.

(*CV*, p. 62)

I. THE 'OLD' AND THE 'NEW'

Wittgenstein's conception of language as an activity constituted by socially constructed rules is a persuasive and influential one. Locating the sources of meaning squarely within the realm of the social world, shifting the centre of gravity away from the privacy of consciousness to the public sphere of regulated practice, is now an all too familiar move in contemporary thought. But the wider implications of Wittgenstein's version of this bold reversal, moving the locus of signification from the inner world of consciousness to the outer sphere of regulated practice, has escaped close scrutiny. This is especially true of issues surrounding the historicity of language-games. Problematic questions regarding the relationship between current and past practices, between contemporary language-games and those no longer current, often escape attention in the philosophical literature. The reference to the 'old' and the 'new', one of the few direct allusions in Wittgenstein to temporality as a problem, signifies awareness of the tension between language-games of the past and the present. Can language-games embrace the 'new', in linguistic novelty, neologisms, literary and metaphorical expressions, with only the resources of restrictive rules? How, on the Wittgensteinian model, can one explain the latitude within which the countless transgressions of the 'old' (that is, current) practices in literature and everyday speech and writing are effected? Wider questions pertaining to assumptions about temporality and change, questions surrounding the larger network of socially derived pragmatics of meaning, and how they might be understood, need to be addressed. Unease about language's relationship to its own history is hard to ignore when little more stabilizes meanings than the network of customary practice. Evidently Wittgenstein felt a sense of disquiet and was aware of, yet unable to overcome these puzzles, as the paradoxical reflection on the 'old' and the 'new' indicates. A move to the social realm of language is inadequate without a concomitant move to a more continuous and holistic narrative within some version of the historical. Further movement in this direction brings out more emphatically the tensions between the 'old' and the 'new', not by way of a suggested resolution but by making the tensions more productive than paradoxical.

Wittgenstein is not entirely blind to a historical perspective. He places language-games within the context of the customary: 'A person goes by a sign-post only in so far as there exists a regular use of sign-posts, custom' (*PI*, §198), and 'To obey a rule, to make a report, to give an order, to play a game of chess, are *customs* (uses, institutions)' (*PI*, §199). Customs are more than routine activities in institutional contexts; they are the vehicles through which a culture's past has its effect upon the present. Customs, by their very nature, are constituent parts of a wider association, tradition. Customs (including rules and codes of procedure) are socially embedded, hidden within the fabric of daily life, and yet for all their regulative power are unavailable to rational reflection; this much Wittgenstein evidently acknowledges. Yet a more detailed investigation of the customary must surely reckon with the sense in which current practices extend back into the recesses of the past. Further questions concerning the nature of the connection between customary activities in the past and those in the present, and whether this reveals anything significant about a culture's self-understandings are absent from Wittgenstein. These issues are of vital importance to Gadamer's version of the customary, that is, tradition.

Gadamer's hermeneutics works within the strictures of conventionalism whilst disclosing the essential historicality forms of linguistic agreement presuppose. A comparison between Wittgenstein's 'language-games' and Gadamer's linguistic 'horizons' is instructive. The comparison serves to show a rift between the two approaches. With the inclusion of a historical perspective Gadamer comes to an understanding of the relationship between linguistic rules and their application. This is done without violating the patterns of everyday language. Language-games for all their differences display an essential unity.

II. THE HISTORICALITY OF LINGUISTIC RULES

In his review of *Truth and Method*,[2] Jürgen Habermas contrasts Gadamer's hermeneutics with Wittgenstein's pragmatics of language exposing the distance between them. Habermas takes up a critical attitude to Gadamer in the remainder of the review and initiates a lengthy debate around issues concerning the shortcomings of a revived notion of tradition and its threat to an Enlightenment understanding of social critique, but his initial sympathies are with the general anti-positivism of philosophical hermeneutics. The problem for Habermas is that Wittgenstein sustains, throughout his later work, a residual commitment to formalized languages adopting a critical stance much like the position argued for in the previous chapter of this work. Gadamer, Habermas claims, has the edge over Wittgenstein in so far as 'hermeneutic self-reflection goes beyond the socio-linguistic stage of language analysis'.[3]

Giving a clear acknowledgement to Wittgenstein's achievement in the later work Habermas continues:

> When the transcendental construction of a pure language was shattered, language gained a new dimension through the pluralism of language-games ... [b]ut Wittgenstein still conceived of application too narrowly. He saw only invariant linkage of symbols and activities and failed to appreciate that the application of rules includes their interpretation and further development.[4]

In considering some of the implications of Wittgenstein's failure to widen the sphere of application, Habermas offers incisive criticism placing emphasis upon a perceived failure to bring out the historical dimension to language-games:

> Language spheres are not monadically sealed off but are inwardly as well as outwardly porous. The grammar of a language cannot contain a rigid designation for its application. Whoever has learned to apply its rules has not only learned to express himself but also to interpret expressions in this language. Both translation [outwardly] and tradition [inwardly] must be possible in principle. Along with their possible application, grammatical rules simultaneously imply the necessity of interpretation. Wittgenstein failed to see this; as a consequence he conceived the practice of language-games unhistorically.[5]

By participating in a language-game one acquires the ability to apply its 'grammar'. Application is a two-way street wherein meanings are expressed and interpreted. The necessity for interpretation extends beyond everyday

dialogical exchange to the broader vistas of translation, presumably horizon-
tally across cultures and forms of life, and vertically within traditions. For
Habermas, because Wittgenstein neglects the interpretive dimension so
evident in hermeneutics, he distorts the language games by neglecting the
historical dimension.

The previous chapter spoke of the vestigial commitment to a 'logics of
language' in the later work despite Wittgenstein's radical questioning of the
Tractatus. 'Blind' allegiance to rules (*PI*, §§217, 219) was identified as the
nodal point where the commitment to socially produced language-games
failed to interconnect with the plurality of meanings. The socially enshrined
agreements sustaining meaning on Wittgenstein's account lack flexibility,
needing to be what Habermas terms 'outwardly porous'. Inflexibly
conceived, the language-games are no more than (blind) repetitive re-enact-
ments of the already given. There needs to be some dynamic, organic, overarching medium within which language-games of the present participate in
past language-games and from within the resources of the present advance,
change, and innovate.

Richard Rorty suggests an evolutionary answer to the problems
surrounding language's own history, a solution worked out from within a
pragmatic but generally Wittgensteinian framework. In the essay 'The
contingency of language'[6] Rorty plots a middle course between complete
arbitrariness and a capitulation 'to the idea that language has a purpose'[7] by
historicizing language-games and meeting some of the challenges outlined
above. The suggested solution is to view historical movement as a series of
non-teleological moves, not unlike the arbitrary 'process' of natural selection.
Likening language to the history of natural organisms, Rorty says, 'our
language and our culture are as much a contingency, as much a result of
thousands of small mutations finding niches (and millions of others finding
no niches), as are the orchids and the anthropoids'.[8] In turning to Darwin (or
a Davidson-inspired 'linguistic Darwinism') Rorty locates historical change
within the limits of language itself without resorting to a grand teleology,
either Hegel's or something akin to Jean-François Lyotard's idea of the
'meta-narrative'. For all its ingenuity there seems to be a hint of the
'monkeys and typewriters' argument here, a flawed attempt to derive pattern
and structure from pure randomness. Admittedly this position is an advance
on Wittgenstein, showing as it does an acute awareness of the temporal
problem. However, although Rorty gives a plausible account of language's
transformations he has not touched upon the question of historicality itself.
Contingency and chance make way for an explanation of the slow accretion
of linguistic forms but the history of development does not indicate how (or
if) the past affects the present and how (or if) the language-games of the

present are resourceful enough to drawn in the language of epochs and cultures long dead. The interpretive and expressive dimension to language, seemingly lacking in the Darwinian picture of language, is invariably encompassed by the overtly historical. The blind evolutionary process Rorty outlines has more in common with natural as opposed to human history. Linguistic development needs to be located within an arena of human projects and endeavours, within a general narrative of changing cultural self-understanding. A dynamic link between past and present is best captured in the idea of tradition.

'Language-Games' and 'Horizons'

The idea of the horizon is a familiar one in the phenomenology of Husserl, where it has a specifically perceptual application, recognizing an initial failure to perceive objects in their totality. The horizon is extensively used in Heidegger's *Being and Time*, where it is disconnected from the perceptual field, becoming more a position from where questioning can take place, and an indication of the limits available to interrogation. Heidegger's 'horizon' owes much to Husserl but incorporates and extends the Nietzschean idea of interpretation as 'perspective'. With Gadamer the horizon takes a uniquely linguistic turn although a visual analogy is evident. Likening understanding to the various ways of seeing Gadamer explains what he takes the horizon to be:

> Every finite present has its limitations. We define the concept of 'situation' by saying that it represents a standpoint that limits the possibility of vision. Hence essential to the concept of situation is the concept of 'horizon'. The horizon is the range of vision that includes everything that can be seen from a particular vantage point. (*TM*, p. 302)

Running over the references to 'horizon' in the history of philosophy, Gadamer notes that 'the word has been used ... to characterize the way in which thought is tied to its finite determinacy, and the way one's range of vision is gradually expanded' (*TM*, p. 302).[9] Gadamer here brings out the appropriateness of the horizon as a metaphor for thought, and by extension language use. A deeper engagement with language enhances an individual's increased articulacy, expanding the range of possibilities, for '(the horizon) expresses the superior breadth of vision that the person who is trying to understand must have' (*TM*, p. 304). And yet there are limitations, recalling the early Wittgenstein's 'The world is *my* world: this is manifest in the fact that the limits of *language* mean the limits of *my* world' (*Tractatus*, 5.62). But the boundary for Gadamer does not invite thoughts of solipsism; on the contrary, the limit is a check upon unbridled subjectivity.

Every language-user occupies a unique site within language. The horizon is culturally acquired, extending on entry to the already interpreted and structured socio-linguistic environment, where the individual develops a range of abilities through primary, formative encounters with language. Language-games readily transcribe into horizons if the comparison is focused on the element of constraint. Wittgenstein sees the language-user restricted by training and the regularity of use. Yet for Wittgenstein, every time alternative language-games are entered into potentially unfamiliar horizons are opened up, creating a multiplicity of vantage points, a kind of linguistic perspectivism, giving to the horizons an arbitrary quality, as though they are freely entered into. Here the parallel with Gadamer falls apart, for missing from Wittgenstein's horizons are the forms of mutuality and reciprocity, which prevent the collapse into relativism or subjectivity.

Consideration of the language-user's earliest encounters with speech brings out the crucial difference between Gadamer and Wittgenstein. For Wittgenstein, every time the learner enters into a new language-game he or she must undergo a specific training. The demonstration of this is as follows. When forgetting how a language-game is appropriately re-enacted and a word correctly used, Wittgenstein exhorts the perplexed to think back to the original conditions when the word was first encountered and learnt:

> In such a difficulty [that is, when confused about how to continue in a language-game] always ask yourself: How did we *learn* the meaning of this word ('good' for instance)? From what sort of examples? In what language-games? Then it will be easier for you to see that the words must have a family of meanings. (*PI*, §77)

Although Wittgenstein offers the example here as a demonstration of a word's manifold meanings it is actually counter-productive. Recalling past uses of the word 'good' is, in itself, an inadequate guide to current usage. The piecemeal procedure of resorting to specific memories for instances of past use as a guide to current applications will not work. A more holistic picture of language is required and Gadamer's hermeneutical perspective offers an alternative. In learning the rules, one at the same time learns the condition of all possible usage. There is no internalizing of a set of rules for particular language-games, one is not merely acculturated into the specifics of the various language-games but brought into linguisticality itself. In learning the initial language-games, one at the same time develops the capacity to apply the games in new contexts and in relation to new games. This draws upon the Gadamerian idea of the universality of the hermeneutical procedure. He claims that 'the accumulation of vocabulary and the rules of its application establishes only the outline for that which ... actually builds the structure of a language, namely, the continuing growth of expressions into new realms of application'.[10]

All linguistic understanding takes place from within particular horizons. In the first instance, the horizon is strictly regulated by convention and agreement (in some sense given because inherited and unavailable to reflection). Wittgenstein's abundant examples of the many uses to which we put ordinary language never seem to advance much beyond the elementary stage of linguistic appropriation. The mature use of language is modelled upon early training[11] and never takes into account the complex transformations undergone both by the speaker and language itself. The mature use of language embraces the complex discourses of philosophy, politics, art, and religion. Wittgenstein significantly avoids mention of these. It would be negligent to exclude from this list the totality of the human and natural sciences, which he saw, no doubt, as obfuscatory and parasitic intrusions upon the authentic idioms of everyday life.

Without a holistic vision of language, and the *Investigations* is largely concerned with particulars, there is a general failure to see the bigger picture. The narratives of the human sciences, and here we can include rhetorical and poetic uses of language, far from being distortions of everyday language-games become authentic voices in the extended horizons of tradition. The widening of linguistic horizons, across traditions and cultures, is a central feature of Gadamer's hermeneutics.

III. GADAMER AND THE HISTORICALITY OF LANGUAGE

Gadamer develops insights into the ways language acquisition and use advance, how horizons extend, not by simple repetition, but through a capacity to widen limits and transcend the rules (whilst keeping the rules in play). The key to unravelling this difficulty is in appreciating the dialogical and conversational nature of linguistic horizons.

Gadamer looks to speech rather than writing as language's basic condition.[12] The written word, removed (in writing) from the original context of utterance lacks the qualities present in live speech. Gadamer adopts a Platonic suspicion towards the polysemic dangers associated with the written word. If spoken language itself is at a distance from the things themselves then written words are yet another level of alienation. Part of the original task of hermeneutical retrieval, and it is one Gadamer continues, is to revitalize lifeless inscription returning it to its condition of live speech. Gadamer says:

All writing is a kind of alienated speech, and its signs need to be transformed back into speech and meaning. Because the meaning has undergone a kind of self-alienation through being written down, this
transformation back is the real hermeneutical task.... The spoken word
interprets itself to an astonishing degree, by the manner of speaking, the
tone of voice, the tempo ... and by the circumstances in which it is
spoken. (*TM*, p. 393)[13]

In the everydayness of articulation and dialogue, horizons meet and interact.
To accommodate another horizon, be it another language-user or a
text, the speaker ceaselessly interrogates and interprets what is being
said. Ultimately, for Gadamer, all authentic use of language involves interpretation as one both seeks to understand and be understood. Interpretation
(and translation) are not reproductive acts, they are *productive* and hence
creative.

There can be no standing outside the historically given horizon. The
horizon offers the conditions of possibility for understanding what another
is seeking to say. This involves translating something initially 'foreign' (that
is, outside the individual's horizon) into something familiar, not by defusing
alterity but by searching for what unites the speakers. The rules sustaining
horizons are modified, unnoticed by the individual language-user as the
range of linguistic application extends.

The necessity for interpretation is not always apparent as, in day-to-day
linguistic exchanges, speakers frequently glide effortlessly on the surface of
language, as it were, especially when the language-game is routine,
familiar, and unproblematic; where meanings offer no resistance. The
procedure of naming and passing slabs, as in the 'primitive' language-game
of the *Investigations*, would be a case in point. When language becomes
opaque, when what the other is seeking to say initially defeats, evades
comprehension, the usually invisible act of interpretation comes to the
fore. Impeding a dialogue between the reader and poem, for example, is
the new and unfamiliar, disruptive of existing linguistic practice. The
situation is invariably normalized when a new, but temporary, resting-
place is achieved. Prejudice, the condition of judgement, limits the horizon
and yet at the same time extends it. Unlike Wittgenstein's rules (of
language-games), prejudices are extended and changed in every linguistic
encounter.

For Gadamer, horizons participating in dialogue are transfigured. The
initial prejudices, regulating what can be said, modify. A dialectical, that is
hermeneutic, oscillation between the rules and their application takes place.
The range of applicability of words and sentences is regulated, but the appli-

cations themselves amend the rule. Once again, it is possible to expose the
limitations of Wittgenstein's position; whereas he sees a more formal relationship between rules and application, Gadamer sees them as an illustration
of the 'hermeneutic circle'.

Part of the dynamic of language, its interpretive possibilities, compels it
into ever-new formulations, expanding and shifting horizons. Another force
is at work: play or playfulness, something language, by its very nature, is
given to. Following Heidegger, Gadamer speaks of language as essentially
'apophantic', that is 'world-disclosive'. Opened up is the human world and
an arena of concerns, things that matter to those operating within the disclosure. A prime motivation for using language is not transparent communication; this is a modernist fantasy, but reflexive dialogue with others. It may
not be immediately obvious, when language is functioning as little more than
a means of communication, but all language is indirectly a dialogue addressing central concerns. All concerns or matters at issue (from the point of
view of the horizon) motivate the linguistically mediated self, with its
ongoing and inconclusive quest for personal meaning. Man, the 'language
animal', is fundamentally motivated not by a desire for idle communication
or the attainment of an illusory objective knowledge but for self-understanding.

At another level, namely the totality of language, concerns are the enduring
questions endlessly posed and reformulated throughout the historical disclosure of language. Questions about the nature of justice and the good, for
example, are perennially addressed in Western culture. There can be no definitive answers. The current language-games offer no more than provisional
possibilities, new ways of formulating time-honoured questions. Wittgenstein's idea that these philosophically motivated meta-questions are no more
than violations of ordinary language indicates once again a fraught relationship to the historical.

Admittedly, grand narratives like that of the unfolding and coming to self-
consciousness of Spirit, are unwarranted or at least depend upon superfluous
assumptions (about progress or an inner telos or development). Wittgenstein
performs a valuable service in rejecting dubious forms of historical explanation, as he says, 'there is nothing more stupid than the chatter about cause
and effect in history books; nothing is more wrong-headed, more half-baked'.
(*CV*, p. 62)[14]

Against the 'half-baked' 'chatter' of historical theory Wittgenstein presents
an alternative. In his hostility to the methodology of early anthropology, in
his 'Remarks on Frazer's *Golden Bough*', he returns to the idea of the picture.
Here the picture is used as a way of grasping the bigger picture without
recourse to causal hypotheses:

The historical explanation, the explanation as an hypothesis of development, is only *one* way of assembling data.... It is just as possible to see the
data in their relation to another and to embrace them in a general *picture*
without putting it in the form of an hypothesis about temporal distance.
(My emphasis) (*PO*, p. 131)

Wittgenstein's aversion to Frazer's enthusiasm for scientific rationalism and
progress clearly connects to the quotation above. 'Frazer is much more
savage than most of his savages' he says and 'his explanations of primitive
practices are much cruder than the meaning of the practices themselves'
(*PO*, p. 131). This gives the background to the resistance to historical
explanation dependent upon a crude causal model. Wittgenstein acknowledges the difficulty of making sense of ancient rituals and practices,
Frazer's principal objective in *The Golden Bough*, but explaining the past as
a vulgar and unrefined version of the present, a tendency Wittgenstein no
doubt detected in much culturally imperialist historical science, he sees as
capricious and arbitrary. So-called 'savages', he explains, 'are not as far
removed from the understanding of a spiritual matter as a twentieth-
century Englishman' (*PO*, p. 131). The sense of being privileged in the
present is questionable; especially when we realize that forgotten ideas and
practices exemplify greater wisdom and 'understanding'.[15]
   All of this makes sense but Wittgensteinians still need to confront that
cluster of intractable questions about language's potential for bridging the
historical divide, that is, the distance between the language-games of the
present and the past.
   Historically conditioned concerns constitute another dynamic within
language. Only from the framework of inherited questions is language
capable of change. Rules delimit concerns yet the concerns themselves reflect
back, bringing about ever-new applications. The character of concerns is
changed by the rule. The concerns reveal the limitations of the rules and
further extend them.
   Gadamer speaks of a 'fusion of horizons'. Horizons are fused in every
linguistic encounter, in day-to-day dialogical exchanges. Mutual concerns
draw the participants into dialogue and in the transaction both language
and horizons are transformed. A 'fusion of horizons' takes place when one
inevitably and unwittingly encounters the language-games of the past: 'To
bring about this fusion in a regulated way is the task of what we called
"historically effected consciousness"' (*TM*, p. 307). For Gadamer, past
language-games are not inert repositories of redundant meaning, as for
Wittgenstein; on the contrary, they sustain their effects in the present.
Without past meanings current meanings would be impossible, hence Gada-

mer's idea that consciousness in the present is always an effect ('historically effected consciousness') of the language-games of the past, constituting the tradition.

An unbridgeable historical distance does not separate language-games from the present; they are, like current language-games, part of an ever-extending totality, the tradition. The current web of meanings is never simply a given starting point being itself the effect of former language-games. The past continues to resonate in the present.

Gadamer gives useful examples of the way past meanings continue to reverberate and have an effect in the present in his collection of essays *The Enigma of Health* (1996). Gadamer is ceaselessly vigilant to abandoned and forgotten nuances of meaning in hermeneutical reflections upon the language of health, illness, and medical practice.[16] Part of Gadamer's purpose is to illustrate how echoes and traces of words are still, albeit in sedimented form, maintaining an influence in the language of the present. Listening to the reverberations of lost or inert prescientific meanings, a difficult but not impossible task even in the modern age, enriches the level of reflection and understanding, making one more mindful of what has been forgotten in the present age. A frequently used illustration in these essays, because it bears directly upon the medical lexicon, is the notion of 'treatment'. To draw attention to the all too easily neglected interpersonal aspects of the doctor's expertise, Gadamer, in the essay 'Philosophy and medical practice', reminds us of forgotten nuances to common medical terms. His strategy is to retrieve forgotten meanings and awaken the reader to a less instrumental under-standing of the physician's art:

> The German word *Behandlung* is a rich and significant word for 'treating' people and 'handling' them with care. Within it one hears literally the word 'hand', the skilled and practised hand that can recognize problems simply through feeling and touching the affected parts of the patient's body. 'Treatment' in this sense is something which goes far beyond mere progress in modern techniques. (Gadamer (1996), p. 99)

Meanings enshrined in the historical texts of the past have their own horizons and they can be productively encountered from the present. Ancient texts are not alien and radically other, they have their own horizons, they share common concerns, and they stand within an all-encompassing tradition. Interpretive dialogue with the past is always possible, in fact, unavoidable.

The continuity of language, a capacity to absorb and generate endless novelty and change, brings everything within the ambit of tradition. Gada-mer's vision of language as essentially historical and continuous runs against the Wittgensteinian idea of fragmented and discontinuous language-games. Of course language, for Gadamer, in one sense, is discontinuous: in the interpretation of a written or spoken 'text' (dialogue) the speaker is always caught within a tension between the familiar and the unfamiliar. Although the prejudicial horizon of the speaker is incessantly disrupted, the 'fusion of horizons' enables a negotiation of the strange and unfamiliar. To some critics Gadamer overestimates the degree to which his hermeneutics reaches out to, and ultimately neutralizes, the unfamiliar. This thought is at the heart of the deconstructive rejection of philosophical hermeneutics; Gadamer's extension of horizons to effortlessly fuse even with those horizons across disparate traditions and cultures is taken to be a glib and politically reactionary denial of an ineradicable alterity. Gadamer is frequently taken to task for emphasizing what unites rather than separates us.

Fusing of horizons overcomes a huge difficulty encountered in literary, philosophical, and historical studies, namely, the location of the interpreter with respect to the past.

Deep contextualism obliterates any sense of a problematic in the present as the interpreter submerges in the past. The rational reconstructor simply ignores context and adopts the 'view from nowhere' as a way of interpreting past texts as though the distance of history was irrelevant. 'Fusion of horizons' acknowledges the embeddedness of the interpreter in the present, allowing for the horizon of the interpreter to expand and embrace the horizon of the past text. Gadamer states, 'In a tradition this process of fusion is continually going on, for there old and new are always combining into something of living value, without either being explicitly foregrounded from the other' (*TM*, p. 306).

Meaning is never fixed; it slips as the tradition changes. The incompleteness of meaning is realized in the dialogical fusion of horizons. This idea is obviously scandalous in certain quarters and one of the first English-language reviewers of *Truth and Method* took Gadamer to task on what was termed 'the indeterminacy of meaning'. Central to E. D. Hirsch's criticism is the perception of a failure on Gadamer's part to distinguish between 'meaning' and 'significance'. Hirsch writes,

> There is a difference between the meaning of a text (which does not change) and the meaning of a text to us today (which changes). The meaning of a text is that which the author meant by his use of a particular linguistic symbol.[17]

For Hirsch meaning never changes because authorial intention is permanently fixed but the significance of a text, the history of its fortunes within the literary canon is susceptible to the kind of indeterminacy Gadamer defends. Hirsch rejects here the fundamental hermeneutical principle that the author does not have a privileged access to the 'true' meaning of his or her text.

IV. WITTGENSTEIN AND TRADITION

There is an uneasy tension in Wittgenstein's later work around the whole question of the historicality of language. When spelt out it appears to undermine much of what was said earlier about his resistance to the historical. The tension is as follows. The agreements sustaining language are provisional and given to unaccountable changes. There is nothing, in principle, to connect current and former language-games, but there is an intriguing counter-thrust in the section in the *Investigations* on rule-following which tends to pull against the 'language-as-discontinuous' theme.

Wittgenstein shifts almost unnoticed from talk of more or less arbitrary rules and agreements to a completely new thought. Language-games are no more than customary activities (*PI*, §198).

In describing regularities, especially those built into language, as customs seems to bring Wittgenstein close to a new position, one thematizing the continuity of tradition. In rejecting the possibility of psychological or epistemological grounding, Wittgenstein gives language a foundation in social consensus: agreements are held fast by customary activity. In embracing the idea of the customary Wittgenstein succeeds in avoiding discontinuity; significantly, he is able to bring together the various games within an all-embracing concept. Since customs have their origins in obscurity there is some sense here of the historicality of language.

By resorting to the notion of custom Wittgenstein emerges not as a postmodern nihilist, delighting in endless difference, but as a closet traditionalist, subsuming all activity under the mute category of custom. The price to be paid for this kind of historicizing of language is very high. Language-users become unwitting victims of tradition. There is no shifting sand of contingent agreement, only the solid bedrock of inflexible custom.

By changing the foundations of language from social consensus to custom, echoes of Gadamer's appropriation of tradition re-emerge. Nevertheless, the shortcomings of Wittgenstein's failure to adopt a more hermeneutically sensitive position are as apparent here as elsewhere; again the comparison with Gadamer falls apart. Wittgenstein treats customs as though they were unwavering attributes of the language-game, regarding them like rules, that is, as rigid limits circumscribing linguistic possibilities. A very different way of talking about customs, and this is indeed close to Gadamer but unavailable to

Wittgenstein, is the one offered by the English political philosopher, Michael
Oakeshott:

> Custom is always adaptable and susceptible to the nuance of the situation.
> This may appear a paradoxical assertion; custom, we have been taught, is
> blind. It is, however, an insidious piece of misobservation; custom is not
> blind, it is only 'blind as a bat'. And anyone who has studied a tradition of
> customary behaviour (or tradition of any sort) knows that both rigidity and
> instability are foreign to its character.[18]

Implicit in Oakeshott's conception of custom is its openness and flexibility,
its adaptability to 'the nuance of the situation'. Custom here preserves a
manner of behaviour, including linguistic performance; at the same time it is
open to change and innovation. Oakeshott locates custom within the
extremes of 'rigidity' and 'instability'. This is not unlike Gadamer's
(Hegelian) traditionalism where the strains between the givenness of
language and the ever-new needs of each unique situation carry tradition
forward.[19]

Language is irredeemably implicated in its own history and Wittgenstein's
move to the customary is no more than a token appreciation of this fact. The
practical contexts of language, the life-blood of language-games and the
cultural space within which they are enacted, are part of a wider historical
picture, tradition. Wittgenstein's service to contemporary thought is to
acknowledge the specificity of language. Yet only by situating language-
games within the broader ambit of a totalizing power, tradition, is it possible
to uncover the richness of language's interpretive dimensions, its ability to
embrace the 'old' and the 'new'.

Criticism in this chapter focuses on a failure in the later Wittgenstein to
connect current linguistic practices with the past. Attention to this short-
coming is made possible by adopting Gadamer's hermeneutical perspective.
The relationship between current practices and those of the future presents
further problems to the Wittgensteinian picture of language. Forms of
linguistic novelty and innovation, most evident in the power of the poetic to
forge ever-new meanings and experiences with language, require investigation. Viewed hermeneutically language constantly overreaches itself into
every new form of expression; this is an issue of great concern to Gadamer,
particularly in his work after *Truth and Method*, but warrants scant attention
in Wittgenstein. Before focusing on this question I present, in the next
chapter, a brief excursus on Saint Augustine. Significantly both Gadamer
and Wittgenstein regard Augustine as a key figure in the history of philosophy. In radically opposing ways they assess the significance of Augustine's
contribution to the philosophy of language. The evidently different

approaches to Augustine serve to underwrite contrasts already noted in this
study.

NOTES

1. Wittgenstein (1979), p. 82.
2. J. Habermas, 'Review of Gadamer's *Truth and Method*' in Wachterhauser (1986),
   pp. 243–76.
3. Wachterhauser (1986), p. 248.
4. Wachterhauser (1986), p. 248.
5. Wachterhauser (1986), p. 249.
6. In Rorty (1989), pp. 3–22.
7. Rorty (1989), p. 16.
8. Rorty (1989), p. 16.
9. There is a long tradition of overlapping the activities of seeing and understanding, from adopting 'points of view' to gaining 'moments of insight'. For
   detailed examination of visuality in the history of Western thought see Levin
   (1997). A connection with Wittgenstein is important here. Despite dropping his
   earlier 'picture' theory of language there is repeated mention in the later work of
   thinking as 'picturing'. For an enlightening discussion of the importance of the
   visual in Wittgenstein see Genova (1995).
10. Gadamer, *PH*, p. 85.
11. In the early stages of the *Investigations* 'training' and 'teaching' are used inter-
    changeably and play a large role in describing initial language acquisition. But
    perhaps these are too regimented and formulaic to fully grasp what happens in
    the earliest encounters with language? Aristotle's 'habituation' comes to mind
    here and perhaps language-acquisition is little more, in the first instance, than
    acquiring habits? Certainly habits are picked up within the loose and unregulated
    structures of play.
12. When reading Wittgenstein one gets the strong feeling that the language-games
    are invariably spoken rather than written; either in the silent speech of thought
    and 'inner' monologue or in the imaginary dialogues peppered throughout the
    Investigations. There are few instances in the later work where Wittgenstein
    differentiates between speech and writing – as though what pertains to one
    pertains to the other.
13. Gadamer is aware of Derrida's questioning of phonocentrism. On this matter see
    H-G. Gadamer 'Letter to Dallmayr', in *DD*, pp. 93–101.
14. Wittgenstein's reaction to causality in history is not unlike his attitude to Freud.
    According to Jacques Bouveresse, Wittgenstein felt Freud had got into a
    'horrible mess' because he did not distinguish between reasons and causes. There
    is an obvious connection between bad history and a mistaken understanding of
    human action here. See J. Bouveresse, *Wittgenstein Reads Freud* (Princeton: Prin-
    ceton University Press, 1995), Chapter 4, 'Reasons and causes', pp. 69–82. Also,
    Freud, like Frazer, was for Wittgenstein at his most unconvincing when he
    resorted to pseudo-science.
15. The Wittgensteinian Peter Winch pursued many of these ideas in his work. See

his 'Understanding a primitive society' in B. Wilson (ed.) *Rationality* (Oxford: Blackwell, 1970) and *The Idea of a Social Science and Its Relation to Philosophy* (London: Routledge & Kegan Paul, 1958). It is significant that Winch's work has often been seen as an attempt to appropriate Wittgenstein in the service of hermeneutics. On this matter see Howard (1982), especially pp. 72–85 in the chapter on 'Analytic hermeneutics'.

16. Gadamer's work, since the publication of *Truth and Method*, demonstrates the applications of philosophical hermeneutics to specific forms of praxis. Having elaborated upon the interpretative practices of *inter alia* law, literary criticism, and education, in *The Enigma of Health* he focuses upon medical practice. Like the earlier studies in 'applied hermeneutics', Gadamer illustrates, in this collection of thirteen essays, the relevance of the central themes in *Truth and Method* to a specific area of practice. One of these themes relates to the origins and consequences of modernity's commitment to a hyper-rational, and hence distorted, version of the ancient *techne*. Nowhere are these consequences more evident and potentially disastrous than in the realm of everyday practice.

In our scientific age, the forms of practical knowledge, derived through historically conditioned activity, run the risk of obliteration as they get filtered out by a methodized, theoretical world picture. The dangerous legacy of post-Cartesian thought is an intensification of the forgetting of practice we encounter when theory and *techne* are threatened with merger.

Another important theme from *Truth and Method*, concerning what Gadamer calls 'effective history', that is, the continued effect of the past upon the present, also comes to the fore in this collection of essays. The hermeneutics of effective history, present in all authentic thinking, resists the gravitational effect of attempts to foreclose genuine understanding. *The Enigma of Health* offers a vivid illustration of how these tension-ridden themes work together in the specific arena of medical practice.

The contemporary medical practitioner has access to the most sophisticated technology, whether it be life-support systems, the wherewithal for organ transplantation, or computer programmes for diagnosis. A proliferation of research and development has put at the doctor's disposal an endless array of drug therapies. More and more, medical science becomes medical technology as new forms of knowledge are transposed and applied, transforming the doctor into a politically powerful technologist – a technologist of the body. In order to plot the course of this radical change, and to reflect upon its limitations, we need to think through a web of ideas concerning the real nature of technology, its origins in the Greek notion of *techne*, and the connection between *techne* and *praxis*: this Gadamer does in the first essay in *The Enigma of Health*, 'Theory, technology, praxis'. Drawing upon Aristotle's account of practice in the *Nicomachean Ethics*, Gadamer shows how the technologization of knowledge in the modern world distorts the traditional theory/practice relationship.

For the ancient craftsman, the productive process involved the application of knowledge to a preplanned object. The artefact emanated from the practical skill (*techne*) of the artisan. Even for Aristotle, the doctor occupied a special place because his practical skill was not directly applied to the construction of an object. Medical art produces nothing in the literal sense: health is not an object.

Medicine, and this is one of the central insights Gadamer brings to an understanding of the modern world, can never be reduced to a mere skill. What the doctor seeks to bring about is health, but its return is never a direct consequence of applied skill since skilfulness only relates to the production of artefacts.

Medical practice is, if one thinks back to its primordial sense, the *art* of healing. What the modern world is in danger of neglecting is the sense in which the real expertise of the doctor assists rather than controls the natural healing process. The doctor requires a special kind of (phronetic) judgement in aiming to restore the essential balance or equilibrium of the patient. The doctor should have no illusions that he or she is curing the patient with interventionary techniques. At best he or she can, with solicitude, tentatively apply general medical knowledge to this particular (that is, unique) individual. Medicine is both an art and a skill. The artistry displays itself as the doctor seeks to interpret the imbalance in the patient and guides the process whereby the patient recovers a lost equilibrium. Balance is required of the doctor in that he or she needs to make a fine discrimination between what will assist the patient and what needs to be left to the 'open domain' of nature. The illness of the patient presents the doctor with a hermeneutical problem.

So easily the doctor's intervention can be fractionally too much or too little, bringing about a complete reversal of the intended effect. Gadamer likens the doctor's art to Rilke's description of the acrobat where, 'the pure too little incomprehensibly transforms itself, springs over into the empty too much' (p. 36). In our scientific age, Gadamer suggests, the fine discriminations of the doctor are limited because technology artificially reduces the necessity for judgement. As Gadamer says, 'the more strongly the sphere of application becomes rationalized, the more does proper exercise of judgment along with practical experience in the proper sense fail to take place' (p. 17).

The true enigma of health is this: when all is said and done the doctor is not fully in control, neither is he or she ever in a position to completely understand the nature of health, the body, and healing. The true concern of the practitioner is not the general nature of health but the restoration of the equilibrium of a particular, unique individual, in his or her care. Ultimately health cannot be explained entirely from within the province of the scientific world. 'Illness is a social state of affairs. It is also a psychological-moral state of affairs, much more than a fact that is determinable from within the natural sciences' (p. 20). More fundamental than general scientific understanding for the doctor is the range of ethical concerns relating to the care the practitioner demonstrates towards the patient and the care the patients exercise upon themselves.

17. *Validity in Interpretation*, Hirsch (1967), p. 255. (For his trenchant critique of Gadamer see Appendix 2: 'Gadamer's theory of interpretation', pp. 245–64).
18. 'The Tower of Babel', Oakeshott (1991), p. 471.
19. For a detailed account of the proximity between Gadamer and Oakeshott on tradition see Lawn (1996), pp. 267–77.

CHAPTER 6

A Competition of Interpretations:[1] Wittgenstein and Gadamer Read Augustine

In the beginning was the Word, and the Word was with God, and the Word was God

(John 1:1)

I. INTRODUCTION

The writings of Saint Augustine are a common reference point for Gadamer and Wittgenstein. Part One of the *Investigations* famously begins with an extended quotation from Augustine's *Confessions*, exemplifying what for Wittgenstein is a now orthodox, but mistaken, attitude to language and its acquisition. Augustine is rebuked for an allegedly primitive and simplistic identification of word and object. On the Wittgensteinian reading a baleful tradition in philosophical writing about language is inaugurated. Augustine is assumed to set in motion the designative theory, discussed in detail in Chapter One. Augustine's major works wholly or partly concerned with language are: *De Dialectica* (On Dialectic); *De Doctrina Christiana* (On Christian Teaching); *De Trinitate* (On the Trinity); *De Magistro* (The Teacher). The *Confessions*, frequently referred to by Wittgenstein in the later work, make only minor and passing autobiographical references to language; this in itself forces one to think he underestimated the full scope of Augustine's achievement in this area and was unaware of the more detailed semiotic and hermeneutical writings.

Notably in Part Three of *Truth and Method*,[2] Gadamer advances a radically alternative reading, for he sees in Augustine, on the contrary, a decisively positive moment in the history of the development of the concept of language. Augustine, far from being a dark force, in fact heroically rescues the living word from overshadowing and obliteration by the wordless powers of human thought. Inspired by Stoic theory he resists the Platonic tendency to downgrade speech, refusing to subsume language under the all-embracing category of reason. Augustine, far from being dismissed as a misdirected ancient, the familiar story in modernist (designative) accounts of the history of philosophy, is elevated in status by Gadamer and treated as the genuine founder of a universal hermeneutics and early proponent of an anti-Platonic philosophy of language. Many aspects of Gadamer's account of language touched on in earlier chapters, relating to its essential incompleteness, its interpretive dimension, and its ability to resist closure in formal propositions, are in fact prefigured in Augustine's work.

Gadamer and Wittgenstein offer widely divergent interpretations of the same historical figure. An obvious question presents itself: how can contemporary thinkers offer such diametrically opposed assessments of the same author? This is a question behind much of this chapter. The early Church father becomes a touchstone for comparing Gadamer and Wittgenstein as well as raising broader questions surrounding the interpretation and reception of historical texts.

Is Wittgenstein's use of Augustinian thought legitimate? Is he, unfairly perhaps, using the specific section from the *Confessions* (on the young Augustine's early encounters with language) to make a general point against a generic 'picture' of the 'essence' of language or is his aim more focused upon the figure of Augustine himself? And, whether he is attacking Augustine or what has come to be known as the 'Augustinian picture of language', are Wittgenstein's criticisms defensible? Is his criticism a glaring example of what happens when historical scholarship and hermeneutical practice are abjured in favour of a context-less inspection of the apparent logic of a position? These and other questions pertaining to Wittgenstein's Augustine critique become all the more vivid and important set against Gadamer's reading of Augustine. This chapter starts with a consideration of the importance of Augustine for Gadamer.

II. AGAINST THE FORGETFULNESS OF LANGUAGE: AUGUSTINE'S 'INNER WORD' AND THE HERMENEUTICS OF THE TRINITY

In Part Three of *Truth and Method*, language, always implicit in the work, becomes the dominant motif. There is a clear shift away from an analysis of the hermeneutical structure of our experiences of art and history to an explicit focus on language. All experience is revealed to be in some sense linguistic. To substantiate his final claim that hermeneutics has a universal dimension, one which the whole work has been leading up to, he considers 'The development of the concept of language in the history of Western thought'.[3] Gadamer argues for the impossibility of positing frames of reference outside language and he seeks to show how this fundamental insight gets forgotten or repressed in the construction of modernist narratives of the history of philosophy. There is no conspiracy theory here, merely the suggestion of a mistaken or infelicitous turn inspired by the differing receptions and appropriation of Plato's work. Gadamer embarks on a detailed historical analysis of the unfolding of the concept of language to demonstrate what he refers to as 'the forgetfulness of language'; the various ways language is forgotten or forgets itself. In the modern post-Christian world, crucial chapters in the story of the unfolding of language are neglected; the importance of Augustine is hidden within this general historical amnesia.

The identity of thought and language is disrupted by Plato's interpretation of the *logos* as that which stands behind and above the network of significations. Even though Plato conceived of thought as a 'dialogue of the soul with itself', this is not the linguistic exchange of the Socratic dialogues (or rather conversations); it is the wordless monologue of *dianoia*, thought thinking by and to itself. The prejudice for constructing an ontologically superior level of being beyond everyday language's implication in the world informs the Platonic dialogues.

Gadamer concentrates upon the argument of the *Cratylus*. It is there he identifies, in the debate surrounding the conventional or natural status of language, the genuine starting point for an instrumentalist theory, a theory starting in Plato and reaching a *tour de force* in the modern age. Instrumentality reduces the being of language to 'pure sign' (*TM*, p. 418).

The Greek word *logos* carries with it a variety of senses. Plato is responsible for elevating the term's cognitive dimension in the stress laid upon associations with reason, argument, and thought. *Logos* has other connotations signifying discussion, discourse, and speech. Plato neglects the more linguistic nuances giving priority to the identification of *logos* with reason. Here starts a tendency in Greek thought to elevate the status of rationality whilst underplaying the formative significance of language and neglecting its intimate association with thought. But there is a key moment in the subsequent development of the concept of language where the Greek (Platonic) trend is called into question and significantly reversed. For Gadamer, 'There is, however, an idea that is not Greek which does more justice to the being of language, and so prevented the forgetfulness of language in Western thought from being complete' (*TM*, p. 418).

Recognition of the actuality of language, albeit temporarily, reasserts itself in the most unlikely place, namely, in Saint Augustine's theological reflections upon the mysterious nature of the Trinity. Gadamer takes his cue here from Heidegger. In the 1921 lectures on 'Augustine and Neo-Platonism'[4] Heidegger looked to Augustine's writings on the Trinity (*De Trinitate*) as one of the many sources for his hermeneutical phenomenology and as Jean Grondin has shown[5] the Augustinian influence on Heidegger was substantial. Gadamer, as one of Heidegger's students, was profoundly affected by these and subsequent lectures, and uses his teacher's insights as the springboard for his own position.[6]

III. IN THE BEGINNING WAS THE WORD

In attempting to understand the actuality of God's incarnation and its uneasy relationship to embodiment, connecting this to scriptural accounts, notably in the prologue to Saint John's gospel,[7] Gadamer sees in Augustine the emergence of a new, fundamentally non-Greek idea of language. The crucial move here is the turn away from Greek *logos* to the Stoically derived *verbum*; particularly what Augustine terms the *verbum interius* or 'inner word'. Gadamer argues that in resolving a theological question, namely, how one explains the enigma of the Trinity, Augustine simultaneously throws helpful light on questions surrounding the being of language, questions which, as we saw, the Greek *logos* had failed to disclose.

What, essentially, is the theological problem of the Trinity? The difficulty is in explaining to human understanding the Son's consubstantiality with the Father. Christ's divinity and humanity appear to be contradictory in an obvious way. If Christ is God where is his genuine humanity and if he is human where is his divinity? Grondin expresses this dilemma theologically when he says 'The theory of the Trinity must strike a path between the Charybdis of a pure subordinationism and the Scylla of docetism'.[8] Augustine's defence of the Trinity avoids these heretical outer limits.

There is an analogy between the relationship of thought to language and that between God the Father to God the Son. It is mistaken to suggest, as we saw in the interpretation of the Greek *logos*, that thought and language are ontologically separate; if so how does thought become word? The answer is this. Thought readily becomes word if it is from the very beginning linguistic in some form. In the same way, there is no problem of the Word becoming Flesh or God becoming man if from the very beginning there is true consubstantiality:

> The ... miracle of language lies not in the fact that the Word becomes flesh and emerges in external being, but that that which emerges and externalizes itself in utterance is always already a word. That the Word is with God from all eternity is the victorious doctrine of the church.... (*TM*, p. 421)

So what is the analogy between the Trinity and the thought–language relationship? Thought is essentially verbal; it is the 'inner word' under another description; the relationship between thought and language is a tension between one version of linguisticality and another. At the heart of Augustine is this notion of the inner word. As we will see, in postulating the inner word he does not commit himself to a form of mentalism or psychologism; anything but, despite Wittgensteinian and post-Wittgensteinian attempts to sell this interpretation although, strangely, one of the foremost Augustine scholars in the English language, Christopher Kirwan, offers this crypto-Wittgensteinian thought: 'Augustine has founded his theorizing about language on the underlying principle that its general function is to transmit thoughts from one mind to another'.[9] The inner word is not a source of private meanings transferred to the public realm; on the contrary, it is the necessary universal dimension of language, without which spoken language would be impossible. The inner word is much like Gadamer's 'tradition' in that current linguistic meanings are invariably derived from the resources of customary practice and yet are never reducible to it. The hermeneutical tension between the inner word and a spoken word is analogous to the relationship between current meanings and the tradition.

According to scripture the Word became or was made flesh. The becoming is not a transformation of quality to quality or quality to quantity. God is one yet the Word, *ab initio*, is incarnate. Gadamer shows how Greek embodiment is unlike incarnation: 'Incarnation is obviously not embodiment. Neither the (Greek) idea of the soul nor of God that is connected with embodiment corresponds to the Christian idea of the incarnation' (*TM*, p. 418). The Greek gods, by magical means of embodiment, cunningly assume human form whilst remaining gods and exact their wicked way with mere mortals. The Christian God is not embodied but 'is made flesh', is incarnated and becomes fully human in Christ, without loss of divinity. Although an ineffable relationship, Augustine offers a partial explanation of the central mystery of Christianity:

> (O)ur word becomes an articulate sound, yet it is not changed into one; so the Word of God became flesh, but far be it from us to say He was changed into flesh. For both that word of ours became an articulate sound, and that other Word became flesh by assuming it, not by consuming itself so as to be changed into it.[10]

The relationship between God the Father and God the Son is like the relationship between the inner word and the spoken word. Just as God is consubstantial with the Son without loss of divinity so the inner word is essentially word despite the fact that it is silent, inexpressible, unspoken, universal, and cannot be articulated.

In *De Trinitate* Augustine offers various accounts of the inner word. 'The word that sounds outwardly', he says, 'is the sign of the word that gives light inwardly (the "inner word"); which latter has the greater claim to be called a word',[11] and 'For the thought that is formed by the thing which we know, is the word which we speak in the heart: which word is neither Greek nor Latin, nor of any other tongue'.[12] The inner word somehow makes the spoken word possible and yet is not identical to it. The (hermeneutical) distance between the spoken and the inner word provokes speech: 'When … there is something which you wish to say the very conception of that in your heart is a word not yet uttered'.[13]

The inner word cannot be fully articulated for it is in some inexpressible sense a reflection of the word of God (which is One) and, for Augustine, enigmatic. At the same time, the spoken word is, in some unaccountable sense, a reflection of the inner word. The nature of this reflection Gadamer later calls 'speculative' (from *speculum*, mirror image) echoing Hegel's reference to the dialectical and hermeneutical qualities of the speculative.

Particularly in the light of what has come to be known, via Wittgensteinian scholarship, as the 'Augustinian picture of language', much has been written, especially by analytic philosophers, against Augustine's language theory. The notion of the inner word is seen as the embryo of a now discredited mentalism, namely, that words stand proxy as signs for thoughts, and that ultimately language is the instrument for communicating individual thoughts; this is the very reverse of Gadamer's Augustine interpretation.

Another aspect of Augustine's work that is in receipt of a bad press is an alleged psychologism. In the recently published *Cambridge Companion to Augustine*[14] the distinguished medieval scholar Christopher Kirwan perpetuates the view that Augustine's 'inner words' are no more than private thoughts. In the essay 'Augustine's philosophy of language'[15] Kirwan identifies the inner word appropriately as 'a kind of languageless word'.[16] This is dismissed and replaced by 'Speech-thought isomorphism':

> For language to be a possible method of thought transmission, thoughts must be analysable into constituent elements, each one signified by a distinct word. There must be a one-one correspondence between the elements of a sentence, which are words, and the elements of the thought signified by that sentence.[17]

The 'language-less word' idea is precisely the one Gadamer picks up on in *Truth and Method* as that crucial moment in the history of Western philosophy when language is roused from its self-forgetfulness: Kirwan's 'speech-thought symmetry' perpetuates a piece of mystification. The inner word is the languageless word, without which language itself would be impossible.

And further, taking his lead from Augustine's inner word and refining it in the light of Schleiermacher's hermeneutics and Heidegger's existential phenomenology, Gadamer is able to construct his own picture of language, one at variance with the standard picture of language as calculus, as the ordered schema representing the ordered structure of the world. Gadamer is clearly offering an interpretation of Augustine as a proto-expressivist.

Augustine repudiates the idea that the word, as in Plato's *Cratylus*, is merely conventional. For Augustine the word is a sign, and he is a semiotician long before Peirce, Eco, and the structuralists, but he takes the sign to be more than a mere convention. The sign is not a random cipher made meaningful within the arbitrary structures of a man-made language, an idea we might attribute to Wittgenstein amongst others; the sign is intimately connected to something beyond itself, ultimately to the Word of God and immediately the world.

Locating the meaning of the word beyond the manipulative structures of individual human consciousness was central to Heidegger's hermeneutical phenomenology of language in *Being and Time* and it is taken up and extended in Gadamer. Against the arbitrary system of signs is the thought that the being of things, and not the consciousness of individual manipulating of idiolects, makes language possible. Does Augustine's prioritizing of the being of objects over and above the consciousness of language-users make for a discredited word – object realism? Is this not precisely the kind of argument Wittgenstein subjected to sustained criticism in the *Investigations*? The whole thrust of the opening paragraphs of the *Investigations* is a denial of strict designation as witnessed in *PI*, §13, 'When we say: "Every word in language signifies something" we have so far said *nothing whatever*'.

The inclusion of the 'inner word' frees Augustine from accusations of a dependence upon designation. The tension between the 'inner' and the 'spoken' word is precisely Augustine's escape route from any possible insinuation of reductionism. The inner word is not temporally locatable yet the spoken word is irredeemably tainted by its own specificity and historicality. Speaking, thinking, and writing are all performative acts within a specific historical tradition or socio-cultural space. Any utterance is unique to its time and place, that is, its context, yet it draws upon the wider domain of tradition. Language, on the Augustine (and Gadamerian) picture, is the dynamic movement between extremes.

For Augustine, there is universality about language to which the inner word bears testimony. There is an imprecise dimension to the word irreducible to its context. The inner word, a reflection of the word of God, brings together all natural languages, points to the thought, the inner dialogue, without which there would be no speech. At the same time, the inner word represents the being of the thing, the matter at issue, *die Sache*, as Gadamer has it. Gadamer sees language in terms of what it is about. If language is 'object directed' what are the intentional objects of language? For Gadamer, Augustine has this right when he speaks of the aspect of the world by which language is anchored. The inner word reveals the true being of a thing. Again this does not lead Gadamer into an antiquated 'realist' philosophical position. Brice Wachterhauser sees a suspension between realism and a kind of historicism:

> Gadamer understands the need for a consistent realism, which maintains that our disputes must be about what is real in some sense independently of the inquirer's mind and place in history, and at the same time, he dedicates his thinking to working through the issue of historicity for our understanding of this realist truth.[18]

Language is hermeneutically suspended between the universality of the inner word, which can be likened to the totality of meanings within tradition, and the deep historical and cultural dependency of the spoken word applied within a specific context. Here is not so much a re-enactment of the ancient problem of the One and the Many (or the intractable philosophical question of the Universal and the Particular) but a 'playful' (as Gadamer may express it) interchange between extremes. At work in the hermeneutics of the Trinity is precisely this tension. God, like linguistic meaning, remains unidentifiable with a particular time and yet is ever-present in human history and temporality by way of consubstantiality with Christ.

Drawing together various disparate threads we might present in a more panoramic form Gadamer's Augustinian picture of language. Most fundamentally we witness a re-emergence of a now familiar theme, the rejection of the modernist philosophical myth that language divides neatly into discrete entities called propositions and the associated fable that these make truth-functional claims about the world. Gadamer dismantles the fallacy of the formal proposition as the essence of language in his analysis of the development of the concept of language in *Truth and Method*. In following Heidegger, Gadamer shows how the account of language as proposition, under the influence of Greek, mainly Platonic thought, took hold.

Revealing Augustine (and subsequent scholasticism)[19] as a key moment in a backwards movement away from Greek instrumentalism Gadamer finds authority for his alternative to the logic of the proposition. For Augustine, language is essentially non-propositional, because propositions are, in terms of Aristotelian logic, timelessly the case. For Augustine and Gadamer the spoken, as opposed to the inner, word is temporally constrained and incomplete. The hermeneutical movement between the spoken and the inner word is a continuous dynamic between a single interpretive act and the totality of the tradition. Augustine indirectly affirms the thorough linguisticality of our interpretive appropriations of the world in seeing in the inner word not the abstract timelessness of Platonic thought but a dialectical tension between the universality of the inner word and the temporality of the spoken words of everyday discourse.

Where does this all lead? Certainly the conception of language presented by Gadamer and his interpretation of Augustine and Plato goes manifestly against the grain of designative theories. Gadamer replaces the proposition as the central figure of language with dialogue. As Grondin makes clear,

> The inner word 'behind' the expressed word means nothing else but ... dialogue, this intimate connection of language with our enquiring and self-enquiring existence, a dialogue that cannot completely reproduce any proposition. In the words of Gadamer: 'What is explicitly said is not everything. What is unsaid first makes what is said into a word that can reach us.'[20]

IV. WITTGENSTEIN'S AUGUSTINE

Wittgenstein's understanding of Augustine is diametrically opposed to the reading Gadamer offers. It is almost as if they discuss different thinkers, such is the gap between interpretations. As if to demonstrate the importance of Augustine for his work Wittgenstein commences the *Investigations* with a lengthy quotation from Augustine's *Confessions*, a book he regarded highly as a spiritual classic although, as we will see, he had reservations about the account of language it advances. According to his friend Maurice Drury, Wittgenstein once described the *Confessions* as 'the most serious book ever written' (quoted in Rhees, 1984, p. 90). And Norman Malcolm in his *Memoir* remembers how '(Wittgenstein) revered the writings of Saint Augustine ... he decided to begin his *Investigations* with a quotation from the latter's *Confessions*, not because he could not find the conception expressed in that quotation stated as well by other philosophers, but because the conception *must* be important if so great a mind held it' (quoted in Kerr, 1997, p. 39).

There is little serious scholarly engagement with Augustine's writings, although Wittgenstein clearly thinks his views significant. Augustine is used as a representative of a view of language Wittgenstein will, throughout the early part of the *Investigations*, hold up to scrutiny and criticism. Whether the critique is fair to the historical Augustine is another matter. The *Investi-*

gations commences with a lengthy extract from Book 1 of the *Confessions*, describing Augustine's memory of his earliest encounter with language. This is quoted in full:

> When they my elders named some object, and accordingly moved towards something, I saw this and I grasped that the thing was called by the sound they uttered when they meant to point it out. Their intention was shown by their bodily movements, as it were the natural language of all peoples: the expression of the face, the play of the eyes, the movement of other parts of the body, and the tone of voice which expresses our state of mind in seeking, having, rejecting, or avoiding something. Thus, as I heard words repeatedly used in their proper places in various sentences, I gradually learnt to understand what objects they signified; and after I had trained my mouth to form these signs, I used them to express my own desires. (Quoted in the Latin original and in this translation in *PI*, §1).

Augustine is taken to inaugurate, or at any rate perpetuate, what is for Wittgenstein a misguided, but historically influential, view of language and its acquisition. Wittgenstein rejects the detail of Augustine's claims, initially, by questioning their authority as 'a picture of the essence of human language' (*PI*, §1). Augustine, apparently, assumes an essence to language and this leads him into muddle and confusion.

Augustine is assumed to be guilty of a kind of reductionism based on the assumption that 'every word has a meaning' and 'this meaning is correlated with the word' being 'the object for which the word stands' (*PI*, §1). To portray language as a totality of monadic, isolated meanings made possible by an unambiguous correlation between word and object is a massive oversimplification. This naive view of language has seduced many a philosopher since Augustine; even Wittgenstein, in his earlier Tractarian incarnation, fell victim to its charms, as he freely admits. What is wrong with the theory of meaning implied in Augustine's position, as set out in the *Confessions*? For Wittgenstein there is yet another kind of reductionism at work. Augustine's view, because it erroneously takes all language to be *au fond* concerned with naming, also depends upon a simplified code consisting 'primarily of nouns like "table", "chair", and "bread"' (*PI*, §1). Even a superficial reading of Augustine's *De Dialectica* shows Wittgenstein to have underestimated Augustine. The introduction of a distinction between 'simple' and 'complex' words is evidence of a level of sophistication Wittgenstein ignores. He further underestimates Augustine when he states in *Philosophical Grammar* (p. 56):

When Augustine talks about the learning of language he talks about how we attach names to things, or understand the names of things. *Naming* here appears as the foundation, the be all and end all of language.

This begs the question: how do relational and abstract terms then become meaningful? 'And', 'every', and 'although' have a place in sentences but they are not underwritten by objects for which they stand proxy. Wittgenstein uses his own examples:

> Augustine, in describing his learning of language, says that he was taught to speak, learning the names of things. It is clear that whoever says this has in mind the way in which a child learns such words as 'man', 'sugar', 'table', etc. He does not primarily think of such words as 'today', 'not', 'but', 'perhaps'.[21]

Elsewhere he demonstrates, with very elementary examples taken from language learning situations, how flawed he takes the Augustinian picture of language to be. The destruction of an object has no bearing upon the sense of objects named in sentences: 'It is clear that the sentence "Excalibur has a sharp blade" makes sense whether Excalibur is still whole or is broken up' (*PI*, §39). If words are only meaningful by virtue of an intimate connection between word and thing named, how is 'Excalibur', and hence, sentences utilizing the name 'Excalibur', persistently intelligible even when the object is destroyed and there is no naming relationship? Wittgenstein clearly takes this to be an unanswerable question for Augustine.

Wittgenstein proceeds, in an unsystematic way throughout the early stages of the *Investigations*, to tease out some of the implications of this position. Not only is the strategy to discredit Augustine but it is also to make plausible the Wittgensteinian alternative outlined in the discussion of rules. If Augustine's first mistake was to identify word and object as the matrix for all meaning, he compounds the error by assuming the naturalness of what Wittgenstein terms 'ostensive definition' and 'ostensive teaching of words' (*PI*, §6). The infant Augustine 'grasped that the thing was called by the sound they uttered when they meant to point it out' (*PI*, §1). No amount of repetition of a word, accompanied by the gesture of pointing, will lead, in itself, to the child seizing upon meaning unless, of course, there is an assumption that the child has some innate predisposition, by *anamnesis* perhaps, to instinctively connect word uttered with finger pointed. For Wittgenstein, there is no such prenatal ability, yet Augustine, he claims, depends upon it.

Ostensive definition is a socially regulated activity and has to be genuinely mastered in a cultural context – obviating the need for explanations involving innateness. Without such an admission we would be compelled to assume that the child came into the world with a sophisticated and developed control of language (and the world) ready formed. We get some sense of this criticism when Wittgenstein comments:

> Augustine describes the learning of human language as if the child came into a strange country and did not understand the language of the country; that is, as if it already had a language, only not this one. Or again: as if the child could already *think*, only not yet speak. And 'think' here would mean something like 'talk to itself'. (*PI*, §32)

The child's untutored mastery of the practice of pointing, ostensive definition, gives the sense of innate linguistic competence, a predisposition, preceding the actual acquisition of language. Learning what a word means from the activity of pointing is, like rule-following, a custom. The association of word and object is not innate but socially taught and culturally acquired.

This leads to another of Augustine's supposed mistakes: the assumption that the child comes into the world with a ready-formed capacity to think and make connections, with reason already in place. By way of the innate powers of reasoning, the child readily converts private thoughts into publicly communicable speech.

Wittgenstein starts the *Investigations* with reference to Augustine, thinking him responsible for a mistaken 'picture' of language. The distortion initially assumes an isolated individual to be single-handedly responsible for entry into the linguistic world. Wittgenstein, via the whole edifice of language-games, seeks to reverse this arrangement. Language is always in place; descriptions of its operations start from this fact not from myths of innateness. Wittgenstein's game analogy moves away from the attempt to build up a structure of meaning from the individual resources of the private language-user. Rationality develops in tandem with linguisticality. It makes no sense to say, 'the child could already think, only not yet speak' (*PI*, §32). Here Wittgenstein echoes Hamann's insistence on the priority of speech over thought.

It is equally incoherent to suggest words do no more than name the world. To combat this idea Wittgenstein envisages a simplified language, not unlike the one outlined in the *Confessions*, the 'primitive language game' of builders A and B (*PI*, §2). Even here the expression 'Slab!' is not merely the name for an object. It is also a command, a speech-act, if uttered in a certain way within a pregiven cultural framework. Tone of voice and context are also factors contributing to nuances of meaning. Meaning is constituted and modified according to context of utterance or the many activities that go to make up a 'form of life'. Augustine's rudimentary picture of words as names or signs pointing to objects in the world stands in the way of the Wittgensteinian image of interlocking, culturally transmitted language-games.

The whole 'Augustine picture of language' sketched out above has become the Wittgensteinian orthodoxy and is seldom seriously challenged in the analytic tradition.

V. INTERPRETING INTERPRETATIONS

Does Wittgenstein distort Augustine or are his criticisms misdirected? Anthony Kenny is forthright in criticism. In the essay 'The Ghost of the *Tractatus*',[22] Wittgenstein's assessments of Augustine (and Frege) prove him to be 'unreliable as an historian of philosophy'. Kenny comments upon how, when Wittgenstein 'criticized other philosophers he rarely gave chapter and verse', and 'on the rare occasions on which he quoted verbatim he did not always do justice to the authors quoted'.[23] Wittgenstein plays fast and loose with the ordinary conventions of scholarship although without doubt many of the penetrating insights into the blind alleys of traditional philosophy are a consequence of a fresh, because untrained, approach. Wittgenstein in a moment of self-reassurance comments: 'It's a good thing I don't allow myself to be influenced' (*CV*, p. 1). This thought actually raises a crucially important question about appropriate methodology in the history of philosophy. Does attention to the fine details of philosophy's history – appreciation of context and problematics – stifle originality in interpretation or is it the necessary breeding ground for creativity?

Wittgenstein projects onto Augustine ideas 'resembling [his] own views rather than the views that are [his] target', claims Anthony Kenny.[24] In the quotation from the *Confessions* at the beginning of the *Investigations*, Wittgenstein focuses on the error of reducing all language to the formula 'meaning is correlated with the word. It is the object for which it stands' (*PI*, §1). Augustine's actual words are translated as follows:

> (The elders') intention (in pointing to objects and uttering sounds) was shown by their bodily movements, as it were the natural language of all peoples: the expression of the face, the play of the eyes, the movement of other parts of the body, and the tone of the voice. (Augustine, *Confessions*, quoted in *PI*, §1)

The reader's attention is not drawn to these acute observations nor are they discussed in the ensuing exegesis; they are simply taken as supporting the view Wittgenstein places in doubt. The irony Kenny no doubt saw relates to Augustine's emphasis upon the expressive relationship between speech and its bodily and gestural form. This affiliation is unambiguously Wittgensteinian. One of the points of the language-game analogy is to draw us away from introspective mentalist accounts of language production and to focus instead on the material conditions and circumstances of utterance. The language-game draws attention to the surrounding activities that serve to contextualize linguistic activity. These activities, described variously by Wittgenstein as practices, ceremonies, rituals, and gestures are precisely those external embodied activities Augustine emphasizes in this passage. *Lebensformen* or 'forms of life' (*PI*, §§19, 23, 241) is Wittgenstein's collective name for the various gestures and performative activities, the living contexts without which language would be meaningless.

Wittgenstein's blindness to Augustine's emphasis upon 'bodily movement', 'tone of voice', and 'play of eyes' is significant. The Augustinian sensitivity to the embodied and gestural is further demonstration of his closeness to an expressive rather than purely designative picture. 'Forms of life', so important in highlighting the horizon of meaning beyond the spoken and the 'literal', bring Wittgenstein close to hermeneutics and yet he undermines this in his partial and overhasty reading of Augustine and in a restrictive understanding of linguistic rules, an issue already discussed in Chapter 4.

VI. WITTGENSTEIN'S NATURALISM

There is a version of naturalism running throughout the later Wittgenstein. 'Commanding, questioning, recounting, chatting are', he claims, 'as much part of our natural history as walking, eating, drinking, playing' (*PI*, §25). And he takes the *Investigations* to offer no more than 'remarks on the natural history of human beings' (*PI*, §415). Naturalism militates against the implicit, soft relativism in the *Investigations* and *On Certainty*. Relativism and linguistic autonomy are the inevitable consequence of making language an enclosed and self-dependent system, making truth and certainty features of nothing other than the arbitrary language-games. The reduction of language to a self-authenticating system is a dominant motif in *On Certainty*, apparent in remarks such as, 'What counts as an adequate test of a statement belongs to logic. It belongs to the description of the language-game.' Arbitrariness is also evident in the claim that 'The *truth* of certain empirical propositions belongs to our frame of reference' (*OC*, §§82–3). The connection between relativism and naturalism is this. Naturalism is a possible bulwark against the excesses of relativism and a stand-in or substitute for the word–world connection the language-game idea aims to destroy. Clearly there is also a version of naturalism running through Augustine. 'Bodily movements' we are told are part of the 'natural language of all people' (*Confessions*, 1.8, quoted in *PI*, §1).

The oft-quoted 'if a lion could talk, we would never understand him' (*PI*, p. 223) is a further affirmation of naturalism, an aphoristic acknowledgement of a common, that is, universal, stock of gestures, indifferent to the specifics of culture. Leonine gestures, whatever they may be, could never find purchase on the uniquely human gestures common to all peoples.[25] The universalism expressed here is curiously out of sync with the rest of Wittgenstein's 'attention to particulars', his fastidious concentration on the specifics of everyday language and his rejection of theory-driven approaches. The commonality of gesture and behaviour more generally constitutes a condition of possibility for translating one natural language into another and acknowledges the opportunity of escaping the prison house of the language-games of a particular culture: 'The common behaviour of mankind is the system of reference by means of which we interpret an unknown language' (*PI*, §206). No such commonality exists between lions and humans, making 'Leonine', like Quine's *gavagai* (rabbits? rabbit time-space sections?), incommensurable with the home language and, in principle, untranslatable.[26] Naturalism seems to be one of Wittgenstein's devices for overcoming the lost grounding of language. Wittgenstein apparently resorts to naturalism to halt the slide into deep relativism. Freeing language from its close connection to the world, although a reaction against his *Tractatus*, and a position he attributes, ultimately, to Augustine, is the thin end of a wedge.

Wittgenstein in the later work radically disconnects language from an intimacy with the world, making it autonomous, creating hermetically sealed and isolated 'world-pictures' relative to others. The direction of Wittgenstein's work derives, in part, from an overhasty and careless reading of Augustine. Gadamer's Augustinianism, I suggest, circumnavigates these difficulties, although the quasi-realism he adopts is not itself unproblematic. The meaning of the 'inner word' is elusive and cannot be fully captured in the spoken word.

Central to philosophical hermeneutics is an interpretive negotiation of opposing tendencies. Gadamer declares 'the true locus of hermeneutics' to be '(the) *in-between*' (*TM*, p. 295). Linguisticality is riddled with tension and conflict. The task of hermeneutics is not to achieve understanding but to 'clarify the conditions in which understanding takes place' (*TM*, p. 295). Principal among the oppositions is universality and particularity, manifesting itself in different guises through the 'polarity of familiarity and strangeness' (*TM*, p. 295). Polar opposition is even a description of the relationship between the (familiarity) of linguistic rules as they are embodied in the tradition and the (strangeness) of the ever-new applications which extend the rules and increase linguistic variety and possibilities. All of this, if we accept Gadamer, was prefigured in Augustine's movement of the fundamentally

Platonic philosophical explanation of the relationship between universals and particulars to the more linguistically oriented one between the 'inner' and the 'outer' word. Easy connections are readily made here and to equate inner with universal and outer with particular is too simplistic. Neither Gadamer nor Augustine adopts this formula although it is clearly Platonic in origin[27] (and may account for the accusations of Platonism levelled against Gadamer). As I understand Gadamer, the inner word, the ineffable voiceless word of God, is transformed into the voiceless word of the tradition. The meaning of the tradition cannot be foreclosed or encompassed in understanding, representing as it does the incomplete totality of interpretations. It forms the background out of which all particular articulations emerge. The inner word, Augustine's 'word of the heart' (what Gadamer actually calls 'the unsaid'), drives on the outer spoken word just as the arteries of tradition connect to the capillaries of live speech. As Gadamer says, 'what is explicitly said is not everything. What is unsaid first makes what is said into a word that can reach us' (Wachterhauser, 1994, p. 146).

Many of the salient features of philosophical hermeneutics: its denigration of the proposition, its use of dialogue and questioning as a model of incompleteness, and, as we shall discuss presently, the word's world-disclosing tendency, come together in the tension between the inner and the outer word.

If the universality of the tradition, Augustine's 'inner word', is not equivalent to Platonic forms, how then does it operate in Gadamer? The element of Platonism is encountered when the universality of the tradition turns out to be more than an arbitrary conventionalist nominal(-ist) relationship to the world. However, Gadamer avoids naive realism. Brice Wachterhauser in a discussion of Gadamer's relation to realism[28] addresses the question of universality. 'Perspectival realism' is Wachterhauser's term to describe Gadamer's position.[29] The perspectival element, no doubt recalling Nietzsche's perspectivism, emphasizes the fact that the world may disclose itself but the disclosure is always partial and limited, 'historically contingent' and 'linguistically mediated' as Wachterhauser puts it.[30] Gadamer is a realist of sorts. The world is knowable despite our inability to escape the clutches of language: 'The multiplicity of . . . worldviews does not involve any relativization of the world. Rather what the world is is not different from the views in which it presents itself' (TM, p. 447).

Wachterhauser discerns four theses in Gadamer and suggests they form the basis for realism:

1. There are different linguistic views of reality.
2. There is no fundamental incompatibility between these linguistic views, qua views, and reality.

3. Each linguistic view can be seen as a finite presentation of reality...
4. Each linguistic view contains potentially within itself all other linguistic views. (Wachterhauser, 1994, p. 156)

Against Humboldt's conception of radically different worldviews Gadamer acknowledges one world and many ways of articulating it (in both senses of articulation). This is consistent with Gadamerian tradition where there are manifold narratives and interpretations of the world but no final description. There are many perspectives and many ways of talking about the world but language is always about something, directed towards some-thing in the phenomenological sense. Language is a double-edged sword, it can both hide and reveal; this much Gadamer learnt from Heidegger. But there is an important distinction to be made here. Heidegger, especially in his work after 'the turn', was constantly vigilant to the foreclosures of modernity, as thought is framed and ultimately silenced by what he termed 'the language of metaphysics'. On this point Gadamer and Heidegger part company. The structures of language are admittedly prejudicial but this does not condemn all linguistic encounters in the modern world to just more metaphysics. All-embracing structures (the subject-predicate form for Indo-European languages, for example) are separate from linguistic rules. This may be what Wittgenstein had in mind with his distinction between 'surface' and 'depth' grammar (*PI*, §664).

Against Heidegger, Gadamer sees reflected within ordinary language a kind of human cunning, constituting resistance to metaphysical entrapment, being more wily and elusive:

> Can a language ... ever properly be called the language of metaphysical thinking ...? Is not language always the language of the homeland and the process of becoming-at-home in the world? And does this fact not mean that language knows no restrictions and never breaks down, because it holds infinite possibilities of utterance in readiness? It seems to me that the hermeneutical dimension enters here and demonstrates its inner infinity in the speaking that takes place in dialogue.[31]

For Heidegger, the metaphysical, including scientific and technological 'Newspeak', increasingly dominating modernity tends to overshadow and eclipse genuine thought and gets in the way of that primordial intimacy between word and world. As the above quotation shows, Gadamer's faith in the 'language of the homeland', incidentally echoing Wittgenstein's trust in the reliability of the language of the ordinary and the everyday ('Our language is alright as it is'), takes Gadamer in a more hopeful direction than the other route to Heideggerian distrust of the infiltration of everyday language by metaphysics. The capacity of language to evade closure and restriction is implied in the Hegelian notion of the speculative. 'Gadamer argues that when one follows Heidegger's turn to language', Kathleen Wright explains, 'one returns to Hegel with the recognition that what Hegel calls the speculative, the inner infinity of reflection, is not bound to his metaphysics and to the end of the self-unfolding of the concept. Instead it is operative universally in and as the speculative structure of language'.[32]

This all seems a far cry from Augustine and Wittgenstein but, I suggest, this is not so. I sought in this chapter to show how Gadamer's understanding of Augustine's distinction between inner and outer word contributes to the broader picture of language offered by a version of philosophical hermeneutics. With Wittgenstein my purpose was to highlight his reading of Augustine and show ways in which a more rather than a less Augustinian account of language would have overcome certain difficulties in his later work. Here I refer to the tendency towards linguistic relativism and the unsustainable idea that language is autonomous in the sense of losing all anchorage.

NOTES

1. Gadamer: 'You described (what you call) a *conflict* of interpretations. I would prefer to speak about a *competition* of interpretations.' In 'The conflict of interpretations: debate with Hans-Georg Gadamer', in M. Valdes (ed.), *A Ricoeur Reader: Reflection and Imagination* (Hemel Hempstead: Harvester Wheatsheaf, 1991).
2. *TM*, the section entitled 'Language and Verbum', pp. 418–28.
3. *TM*, pp. 405–28.
4. These lectures are referred to in J. Grondin, 'Gadamer and Augustine: on the origin of the hermeneutical claim to universality', in Wachterhauser (1994).
5. See Wachterhauser (1994), p. 138.
6. In many of the biographical essays Gadamer speaks of his first encounter with the work of Heidegger in 1922 via his teacher Paul Natorp. Natorp had been sent a manuscript from the young scholar Martin Heidegger. The essay spoke of the hermeneutical problems of interpreting Aristotle and mentioned the importance of Augustine, not to mention Luther, in this regard. See *PH*, p. 200.
7. 'In the beginning was the Word, and the Word was with God, and the Word was God', King James Version of *The Holy Bible*, John, 1:1.
8. Grondin (1994), p. 141.
9. Stump and Kretzmann (2001), p. 202.
10. Oates (1948), p. 847.
11. Oates (1948), p. 847.
12. Oates (1948), p. 846.
13. Augustine, *In Johannis Evangelium Tractatus*, quoted in Stump and Kretzmann (2001), p. 201.
14. Stump and Kretzmann (2001).

15. Stump and Kretzmann (2001), pp. 186–204.
16. Stump and Kretzmann (2001), p. 201.
17. Stump and Kretzmann (2001), p. 202.
18. Wachterhauser (1994), pp. 150–1.
19. For Gadamer's reading of Nicholas of Cusa and his significance for Gadamer see *TM*, pp. 434–8.
20. Wachterhauser (1994), p. 146.
21. *BBB*, p. 77.
22. Vesey (1974), pp. 1–13.
23. Vesey (1974), p. 1.
24. Vesey (1974), p. 1.
25. Gadamer also adverts to gesture when he comments: 'Language ... is not just a language of words. There is the language of the eyes, the language of the hands, and pointing and naming' (H-G. Gadamer, 'Towards a phenomenology of ritual and language', *LLGH*, p. 24).
26. The whole issue of translatability is a problem in Wittgenstein as there is no escaping indeterminacy. Less so in Gadamer where 'Every translation is at the same time an interpretation' (*TM*, p. 384). For a full discussion of the hermeneutical significance of translation see *TM*, pp. 384–9. However, as we will see in Chapter 7, translation of poetry, particularly the lyric, does present problems: 'Poetic speech is not like normal communication ... I think only a poet can translate a poem in his own language. Therefore, in some cases of poetic translation, we should not call them translations at all. They are new creations' (Gadamer, 1980b, p. 23).
27. I have in mind here Plato's distinction between *eidos* as non-linguistic universals and the particularity of written language. The forms are the absolutely real whereas inscribed language merely represents.
28. B. Wachterhauser, 'Gadamer's realism: the "belongingness" of word and reality', in Wachterhauser (1994), pp. 148–71.
29. Wachterhauser (1994), p. 154.
30. Wachterhauser (1994), p. 154.
31. H-G. Gadamer, 'The language of metaphysics', in Gadamer (1999a), p. 78.
32. K. Wright, 'The speculative structure of language' in Wachterhauser (1986), p. 214.

CHAPTER 7

Ordinary and Extraordinary Language: the Hermeneutics of the Poetic Word

No translation of a lyric poem ever conveys the original work. The best we can hope for is that one poet should come across another and put a new poetic work, as it were, in place of the original by creating an equivalent with the materials of a different language.

(Gadamer, 1986, p. 111)

Translating from one language into another is a mathematical task, and the translation of a lyric poem, for example, into a foreign language is quite analogous to a mathematical *problem*.

(Wittgenstein, *Z*, §698)

I. GADAMER'S POETIC TURN

Gadamer's writings after *Truth and Method* elaborate upon and extend the diverse claims of philosophical hermeneutics. In some of these later essays and lectures emphasis is laid upon the practical application of basic hermeneutical insights to areas as diverse as education[1] and modern medical practice.[2] But another important preoccupation after *Truth and Method* is a sustained focus upon the aesthetics and aesthetic uses of language, more specifically upon the poetic. Linguisticality as a prominent feature of our relationship to the world was worked out in detail in *Truth and Method* and Part Three, 'The ontological shift of hermeneutics guided by language', culminates in a final declaration, which in some ways the whole work had been leading up to, that 'Being that can be understood is language' (*TM*, p. 474). Although hints are evident in the final pages of *Truth and Method*, Gadamer finds the most undistorted affirmations of being in poetry, particularly in that of the modern lyric. Writings on the general nature of poetic language and its connections to ordinary, religious, and philosophical language are collected in the volume *The Relevance of the Beautiful* (Gadamer, 1986). Gadamer also produced a number of interpretive essays on the poetry and poetics of Rilke, George, and Celan, many of which are now translated.[3]

What distinguishes everyday discourse from poetry? A good deal turns on the distinction between 'everyday' or 'ordinary' and 'poetic' language. Gadamer's increasing appreciation of the poetic leads him into interpretations of contemporary poetry, notably the hermetic lyric. 'Play' and 'playfulness', discussed in Part One of *Truth and Method* as hidden or repressed aspects of the truth of the work of art, work most emphatically in the realm of the poetic. When hermeneutically reclaimed, poetic play works against subjectivist modernist versions of the aesthetic of feeling. Gadamer, on his own admission, fails, in *Truth and Method*, to fully thematize poetic play as it warrants no more than a few passing mentions in Parts Two and Three of *Truth and Method*, losing itself in the interpretive turn towards those other facets of hermeneutic truthfulness, historicality and language itself. In the later essays, specifically those reflecting upon the poetic and the aesthetic, 'play' becomes wider and assumes a much greater significance. Play, and this is most evident in the language of poetry, becomes a fundamental characteristic of language itself.

Notions of 'play' and 'language-games' are more obviously associated, in the analytical tradition, with the later work of Wittgenstein, as noticed in earlier chapters. For all his appreciation of language's specificity Wittgenstein seldom thematizes poetic language. There is little explicit rumination on the poetic uses of language in Wittgenstein's later work other than occasional gnomic asides in the *Investigations* and elsewhere.

The Wittgensteinian silence about the poetic is significant. The attempt to move away from a logic-driven picture theory of meaning in the *Tractatus* to the more informal, loosely textured pragmatics of language in the *Investigations* represents a return to 'the rough ground' of ordinary language. But the picture of a full living language is still incomplete without the rhetorical and metaphorical voices. More than embellishments they are the lifeblood of everyday speech and writing as the search for ever-new meanings emerges from the tradition. Nowhere is this more evident than in the quest for personal meanings in the poetic, where ordinary language is unhinged from its everyday patterns and finds ever-new modes of expression. The inner flexibility of language-games, their capacity to transform and extend themselves, to work in new uncharted regions is an aspect of the poetic largely unheeded by Wittgenstein.

Despite the paucity of explicit reference to the poetic the thought occurs that Wittgenstein is not totally unaware of the poetic dimension. The move to an increasingly compressed and aphoristic style, the whole thrust of the later work as an exercise in freeing up language, may be a point of entry for considering an indirect engagement with the poetic. Wittgenstein's complex relationship to the figurative will be revisited in the light of Gadamer's treatment of everyday and poetic language.

III. GADAMER ON ORDINARY, EVERYDAY LANGUAGE

In the essay 'Philosophy and poetry'[4] Gadamer draws a striking analogy between words and money:

> (Valéry) contrasted the *poetic* word with the *everyday* use of language in a striking comparison that alludes to ... the gold standard: *everyday language* resembles small change which, like our own paper money, does not actually possess the value that it symbolizes. The gold coins ... on the other hand, actually possessed as metal the value that was imprinted upon them. In a similar way, the language of poetry is not a mere pointer that refers to something else, but like the gold coin, is what it represents. (My emphasis). (Gadamer, 1986, p. 132)

In another reference to the same Valéry conceit, in 'Composition and interpretation'[5] Gadamer claims that 'ordinary language resembles a coin that we pass round among ourselves in place of something else' and, 'everyday language ... *points to something beyond* itself and *disappears* behind it' (Gadamer, 1986).[6] Returning to the gold analogy in later life Gadamer says in the 'Reflections' essay, 'language emerges in its full autonomy ... language just stands for itself: it brings itself to stand before us'. Whereas '[o]rdinary language resembles a coin that we pass round among ourselves in place of something else', he claims 'poetic language is like gold itself' (Hahn, 1997, p. 39).

Just as paper money is only valuable to the extent that it is underwritten by something of intrinsic worth, gold,[7] so the ordinary word 'does not actually possess the value that it symbolizes'. There are possible ambiguities lurking here. Does the analogy suggest that ordinary words have no value without poetic words (and the meanings of ordinary words change as poetic words change)? Or is the assumption that ordinary words are of inferior value because they are no more than tokens, whereas poetic language is what it is? Ambiguity aside, the purpose of the analogy is to suggest that in the everyday uses of language the words themselves (as sounds and structured patterns of meaning) are a medium, through which pass the matters at issue, the subject matter of the exchange. On the other hand, the poetic word does not disappear behind the matter at issue but is manifest as the matter at issue itself.

What can we say of the *disappearance* of language? In rejecting an account of meaning based upon the truth-functionality of propositions, Gadamer looks to the mutuality of understanding, to the 'fusion of the horizons', as he

termed it in *Truth and Method* (pp. 306–7 and 374–5). Meaning is not something self-sufficient or standing over and above words. Participation in the
creation of meaning accompanies the very act of speaking. Because ultimately
every assertion is an answer to an implied or actual question, meaning
conforms not to the logic of the proposition but to the 'logic of question and
answer' (*TM*, pp. 369–79). Although language is regulated by sometimes
strict, sometimes loose, semantic rules, it is flexible enough in its application
to generate possibilities overreaching and extending the original rules. In
ordinary language this self-transformation is minimal and unnoticed.
Language is at its most transparent when the logic of question and answer is
at its least searching and understanding at its least problematical, in the
routine exchanges of everyday conversation, for example. The situation
dramatically changes when the opaque self-presentation of poetic language
disrupts and complicates the normally smooth flow of understanding.

Living language requires more than conformity to semantic rules, as
Chapter 4 established. To understand and make ourselves understood is also
an ethical matter. 'Good will' even comes into play,[8] echoing Donald Davidson's principle of charity,[9] Gadamer assumes a hermeneutics of trust (against
the 'hermeneutics of suspicion') and a willingness to accommodate the voice
of the other: 'Social life depends upon our acceptance of everyday speech as
trustworthy', he says, 'we cannot order a taxi without this trust. Thus understanding is the average case not misunderstanding', he says in an interview
entitled 'Writing and the living voice' (Gadamer, 1992, pp. 63–71). As an
explicit riposte to deconstruction he continues, 'And Derrida, for example,
when he takes a different view (presumably that *misunderstanding* rather than
understanding is the average case) is speaking about literature. In literature
there is a struggle to bring something into expression beyond what is
accepted' (Gadamer, 1992, p. 71). 'The struggle . . . beyond what is accepted'
is what literature in general and poetry in particular engages in as an expan-
sion of the meanings of the everyday.

Evidently poetic language is not limited to the language of poetry although
poetry, especially modern hermetic lyric poetry is language at its most poetic.

Gadamer constructs a kind of literary hierarchy 'ascending from lyric
poetry through epic and tragedy . . . leading to the novel and any demanding
prose' (Gadamer, 1986, p. 136). Attention is drawn not simply to a literary
taxonomy but to degrees of interpretation and translatability. The language
of the novel, being close to the structures of everyday speech is the least
problematic as it minimally draws upon interpretive resources and depends
on the kind of trust underpinning everyday transactions (like hailing a taxi).
At the other extreme, the lyric poem flatly resists easy transliteration. 'No
translation of a lyric poem ever conveys the original work,' he observes in the

essay 'On the contribution of poetry to the search for truth'.[10] 'The best we can hope for is that one poet should come across another and put a new poetic work, as it were, in place of the original by creating an equivalent with the materials of a different language' (Gadamer, 1986, p. 111).

The Poem as 'Eminent Text'

Frequently Gadamer speaks of 'eminence' as a quality of poetic works. Here, 'poetic compositions are text in a new kind of sense: they are text in an *eminent* sense of the word ... In this kind of text language emerges in its full autonomy. Here language just stands for itself: it brings itself to stand before us.'[11] The poetic word is eminent. It literally sticks out, protrudes in the literal sense (e-minent).

In ordinary language words disappear into their functionality, vanishing in the face of the matters at issue. In poetic language words take on a life of their own, in this sense. In ordinary language, the language of 'the homeland' referred to by Gadamer,[12] we are more attentive to the 'message' than the 'medium'. But with the poetic, the word's 'corporeality', as Gerald Bruns terms it,[13] shines forth. The physicality of words, through their sounds, modulation, tonality, tempo, dynamics, superfluous factors in the exchange of information of everyday speech, comes to the fore in the poetic utterance. The poetic word, in transcending mere information, disrupts the everyday (and our situatedness within it). In *Truth and Method* Gadamer points to a hermeneutical experience of 'being pulled up short' (*TM*, p. 268) in an encounter with a text. We are suddenly alienated from the text's meaning as it thwarts our expectations. The experience of novelty with a text is dramatically heightened in the lyric poem.

In ordinary language there is invariably an element of inventiveness present. All interpretation is production of meaning rather than straightforward reproduction (or, as I spoke of earlier with respect to rules, re-enactment). The constant turning of the 'hermeneutic circle' destabilizes meaning and shows it to be in motion, never unitary or foreclosed. This inventive, self-transformative quality is heightened and intensified in the poetic utterance and links in to the 'speculative' dimension of language mentioned in relation to Gadamer's reworking of Hegel in Chapter 3. In lyric poetry particularly, Gadamer claims, 'the poet releases the multidimensionality of the associations of meaning which is suppressed by practical unity of intention in logically controlled, one-dimensional everyday speech'.[14] As if to demonstrate the truth of his claim Gadamer, in his essay 'Who am I and who are you?' a reading of Paul Celan's poetic cycle, 'Breath turn' or 'Breathcrystal' (*Atemkristall*), analyses the ways the reader's sense of individuation and identity is

disoriented and unsettled in the engagement with these verses. He says, 'we
do not know at the outset, on the basis of any distanced overview or preview,
what *I* or *You* means here (in Celan's poems) or whether I is the I of the poet
referring to himself, or the I that is each of us, This what we must learn'.[15]
The whole question of who is addressing whom in the decontextualized zone
of the poetic, where language is effectively unhinged from its customary sites,
raises important questions for philosophical hermeneutics. With the usual
semantic reference points distorted and dislocated in the poem the hermeneutical task is more demanding as Gadamer admits. Words extend themselves,
moving into new and hitherto unknown spaces in the tradition.

Meaning is ultimately a dialogue, a negotiation between poem and reader.
'In a poem', Gadamer says in the 'Reflections' essay, 'with *whom* does ...
communication take place? Is it with the reader? With which *reader*? Here
the dialectic of question and answer which is always the basis of the hermeneutic and which corresponds to the basic structure of the dialogue under-
goes a special modification' (Hahn, 1997, pp. 39–40). Quite what this special
modification is he does not make explicit but he says, a little later in this
essay, something worthy of note.

> As I look back today I see one point in particular where I did not achieve
> the theoretical consistency I strove for in *Truth and Method*. I did not make
> it clear enough how the ... basic projects that were brought together in the
> concept of play harmonized. ... On the one hand there is the orientation to
> the game we play with art and on the other the grounding of language in
> conversation, the game of language ... I needed to unite the game of
> language more closely with the game art plays. (Hahn, 1997, pp. 41–2)

Poetic language is not the only instance of language at play for the playful
element is never far away even in the routine enactments of daily conversation: yet it stands for language at its most playful. Gadamer succeeded in
suggesting this in his historical survey of the origins and development of the
modern aesthetic, in Part One of *Truth and Method* (see particularly *TM*, pp.
101–11). Only in the later work, as he recently confessed, did he see how this
'playfulness' is a description of all linguistic activity, with language at its
most playful in the poetic. It is worth noting, especially when comparing
Gadamer to Wittgenstein, that 'play' and 'playfulness' are not the same. Play
could be taken as no more than regulated activity. On the other hand playfulness resists codification, we might even say it is playful by virtue of the resistance to codification. But play and playfulness are not just dimensions of life
and language; they achieve a special status in art. All art, and here we include
the poetic, is play but here especially the activity of play always becomes
more than itself in what Gadamer terms 'transformation into structure' (*TM*,

p. 110). Play transforms the players and itself as it discloses some structural dimension of reality for 'the transformation is a transformation into the true' (*TM*, p. 112). Once again the idea of poetic play as disclosure, an opening up of the real, is emphasized.

This enriched notion of play puts Gadamer's account of language in a new light. Those who see in his work little more than a seamless monological and self-affirming (Hegelian) tradition, blind to difference and alterity, ignore his attempt to realign the poetic in his hermeneutics. The playfulness of the hermeneutical dialogue, the fact that it can never make implicit meanings completely explicit, and the fact that the unsaid is always more extensive than the said indicate a constant measure of difference. The element of play in dialogue, eliminating the possibility of closure and identity, is strong evidence that alterity and difference outflanks identity of meaning in Gadamer. If this is the case the reduction of Gadamer's hermeneutics to just another version of Hegelianism in a more modern idiom is questionable.

IV. WITTGENSTEIN ON THE PLAY OF LANGUAGE-GAMES

Despite closeness to Gadamer on the nature of ordinary language, Wittgenstein has much to learn from philosophical hermeneutics, specifically around the whole question of the literary, the poetic, and the self-transformative dimension to language and play. Recently Gadamer reread Wittgenstein and acknowledged an increasingly important influence on his own work especially in the period after *Truth and Method*. But he is not uncritical, as he reveals in the autobiographical 'Reflections' essay.

> Of course the result of this proposed reduction of philosophy to a praxis-context [in the later work, CL] remained for him a negative one. It consisted in a flat rejection of all the undemonstrable questions of metaphysics rather than a *winning back* of the undemonstrable questions of metaphysics, however undemonstrable they might be, by detecting in them the linguistic constitution of our being-in-the-world. For this, of course, far more can be learned from the word of the poets than from Wittgenstein. (Hahn, 1997, p. 39)

For all his admiration of Wittgenstein and belief that hermeneutics shares much in common with the later work, Gadamer is ultimately critical of 'leading all speaking back to the context of life-praxis' and going no further. Wittgenstein's language-games fulfil a primarily negative purpose in rejecting the 'undemonstrable questions of metaphysics' but, for Gadamer, this is not

the end of the matter. Hermeneutics advocates a further stage beyond metaphysics; a 'winning back', that is a retrieval of the questions and concerns at
the heart of metaphysics. This is achieved not by lapsing back into an
illusory transcendence but by 'exploring the linguistic constitution of our
being-in-the-world'. It is not immediately obvious what Gadamer has in
mind here but there is the suggestion, especially when the remark is linked to
the reference to 'the word of the poets', that the poetic word wins back in a
more authentic way what was sought for in metaphysics. Gadamer speaks of
the 'infinite possibilities of utterance' and the 'inner infinity ... that takes
place in dialogue'.[16] An exploration of language's infinite possibilities is
another description of what happens in the playful dialogue of everyday
speech as new positions are taken up, explored, and scrutinized. This is also
what takes place, albeit in a more intense form, in the poetic.

Wittgenstein's language-games miss out this essential playfulness. For
Gadamer, the language-games have some kind of purpose, even if it is not
always immediately evident to the players what that might be. But what, for
Wittgenstein, is the point of enacting the language-games? Let us return
briefly to the discussion of language-games in the *Investigations*. We are
asked to

> Consider for example the proceedings that we call games. I mean board
> games, card games, ball games, Olympic games, and so on. What is
> common to them all? – Don't say 'There must be something common, or
> they would not be called games' – but *look* and *see* whether there is anything
> common to all. – For if you look at them you will not see something that is
> common to *all*, but similarities, relationships, and a whole series at that.

One reason why the game analogy is introduced is to draw attention to
variety. This is the antidote to that 'craving for generality' that searches for
unitary principles or essence. There is no essence of the game, there are just
a vast variety of different games. The diversity is extended when we

> Look for example at board games, with their multifarious relationships.
> Now pass to card games; here you may find correspondences with the first
> group, but many common features drop out and others appear. When we
> pass next to ball games, much that is common is retained but much lost. –
> Are they all amusing? Compare chess with noughts and crosses. Or is there
> always winning and losing, or competition between players? Think of
> patience. In ball games there is winning and losing; but when a child
> throws his ball at the wall and catches it, this feature has disappeared....
> And we can go through the many, many other groups of games in the same
> way; we can see how similarities crop up and disappear. (*PI*, §66)

In *Truth and Method* the ideas of 'play' (*Spiel*) has, on the face of it, an uncanny likeness to Wittgenstein's 'language-games'. There are clearly affinities between Gadamer's use of 'play' and 'playfulness' and Wittgenstein's language-games; nevertheless, it is important to take note of the appreciable differences. In *Truth and Method* 'play' appears initially in the context of the discussion of art, drawing upon Johann Huizinga's *Homo Ludens*.[17] As well as its antecedence in Huizinga Martin Kusch traces its immediate origins back to Heidegger, and before that to the idea of 'the play of life' in Kant's *Critique of Judgment*:

> Gadamer employs the concept of *Spiel* in order to vindicate Heidegger's idea that language speaks to us. Interestingly enough, Heidegger himself had earlier used the notion of *Spiel* for precisely the same purpose. In fact Gadamer's analysis of *Spiel* was anticipated as early as 1928/1929 in (Heidegger's) unpublished lectures entitled 'Introduction to Philosophy'.[18]

Kusch goes on to relate how Heidegger took as his starting point 'Kant's notion of the *Spiel des Lebens*', suggesting '*Dasein's* Being-in-the-world be conceptualized as a *Spiel*.[19] As another historical aside it is interesting to reflect on the many modern thinkers who have incorporated the idea of 'play' and the 'game' into their own thinking: as well as Gadamer and Wittgenstein we could include Jean-François Lyotard's 'gaming' and 'agonistics' and Derrida's use of play in 'Structure, sign and play in the discourses of the human sciences'.[20]

In seeking to distance himself from what he takes to be the Kantian subjectivization of the aesthetic Gadamer shows how there is another tale to be told. Starting from the use-value of a term, he makes this observation: 'If we examine how the word 'play' is used ... we find talk of the play of light, the play of the waves ... In each case what is intended is the to-and-fro movement that is not tied to any goal that would bring it to an end' (*TM*, p. 103).[21] To-and-fro-ness is a feature of all play; if we link this to the play of games another feature of play comes to light: 'Play is not to be understood as something a person does ... the actual subject of play is obviously not the subjectivity of an individual ... *the primacy of play over the consciousness of the individual* is fundamentally acknowledged' (*TM*, p. 104). The game highlights the impossibility of a language dominated by the speaking subject, a language reflecting the mind of the utterer: the game of language always overshadows, outmanoeuvres even, the speaker.

Wittgenstein failed to appreciate a vital aspect of play: its essential playfulness, its to-and-fro-ness, its dynamic, and its seemingly unpredictable (yet structured) dialectic. Neglected in Wittgenstein is the way the game captivates and fascinates, the way it draws us into itself, its 'ludic', that is, playful, aspect, which readily but unaccountably flips over into its opposite, serious-ness. 'Play fulfils its purpose', Gadamer tell us, 'only if the player loses himself in play' (*TM*, p. 32).

Observe the way games, chess, for example, or more dramatically poker, move. They develop not by degrees, but suddenly, unaccountably perhaps, from mere idle diversion to urgent matters of life and death. The sudden movement is from one extreme to another, from the diversionary to the serious. The unpredictability is hardly epiphenomenal; rather it is right at the heart of the play of the game. Playing is not just gaming but playfulness. Further, playfulness engages our resourcefulness and yet out-plays it as non-purposive rationality: 'The distinctive thing about human play is its ability to involve our reason, that uniquely human capacity which allows ourselves to set ourselves aims and pursue them consciously, and to outplay this capacity for purposive rationality' (Gadamer, 1986, p. 23).

Wittgenstein neglects the *experience* of the game. Despite the radical move from the rigour of the *Tractatus* to the increased informality and imprecision of language-games in the *Investigations*, Wittgenstein seems unwilling to venture beyond the level of mere description. In the exhortation to 'Look and see' (*PI*, §66) the differences in the games, and by extension, the language-games, Wittgenstein ignores the fact that 'looking and seeing' is itself a language-game. In other words, there is more than a suggestion that the game can be comprehended from a privileged position *outside the game*. This would be all of a piece with what appears to be the absence in Wittgen-stein of an acknowledgement of one of the subjective elements of the game, the self-understandings of the players.

Gadamer, on the other hand, describes, phenomenologically, the experi-ence of the game. The playful to-and-fro-ness of the game, its capacity to surprise the players with the unexpected, is absent in Wittgenstein. The element of surprise, a regular feature of play, is captured by Gadamer in his use of Rilke's description of the acrobat's fine sense of judgement where 'the pure too little incomprehensibly transforms itself, springs over into the empty too much'.[22] Wittgenstein's descriptions of language, with their stress upon strict rule-governedness, distort the very openness he seeks to expose, further presenting a picture of language as repetition and re-enactment.

Let us return to the idea of blind conformity to rules (*PI*, §34). Interpreted as a comment on the use of linguistic rules, this only makes sense if we see the game as an implied enforcer of the agreements, which constitute a parti-cular linguistic practice. The language-game, if it conforms to the 'blind obedience' model here, is no more than a constant restatement of the rules. This places restrictions upon the game. On this account is language ever able to expand into new areas of meaning, to transform and transfigure itself?

Here language lacks anything approaching novelty and inventiveness and the element of surprise mentioned above. Language is locked into an eternal present, failing to embrace the language-games of the present and the past, no doubt validating those frequently heard charges of Wittgensteinian relativism. Focusing upon the strict rules of the game rather than the capacity of the game, through the to-and-fro-ness of play, to slip from frivolity to seriousness, to change unpredictably, fails to make the connection between playfulness and the capacity of language to transform and self-transfigure.

To what extent is Wittgenstein's understanding of 'play' relevant to his failure to consider poetic, language in the later work? There are occasional reflections on particular poets, notably in *Culture and Value*. On the evidence of the published works Wittgenstein makes few references to poetry or poets. *Culture and Value* collects together a selection of observations and *aperçus* on poets. Mention is made of Goethe, Grillparzer, Lenau, Schiller, Milton, Shakespeare, and Longfellow amongst others. Wittgenstein is known to have supported struggling artists and poets as Marjorie Perloff explains:

> In an impulsive act of legendary generosity, he [Wittgenstein] bequeathed, in 1914, one hundred thousand kronen [roughly the equivalent of one hundred thousand dollars today] ... to the literary magazine *Der Brenner*, instructing [the editor] to distribute the money 'among Austrian artists who are without means.' ... of the three main beneficiaries – Rilke, Trakl, and Carl Dallago – Rilke was the only poet with whose work Wittgenstein was at all familiar. Of Trakl's poems, he wrote ... 'I do not understand them, but their *tone* makes me happy. It is the tone of genius.'[23]

Wittgenstein seldom thematizes the issue of poetic language although the following admittedly fairly isolated remark is revealing: 'Do not forget that a poem, although it is composed in the language of information, is not used in the language game of giving information' (*Zettel*, §160). The comment demonstrates an awareness of the ability of ordinary language ('the language of information') to reach beyond the familiar patterns of use. In many ways this could be a description of what happens in the lyric poem which takes the 'language of information' and forces it into ever new patterns of meaning. The comparison between poetic language and language of information is taken up again when we are offered the following:

> 'When I read a poem or a narrative with feeling, surely something goes on in me which does not go on when I merely skim the lines for information.' What process am I alluding to? – The sentences have a different *ring*. I pay careful attention to my intonation. Sometimes a word has the wrong intonation, I emphasize it too much or too little. I notice this and show it my

face. I might later talk about my reading in detail, for example about the mistakes in my tone of voice. Sometimes a picture, as it were an illustration, comes to me. And this seems to help me read with the correct expression.... I can also give a word a tone of voice which brings out the meaning of the rest, almost as if this word were a picture of the whole thing. (And this may, of course, depend on sentence-formation.) (*PI*, p. 183)

The subjective dimensions to meaning, where nuances are created and destroyed by elements outside the regularities of linguistic rules are alluded to here. Yet it is tempting to suggest that Wittgenstein marginalized the poetic, as an ineffectual discourse (like the machine idling and not pulling anything), that is, like philosophy, in relation to the more workman-like 'living language'. There is some evidence to substantiate this kind of claim but I argue in this section Wittgenstein's avoidance of 'poetic language' is intimately and unavoidably connected to the way he conceives the language-game.

Slightly more cryptic is the likeness between philosophy and poetry: 'I think I summed up my attitude to philosophy when I said: philosophy ought really to be written only as a *poetic composition*' (*CV*, p. 24). The idea of reading Wittgenstein's later work as a poetic composition will be taken up in the next section.

Unfair to Wittgenstein?

Wittgensteinians will, no doubt, take issue with my discussion of the limitations of the description and understanding of the 'language-game' idea. I might stand accused of giving Gadamer all the best tunes. Towards the end of Part Two of the *Investigations*, approximately pp. 194–232, there is a detailed discussion of interpretation and visual perception, initially focused on a discussion of Jastrow's 'duck-rabbit'.[24] In thinking about a possible hermeneutical element in perception Wittgenstein speaks of 'aspects', the 'dawning of an aspect', 'aspect blindness', all as part of the general phenomenon of what he describes as 'seeing as'. A few things are worthy of comment. Were this discussion extended, as it easily might be, from the perceptual to the linguistic, the 'rules-as-blind-obedience' account of meaning I spoke of earlier leads Wittgenstein in a more fruitful and interesting direction. There is evidence that Wittgenstein considered this possibility: 'The importance of this concept [of "aspect blindness"] lies in the connection between the concepts of "seeing an aspect" and "experiencing the meaning of a word". For we want to ask "What would you be missing if you did not *experience* the meaning of a word?"' (*PI*, p. 214). We could also point to the potential closeness between 'seeing as' and Heidegger's 'as-structure of interpretation' in Section 32, 'Understanding and interpretation', in *Being and Time*. Stephen Mulhall[25] has worked in this general area although his discussion of the linguistic dimension to early Heidegger is limited. As well as this Mulhall has little to say on the applicability of Wittgenstein's 'seeing as' to language apart from a brief but useful chapter 'Aspects and language' (Mulhall, 1990, pp. 35–52).

Addressing the question of the poetic, one might construct a positive case for Wittgenstein along the following lines. Whilst staying within the limits of ordinary language in the later *Investigations*, he succeeds in disrupting its everydayness in what Cavell terms an 'everyday aesthetics of itself'.[26] He manages, through artificial language-games as 'objects of comparison', to make existing language-games open up new or hidden meanings in the way that poetic language does in relation to ordinary language. Is this not, for Gadamer, precisely the virtue of the lyric poem? Doesn't Wittgenstein unwittingly force language to transfigure itself, in much the same way as the lyric poet does, by remaining within the confines of the language of everyday speech? Wittgenstein is poetic without resorting to the formal literary devices of poetry.[27] These attempts to throw a lifeline are rather sketchy but do indicate, I think, the direction a Wittgenstein defence would take. However, we might seriously consider the following possibility. Wittgenstein evokes the problem of 'seeing-as' at the end of the *Investigations* precisely because he is unable to account for the capacity of language to change and transform itself.

What of the question of a poetic reading of Wittgenstein (that is, reading Wittgenstein poetically)? In some ways this is a much more interesting line of enquiry. What I have in mind here is the thought that one of the achievements of the poetic word in the lyric is to strain language beyond its usual limits, forcing it into novel formulations and deriving new meanings: all of this within the restrictions of the existing language-games. Could it be that this sense of the poetic is actually one of the more important of Wittgenstein's achievement in his later work? His investigations, like the language of the lyric poem, never stray much beyond ordinary language and yet the effect of his work upon the reader is to open up new lines of enquiry and to produce in the reader a novel experience with language.

This conclusion is faltering. I suspect a rounded judgement of Wittgenstein's relation to the poetic and the ways this might be affiliated to Gadamer will only be possible when the *way* Wittgenstein wrote is given as much attention as *what* he wrote. A brief survey of the literature reveals how little philosophers have attended to questions of style and stylishness. For example, much of the later work is aphoristic, recalling most obviously Pascal and Lichtenberg,[28] and yet little work has been done on the philosophical nature of the aphorism. We can go further and say in fact, in the analytical tradition too little attention is given to the whole question of style and its relevance to philosophical work. Far more work needs to be done on the literary, rhetorical, and stylistic dimensions to Wittgenstein's work. Marjorie Perloff's *Wittgenstein's Ladder: Poetic Language and the Strangeness of the Ordinary*[29] is a step in this right direction. Also worth mentioning in this regard are the studies of Wittgenstein's styles in the work of Stanley Cavell[30] and Fergus Kerr.[31] Conceivably, after a more 'literary' appreciation of Wittgenstein's work we may discern more affinities with Gadamer's distinction between ordinary and poetic language.[32]

Taking Wittgenstein at his word, that his 'philosophy ought really to be written only as a *poetic composition*',[33] the next section concentrates upon a literary reading of the later work using the concept of the tragic.

V. WITTGENSTEIN AS TRAGIC APHORIST

The later work of Wittgenstein presents a variety of hermeneutical problems over and above those encountered in more conventional philosophical writings. The chief difficulty is the simple fact that the later published writings are little more than plunder by his executors from the treasure-chest of literary remains, the *Nachlass*. Herein is contained a huge quantity of note-books and strips of paper (*Zettel*) containing an assortment of opaque and frequently elliptical fragments: imaginary conversations, incomplete observations, memoranda, reminders, jokes, thought experiments, not to mention countless rejected versions of what would subsequently appear as constituent parts of largely invented 'texts' posthumously printed over a period of 50 years after his death.

Until very recently commentators regarded the form of the later work as largely irrelevant to the task of 'philosophical' interpretation, preferring instead to conjure up an imaginary arrangement of 'complete' texts replete with coherent themes and fictitious argumentative stances known as the 'private language argument', 'the argument against solipsism', and the like.

Granted Wittgenstein had in mind the publication of something to be called the *Philosophical Investigations* long before his death in 1951, but its published form, and the nature of the subsequent 'texts,' goes well beyond anything he might have intended. The necessity of interpreting the whole of the later Wittgenstein in terms of the *Nachlass* and not the posthumously published works has been argued for by David Stern in 'The availability of

Wittgenstein's philosophy'.[34] From a hermeneutical perspective I am not totally convinced by the argument that the later work makes more sense when read in the overall context of the *Nachlass*; there remains the interpretive problem of rooting out the insignificant and the uninteresting.

Focusing on these hermeneutical and bibliographical considerations we can question the orthodox approach of treating the ready-made texts as definitive and canonical. Viewing Wittgenstein's later work, not as a traditional philosophical text with a sequential argumentative structure between discrete themes but as a more chaotic and amorphous mixture of loosely connected fragments, a re-evaluation of the nature of the work is irresistible. My thesis about the need for a more literary and bibliographical re-evaluation gains plausibility when the difficulties of construing the totality of Wittgenstein's later work is seen in the light of a historically much earlier interpretive puzzle – how to piece together and, even more problematically, how to interpret, the *Pensées* of the seventeenth-century French religious thinker Blaise Pascal.

There are remarkable parallels between Wittgenstein and Pascal. There is the move away from a general commitment to the rational-deductive method to suspicion of its aims, resulting in the adoption of a more personal, spiritual, even confessional wrestling with faith, certainty, and scepticism. This tendency is reflected in an associated dramatic change in literary style: the early scientific and mathematical treatises of Pascal give way to the new style of the fragments in the same way as the logical precision of Wittgenstein's *Tractatus* is abandoned for the more fragmentary *Investigations*. In both cases the formality of tract and treatise is jettisoned for the less systematic fragment. Any comparison between Wittgenstein and Pascal must acknowledge a glaringly obvious fact, namely, that they were both unable (and unwilling) to complete their masterworks. Wittgenstein and Pascal bequeathed to the world not polished texts but a welter of constantly rearranged fragments. My primary concern is to apply some of the ideas of Gadamer's hermeneutics to the interpretation of the later writings of Wittgenstein. I shall get to this in a roundabout way by examining a neglected interpretation of Pascal and assessing its plausibility and applicability to Wittgenstein, given the commonalities and difficulties of interpretation I outline above. To this end, I want to consider briefly the literary critic Lucien Goldmann's pioneering study of Pascal, *The Hidden God*.[35]

For the Marxist Goldmann, stylistic analysis, where the form of a literary work reveals something about the nature of its content, offers a key to unravelling the *Pensées*. On his interpretation it is so much wasted effort searching for some ideal thematic or conceptual arrangement of the *Pensées*, as though perfect ordering of the text was waiting to be uncovered by painstaking academic detective work.[36] Such agonizing about the precise textual order a revitalized Pascal might give his work had he lived to see it to completion is essentially pointless. Whilst granting that the actual arrangement the work is given conditions the way it is read and understood, Goldmann is at pains to emphasize the aporia at the heart of Pascal. Paradoxically, the solution to the enigma of the *Pensées* is to appreciate the essential wholeness in the work's very incompleteness: the work reveals its meaning via its fractured identity. According to Goldmann, Pascal inaugurated a 'dialectical aesthetic' whereby 'no literary work is valid unless it contains a necessary organic unity between a coherently expressed content and an adequate form'.[37] The Pascalian fragment, albeit unwittingly, represents in literary shape a characteristic of the social life of the epoch and class from which it emerges. Pascal perceives humans as paradoxical and fragmented and this is mirrored in his writing (in both form and content). Goldmann observes:

> In our world, as Pascal sees it, no statement is true unless immediately completed by its opposite, and no action is good without a completely different action which completes and corrects it.... Pascal sees our world as insufficient, as a world without God, a world which crushes man, and which man must necessarily outsoar if he is to remain man.[38]

In the hands of Pascal, the fragment, a literary and philosophical genre to be self-consciously taken up and developed later by Schlegel, German romanticism and beyond, reveals through its form aspects of a vision of human life, more specifically a vision of human limitations. Pascalian fragments bear witness to the frailty of human understanding. The point of the so-called 'Wager Argument' is to show not that it is reasonable to believe in God but, paradoxically, that we must use reason to expose reason's limits. It is rational to enact the wager even though the wager itself sidesteps rational considerations.

The fragmentary nature of Pascal's later work militates against a totalizing vision. His assorted observations and aperçus mock Cartesian rationality, clearly one of the targets of Pascal's rejection of the absurdly untroubled optimistic views of human possibilities, evident in the terse 'Descartes. Useless and uncertain',[39] presaging contemporary antipathies to the father of philosophical modernity.

Belittling reason and exposing the duality of our nature takes us to Goldmann's most potent critical term: the 'tragic'. 'There can be, for the tragic work, only one valid form: that of the fragment.'[40] The fragment is the medium carrying Pascal's 'tragic vision'. The human tragedy is to be suspended between extremes, between 'wretchedness and greatness', between the mind and the heart, between virtue and concupiscence, between the polar opposites of the mere reed and the semi-divine 'thinking reed'. To be caught in the middle, to be unable to resolve the tension by sublating or neutralizing it is the human tragedy.[41] Goldmann marks Pascal down as a tragic thinker because he records so vividly the failure to escape wretchedness or greatness. Pascal is emblematic of a static view of values and thought, inimical to Goldmann's dynamic and progressive Marxist dialectic.

Tragic thought is the Pascalian reaction to the one-sided thinking of either empiricism or rationalism and waits upon the truly dialectical thought of Hegel and the ensuing Marxist tradition.[42] What Pascal, from his limited perspective, failed to grasp was the dynamic movement of ideas from where genuine moments of dialectical synthesis emerge. Given the benefit of dialectical foresight Pascal would have grasped the essential historicality of ideas and understood the movement as a product of social change. In Goldmann's periodization of ideas, tragic thought mirrors the movement of society as it inexorably grows into truly dialectical thought in the inevitable change in material circumstances.

Much of what Goldmann offers as an interpretation of Pascal is shrouded in a rather antiquated historical and dialectical materialism, showing that Goldmann, as much as Pascal, was a product of his time. The idea of Marxist dialectical thought as the *terminus ad quem* of historical development and the assumption that Engels-style dialectics offers a higher stage of development beyond tragic thought makes Goldmann's analysis rather passé. But Goldmann's notion of the tragic offers a potent critical tool for interpreting Pascalian fragments. Crucially, we might place emphasis upon the human tragedy, not as an inexorable consequence of our flawed and paradoxical nature, but as an entrapment within an inevitable stylistic tension. There is the suggestion of this in the Pascalian fragments when he counterpoises the '*esprit de géométrie*' (the geometric spirit) and the '*esprit de finesse*' (the spirit of judgement).[43]

Here we are not necessarily caught within a dual nature but are trapped between competing and opposing interpretive possibilities; a rationalizing calculative tendency ('*esprit de géométrie*'), and the less restricted, even freedom loving, faculty of judgement, within the order of the heart, as Pascal alternatively names the spirit of finesse. And the two are in opposition for 'true morality makes light of morality; that is to say, the morality of the judgement, which has no rules, makes light of the morality of the intellect'.[44]

Against Goldmann, we might say that what makes for tragic thought is not Pascal's misfortune to be born before Hegelian dialectic but his inability to escape or resolve the tension between the calculative, the geometric, and the interpretative and judgemental as mutually tempting and mutually excluding possibilities. Pascal himself realizes that there is no possibility of harmony within human thought; the opposing tendencies will inevitably make for dissonance. The best we can hope for is to sidestep the oppositions and turn to that safe place where contradictions and paradoxes are overlooked, that is, in religious affirmation through faith. But even this is no true resolution as God is a perpetual mystery or, in Pascal's own words, giving the title to Goldmann's own work, the '*Dieu caché*', 'the hidden God'.[45]

What has all of this to do with Wittgenstein? I want to assess the relevance of tragic thought to possible interpretations of late Wittgenstein. In addressing the question of the significance of the *Nachlass* I suggested that a potentially fertile line of enquiry was to read Wittgenstein in the light of the work of Goldmann's Pascal interpretation. And favouring the fragment as the tragic confluence of interpretive possibilities rather than a comment upon human duality, I wonder whether this links up to Wittgenstein? Is he a tragic thinker in the senses outlined above?

Maurice O'Connor Drury, Wittgenstein's long-standing friend, commenting on G. H. von Wright's idea that there is a 'trenchant parallelism' between Pascal and Wittgenstein, responds with qualified approval: 'Certainly Pascal's intensity, his seriousness, his rigorism ... find a parallel in Wittgenstein', he claims.[46] This is about as far as Drury wishes to go with this comparison, offering in the next breath various qualifications (which I quote in full):

> The *Philosophical Investigations* appear to be a haphazard arrangement of remarks and aphorisms such as Pascal's *Pensées* undoubtedly are. It is generally believed that if Pascal had written the book he intended the *Pensées* would have been arranged in an entirely different order from that in which we now have them. But we know that Wittgenstein was constantly rearranging the material found in his book, that he spent a lot of time and thought in obtaining the precise order we now have. To grasp the significance of the *Investigations* it is essential to see the order of development of the thoughts.[47]

For Drury, there is nothing potentially tragic, there is not even anything problematical, about understanding the *Investigations* so long as 'the order of the development' of thoughts is grasped. Such a misguided judgement ignores the incompleteness of the *Investigations*, and 'to see the order of development of the thoughts' is akin to seeing the emperor's clothes.

Wittgenstein wrestled with the structure and order of his projected work eventually concluding that disjointed fragments was all he could ever manage. In the Preface to the jumbled manuscripts he hoped would constitute the *Investigations* he outlines his purpose and the means he intends to use to achieve them, at one point speaking of his work as not fragments but 'remarks' (*Bemerkungen*). He implies that he initially conceived of his later work along the lines of the *Tractatus Logico-Philosophicus*, as a concatenated chain of rigorous reasoning, whereby 'the thoughts should proceed from one subject to another in a natural order and without breaks'.[48] Such a procedure, however, proved impossible. He confesses: 'after several attempts to weld my results together into such a whole, I realised that I should never succeed'.[49] Continuing, 'the best I that I could write would never be more than philosophical *remarks*; my thoughts were soon crippled if I tried to force them on in any single direction against their natural inclination'. He continues, 'And this was, of course, connected with the very nature of the investigation'.[50] A few lines later in the published Preface the philosophical remark is compared to a hastily drawn sketch by an indifferent artist. After a painstaking selection process the more competent sketches could be put together to create an 'album', a sketchbook of journeys across the rough terrain of language. Sadly, the editing part of this task was eventually to be performed not by the author but his literary executors.

All of this must sound familiar and the links to Pascal obvious. An inability to philosophize in strict propositions, an unwillingness to give his ideas an illusory polish, a failure to think beyond the fragmentary and the broken is the destiny of both Pascal and Wittgenstein.

'A main source of our failure to understand', comments Wittgenstein, at §122 in the *Investigations*, 'is that we do not *command a clear view* of the use of our words'; our grammar lacks 'perspicuity'. He continues, 'A perspicuous representation produces just that understanding which consists in "seeing connections"'. And the 'concept of perspicuous representation earmarks the form of account we give, the way we look at things'. Without the possibility of an overview of language, the philosophical equivalent of a theory of everything, the limited vision of the sketchbook will at least encourage us to 'see connections'. So Wittgenstein is able, to some degree, to vindicate the fragmentariness of the later work. But is Wittgenstein's later work 'tragic' in Goldmann's terms? Is there a sense in which he is caught in the middle between tensions and paradoxes? Wittgenstein is trapped between irreconcilable possibilities but does it make sense to call these tragic? Yes. But the notion of tragedy I have in mind is, although in the same district as Goldmann, not quite in the same street.

To view the question of Wittgenstein and tragedy from another direction I turn, briefly, to the work of Stanley Cavell. Not unlike Goldmann's approach to Pascal, Cavell is concerned to tease out and analyse questions of style and stylishness as a way of extending the range of interpretive possibilities in the *Investigations*. In the final section of the essay 'The availability of Wittgenstein's later philosophy' (1962) headed 'The style of the *Investigations*'[51] Cavell points to a central dramatic tension running like a continuous thread throughout the later Wittgenstein. The strain here is manifest as a fraught dialogue, disputation even, between two opposing voices or seductions: he names them the 'voice of correctness' and the 'voice of temptation'. In a later work, 'Declining decline'[52] Cavell's siren voices emerge once more, this time he considers them as part of a 'continuous spiritual struggle'. Now the idea of an Augustinian – or better, for our purposes, a Pascalian – wrestling between countervailing forces is a potentially illuminating one and, interestingly, chimes in with Goldmann's reading of Pascal.

Even a cursory reading of the *Investigations* picks up on the opposing voices struggling to make themselves heard (although Drury seems to have missed them). There is no neat dialogical structure to the *Investigations* with the controlled positioning of philosophical views and a move towards resolution; there are only fragments of conversations, temptations to assert one position rather than another and instant repudiations, subversive counter claims, indecisions, and yet more completely new suggestions. To add to the reader's disorientation there is no obvious controlling authorial or narrative voice unambiguously that of the philosopher. Wittgenstein hides within (or from?) his own fragments.

There is something else 'tragic' about Wittgenstein's later work, and in some ways Goldmann via Pascal and Cavell indirectly adverts to it. Conceivably tragedy derives from a dramatic tension, in turn deriving from a reformulation of Cavell's voices of 'correctness' and 'temptation.' Arguably, despite the plurality of voices, Wittgenstein is frequently driven back to something like the controlling voice of 'correctness' Cavell originally identified. How is this correctness to be described and characterized?

To see the distinction I wish to make we need to reflect upon the two Wittgensteins of the early and later periods. What we can say without a shadow of a doubt is that there is a massive contrast between the *style* of the early and the later work, and this is a difference that makes a difference.

The *Tractatus* is lapidary, compressed, and a closely argued manifesto, authoritative and oracular in tone. Its pronouncements seem severely austere and impersonal with the numbered propositions as part of an elaborately compressed argumentative edifice recalling the concatenated propositions of Spinoza.[53] Against this, the fragments of the later work are largely desultory, teasing, playful, seemingly unstructured, and deeply personal to the point of being confessional, even, as some critics have suggested, guilt-ridden.[54] There is playfulness, absurdity,[55] indecision (plurality of voices), endless stylistic experimentation, in stark contrast to the confident and authoritative tenor and tone of the earlier work.

There is some accounting for this, in part, as the consequence of the new direction Wittgenstein's thought takes, specifically in his elaboration of the novel conception of language; the 'language-game'. This central insight turns on the comparison between language and a game, or rather, collection of games. When seen as a game language becomes more plural, variegated, open and diverse, and lacking in the kind of unitary structure Wittgenstein claimed traditional philosophers had ascribed to it (including himself in his former 'Tractarian' incarnation). This is all true but the move to the language-game itself does not account for the other radical stylistic changes adopted in the later work.

I want to suggest that the conception of language as open and self-transformative represents for Wittgenstein a kind of voice of temptation; a voice I think he frequently repressed in favour of the lingering voice of the earlier work, the 'voice of correctness' of the calculus, of a 'logic-ized' view of the world, language and the philosophical enterprise. This irrepressible craving for order, system, and logical precision corresponds in part to Pascal's *esprit de géométrie* with the freed up picture of language (in the *Investigations*) approximating to the 'voice of temptation', or, translated into Pascalian terms, the *esprit de finesse*. This I take to be one source of anxiety in later Wittgenstein and it is his entrapment within a space between the logical and the interpretive that we might tentatively dub the 'tragic'. For all the novelty and daring of the later Wittgensteinian fragments there is a constant struggle between the strict ('Tractarian') conception of language as a calculus and a more open, playful language.

To test the strength of my claim would demand close scrutiny of the later work, a greater attention to textual detail than current constraints permit. With this in mind I want to point to one of the more obvious examples that spring to mind and hope it makes my point. Let us return to the early part of the *Investigations* (§§198–242), the continuous series of remarks on the general theme of rule-following. Two quite separate positions emerge. On the one hand rules are taken as strict commands admitting of no exception, like rails stretching to infinity (*PI*, §218), or customs (*PI*, §198) and institutions (*PI*, §199), or as orders to be followed blindly (*PI*, §219). Alternatively, rules may be perceived to be more malleable, where every instance of a rule implies a host of possible interpretations. Where is the authentic voice of Wittgenstein amongst these interpretive temptations? Wittgenstein quite explicitly refers to these opposing possibilities as a 'paradox' (*PI*, §201). On my reading of this section Wittgenstein is, in Goldmann's terms, caught tragically between two extreme positions, in this instance between two diametrically opposed ways of conceiving rules. The former speaks Cavell's 'voice of correctness' and the latter offers a more tempting openness, consistent, I might add, with the idea of a game, with all its playful, ludic associations. I suggest that he ultimately draws back, coming down on the side of 'correctness', namely, 'Following a rule is analogous to obeying an order. We are trained to do so: we react to an order in a particular way' (*PI*, §206).

But the position is not wholly unambiguous; Wittgenstein invariably muddies the water with the teasing 'is analogous to' and, on many occasions elsewhere 'is like', and even in the passage just quoted he subverts the initial premise with the unsettling thought that two people (trained to obey orders) might have the same training but react in different ways.[56]

The distinction I offer, then, may not be cut and dried, but it does point to the contours of a basic tension between opposing voices; a tension, I claim, at the heart of Wittgenstein's posthumous corpus. The idea, now commonplace, that there is in the *Investigations* a dispute between Wittgenstein and an 'imaginary interlocutor' (as he or she is frequently named), needs rethinking. It presents the *Investigations* as a coherent text, as a seamless and progressive dialectic between a controlling narrative persona and opposing philosophical positions. I have sought to contest this view preferring instead to disclose an irresolvable, and hence tragic, tension between contrary voices. It is all too tempting to speak of Wittgenstein's later work as a series of posthumous texts, after all we can read, teach, and study the *Investigations*, *On Certainty*, *Culture and Value*, and the like, but this is a temptation we should avoid. Instead of texts we have fragments and these by their very nature are, like the poetic word, ambiguous, paradoxical, and untameable.

NOTES

1. A selection of Gadamer's writings on education, specifically his work on the role of the university in modern life, is collected in Misgeld and Nicholson (1992).
2. The collection of essays *The Enigma of Health* (1996) adopts a critical attitude to modern medical practice. Gadamer traces modernity's increasing dependence upon technology and technological thinking to emphasize the eclipsing of the traditional (hermeneutical) idea of medicine as a healing *art*.
3. For a collection of essays on Gadamer's interpretations of the poetry of Paul Celan see Gadamer (1997a). The introductory essay in this volume, 'The remembrance of language: An introduction to Gadamer's poetics' by G. L. Bruns, is a useful overview of Gadamer's turn to poetry and introduction to his readings of Celan's difficult verse. For an essay on Rilke see Gadamer's 'Mythopoetic inversion in Rilke's *Duino Elegies*' in Gadamer (1994a). Other essays on poetry are to be found in Misgeld and Nicholson (1992), 'Hermeneutics, poetry, and modern culture', pp. 63–131.
4. *TRB*, pp. 131–9.
5. *TRB*, pp. 66–73.

6. Heidegger uses a similar analogy in the essay 'On the essence of truth' (Krell, 1978, pp. 117–41).

7. The gold standard no longer exists but the analogy still stands. Marxist economists would take issue with the idea of gold having an intrinsic value. The high value of gold is largely determined by the immense amount of congealed labour within it.

8. Derrida's third of his 'Three questions to Gadamer' in the 1981 Paris 'encounter' concerns 'the underlying structure of good will'. See Michelfelder and Palmer (1989).

9. 'Charity in interpreting the words ... of others is unavoidable ... just as we must maximize the sense of what the alien is talking about, so we must maximize the self-consistency we attribute to him, on pain of not understanding *him*' (from 'Truth and meaning', in Davidson, 1984, p. 27).

10. Gadamer (1986), pp. 105–15.

11. Hahn (1997), p. 39. Also see the essay, 'The eminent text and its truth', Gadamer (1980b), pp. 3–23.

12. In the essay 'The language of metaphysics' Gadamer asks, 'Is not language always the language of the homeland and the process of becoming-at-home in the world?' (Gadamer, 1994a, p. 78).

13. Gadamer (1997a), pp. 2–11.

14. 'Meaning and the concealment of meaning', in Gadamer, 1997a, p. 167.

15. Gadamer (1997a), p. 70.

16. Gadamer (1994a), p. 78.

17. See *TM*, pp. 104–5.

18. Kusch (1989), p. 250.

19. Kusch (1989), p. 250.

20. Derrida (1978).

21. This search for the understanding of a word through its use is, of course, very like Wittgenstein's procedure, recalling 'The meaning of a word is its use in the language' (*PI*, §43).

22. Gadamer uses this image on a few occasions. In this example it appears in reference to the hermeneutical skill, the fine judgement of the medical practitioner. See 'Apologia for the art of healing', Gadamer (1996), p. 36.

23. Perloff (1996), p. 10.

24. *PI*, p. 194.

25. *On Being in the World: Wittgenstein and Heidegger on Seeing Aspects*, Mulhall, (1990).

26. 'The *Investigations*' Everyday Aesthetics of Itself', Mulhall (1996), pp. 369–89.

27. This is the position Marjorie Perloff adopts in her *Wittgenstein's Ladder: Poetic Language and the Strangeness of the Ordinary*, Perloff (1996). See especially Chapter 6, 'Running against the walls of our cage: towards a Wittgensteinian poetics', pp. 181–218.

28. On the whole question of the importance of the nature of the aphorism and its connection to philosophical thought (and a useful comparison between Lichtenberg's aphorisms and the later Wittgenstein) see Stern (1963). Von Wright has also likened Wittgenstein to Lichtenberg. See von Wright (1982), p. 34.

29. Perloff (1996).

30. See for example his essay 'Notes and afterthought on the opening of Wittgen-
     stein's *Investigations*' in Cavell (1995). On the question of style Cavell detects in
     the *Investigations* the three voices of 'temptation', 'correctness', and 'attainment'.

31. Fergus Kerr in his *Theology after Wittgenstein* (Kerr, 1997) discusses the question
     of style in Chapter 2.

32. A new work entitled *The Literary Wittgenstein* (Gibson and Huemer, 2004) is
     shortly to be published. The publisher's blurb reinforces what I have argued for
     in this chapter: 'Although Wittgenstein said relatively little about literature there
     is growing recognition of the implications of his work for writing, especially for
     fiction and poetry. *The Literary Wittgenstein* is a timely and wide-ranging collec-
     tion of essays addressing Wittgenstein's philosophy in relation to the theory and
     philosophy of literature. It brings together the work of leading philosophers and
     literary theorists and presents the first comprehensive statement of a "Wittgen-
     steinian" criticism.'

33. *CV*, p. 24.

34. In *The Cambridge Companion to Wittgenstein* (Sluga and Stern, 1996).

35. Goldmann 1964.

36. This seems to be what critics like Brunschvicg, Lafuma, and Krailsheimer are
     attempting to do in their various rearrangements of the text.

37. Goldmann, (1964), pp. 193–4.

38. Goldmann (1964), p. 194.

39. Pascal (1966), p. 105.

40. Goldmann (1964), p. 196.

41. In 'Between finitude and infinity: Hegelian reason and the Pascalian heart'
     (Collins, 1995, pp. 1–28), William Desmond, drawing Hegel and Pascal together,
     moves away from Goldmann's 'tragic' reading, offering a more benign and
     optimistic reading of 'the between'. Interestingly, Gadamer speaks of the
     play between a text's familiarity and strangeness as the 'in-between' (see *TM*, p.
     295).

42. In a dramatic fall from grace he also mentions in this context those great thinkers
     Engels and Stalin!!

43. Martin Warner has made much of this distinction in his *Philosophical Finesse*
     (Warner, 1989).

44. *Pensées*, §513, Pascal (1966).

45. *Pensées*, §781, 'Verily thou art a God that hidest thyself' (Isaiah 45:15), (Pascal,
     1966).

46. In 'Some notes on conversations with Wittgenstein', in *Recollections of Wittgen-
     stein*, Rhees (1984), p. 92.

47. Rhees (1984), p. 93.

48. *PI*, Preface.

49. *PI*, Preface.

50. *PI*, Preface.

51. Cavell (1962), pp. 67–93.

52. Mulhall (1996), pp. 321–52.

53. The compressed style of the *Tractatus* echoes the rigid propositions of Spinoza's
     Ethics and *Treatise on the Correction of the Understanding* (*Tractatus de Intellectus
     Emendatione*) was clearly the inspiration for Wittgenstein's own *Tractatus*. Was it

       not G. E. Moore who first suggested the title *Tractatus Logico-Philosophicus* because of the Spinozistic resonances?

54. This point refers to the importance of the confession in Wittgenstein's personal life, as recounted in Ray Monk's *Wittgenstein: The Duty of Genius* (1990). It also links in to the confessional tone in Pascal and Augustine and may explain the attraction of these writers for Wittgenstein.

55. 'Now imagine a game of chess translated according to certain rules into a series of actions which we do not ordinarily associate with a *game* – say into yells and stamping of feet' (*PI*, §200).

56. When referring to language-games is Wittgenstein saying language *is* a game or is *like* a game? Perhaps the central paradox in Wittgenstein is the relationship between ordinary language and the 'language-game': as an expression this is not a part of ordinary language. These questions raise the whole problem of the role of metaphor in Wittgenstein which has been inadequately discussed in the literature. J. H. Gill's *Wittgenstein and Metaphor* (1996) is an important exception but the treatment is very much from the analytic perspective. Christopher Norris's 'The insistence of the letter: textuality and metaphor in Wittgenstein's later philosophy' (Norris, 1983, pp. 34–58) reads Wittgenstein in the light of Derrida's treatment of metaphor.

Conclusion

Currently there is no possibility of a rounded assessment of Wittgenstein. Only with the passage of time and the luxury of greater historical hindsight this affords will we start to make such a task possible. Debates as to which is the greater achievement, the *Tractatus Logico-Philosophicus* or the *Philosophical Investigations*, are far from over although it goes without saying that both works had a profound effect upon philosophical developments in the twentieth century. And even though it is only a little over 50 years since the death of Wittgenstein his influence has waxed and waned considerably during this time. Early verdicts that he must be either a charlatan or a genius have by now been settled; his brilliance is without doubt. As to his legacy and future influence, this is a difficult one to call.

Wittgenstein does not have the central place in philosophy he occupied in the 1960s. Philosophical work on language in the Anglo-American tradition has moved on to new areas of concern. Certain strands of anglophone philosophy of language, over the past twenty years, have witnessed ever greater involvement with philosophy of mind and logic, in part, no doubt, as a result of developments and research opportunities opened up in Artificial Intelligence and cognitive science. If this tendency is a move towards what Heidegger called a more 'technological-scientist' conception of language then it is almost certainly a tendency Wittgenstein also would have found abhorrent. For all the shortcomings of his later work, limitations I have sought to highlight in this work, Wittgenstein was all too mindful of the inadequacies of the Tractatus-type reduction of living language to formal logic and was clearly hostile to approaches to language which depend upon scientific and theoretical frameworks.

Fortunately, there is an opposing tendency in modern philosophy of language which runs against the 'technological-scientist' model and we would do well to dwell on some of its terms for it supports much of what I have had to say in this book. Recent figures in the modern pragmatist and British analytic (and 'post-analytic') traditions continue to work under the shadow of Wittgenstein, using the language-game model and investigations of linguistic rules as a springboard for further study and enquiry. It would be impossible to outline in a few brief sentences what the continuing influence of Wittgenstein is but I want to speak of a couple of areas where I consider recent developments to be in harmony with the account of Wittgenstein I offer in this work. More to the point recent Wittgenstein-inspired developments within analytic philosophy indicate a slow but growing convergence with the work of Gadamer and the hermeneutical and expressivist (that is, largely 'Continental') approaches I advocate in this book.

In recent years there is increasing awareness of the inadequate treatment of history and the historical in Anglophone philosophy. The demise of British Hegelianism at the end of the nineteenth century inaugurated a longstanding suspicion of historicism and historical theory in Anglophone thought. Wittgenstein's historical blindness clearly fed into this suspicion and lent it credibility and support. What passed (and, lamentably, in some cases still passes) for 'history of philosophy' in many universities was a context-less examination of arguments from Descartes to Kant. Any serious reflection upon the historical dimension to philosophy in the Anglophone world was left to fairly marginalized thinkers like Collingwood and Oakeshott and the Continental historicist tradition of Hegel, Marx, and Dilthey. These critical comments apply to Anglophone philosophy in general but they are particularly relevant to its philosophy of language.

With Richard Rorty's groundbreaking *Philosophy and the Mirror of Nature* (1980) things palpably changed. Rorty's account of the genesis of modern epistemology and its dependence upon a representational picture of the mind is a recognizably historical narrative (despite its absence of historical detail!). Significantly, Rorty uses arguments from Wittgenstein both to support his attack upon representation and defend what has come to be known as 'antifoundationalism', a position that Rorty and subsequent thinkers use to bridge the perceived chasm between analytic and Continental thought. In the concluding chapters of *Philosophy and the Mirror of Nature*, although he ignores much of the detail and background, Rorty turns to Gadamer to outline a new vision of philosophy as hermeneutical edification and conversation. Rorty's work is a watershed and in recent years, no doubt under his influence, there has been any number of important historical studies examining philosophy's self-understanding; works designed to locate analytic philosophy within the wider ambit of philosophical thought. And recently there has been a spate of philosophical biographies; part, no doubt, of a general desire to appreciate ideas within their own specific context and take seriously the difficulties textual interpretation raise. Curiously, the relevance of the historical dimension to philosophy of language is still largely overlooked in the Anglo-American tradition, despite the recent interest in analytic philosophy's own past and adoption of a more generally historicist approach. My point here is that a greater appreciation of the work of

Gadamer would allow philosophers of language to understand the historical dimension to their task. My attempt to draw parallels between Wittgenstein and Gadamer should be seen as a modest contribution to that appreciation.

Another welcome development in Anglophone philosophy, also militating against the hard-nosed 'technological-scientistic' model of language, is the interest in the manifest overlap between philosophy of language and literary theory. In some ways this interest was forced upon an initially unwilling philosophical profession. When literary theory burst upon the academic scene some twenty years ago there was a good deal of interest in largely Continental philosophy out of which the whole literary theory interest sprang. Mainstream modern analytic philosophy of language sidelined imaginative writing as well as ignoring questions around the status of rhetoric, metaphor, and figurative language generally. Despite initial hostility to deconstruction from the more entrenched elements within the philosophical establishment it is now familiar terrain. What deconstruction reopened was in some sense no more than an ancient debate about the relationship between philosophy and literature. In some ways, again, the exclusion of literary and aesthetic considerations from Anglophone philosophy had been partially as a result of Wittgenstein's failure to include these issues in his thinking. Now that the deconstructive dust has settled there is a growing philosophical interest in hermeneutics. Gadamer is the crucial place where philosophical and literary, analytic and Continental concerns can be brought together in that fusing of horizons and ceaseless dialogue so central to his thought.

Bibliography

Aarsleff, H. (ed.) (2001). *Condillac: Essay on the Origin of Human Knowledge*. Cambridge: Cambridge University Press.

Apel, K-O. (1980). *Towards a Transformation of Philosophy*. London: Routledge & Kegan Paul.

Aristotle (1976). *Ethics*, revised edition, Harmondsworth: Penguin.

Baynes, K., Bohman, K. and McCarthy, T. (eds) (1987). *After Philosophy: End or Transformation?* Cambridge, MA: MIT Press.

Benjamin, W. (1970). *Illuminations*. London: Jonathan Cape.

Berlin, I. (2000). *Three Critics of the Enlightenment: Vico, Hamann, Herder*. London: Pimlico.

Bernasconi, R. (1986). 'Bridging the abyss: Heidegger and Gadamer', *Research in Phenomenology* **16**: 1–24.

Bernstein, R. J. (1983). *Beyond Objectivism and Relativism: Science, Hermeneutics, and Praxis*. Philadelphia, PA: University of Pennsylvania Press.

Bowie, A. (2003). *Introduction to German Philosophy*. Cambridge: Polity Press.

Brandt, G. (1979). *The Central Texts of Wittgenstein*. Oxford: Basil Blackwell.

Bubner, R. (1981). *Modern German Philosophy*. Cambridge: Cambridge University Press.

Cavell, S. (1962). 'The availability of Wittgenstein's later philosophy', *The Philosophical Review* **52**: 67–93.

Cavell, S. (1995). *Philosophical Passages: Wittgenstein, Emerson, Austin, Derrida*. Oxford: Blackwell.

Collingwood, R. G. (1939). *An Autobiography*. Oxford: Oxford University Press.

Collins, A. B. (ed.) (1995). *Hegel on the Modern World*. Albany, NY: State University of New York Press.

Coltman, R. (1998). *The Language of Hermeneutics: Gadamer and Heidegger in Dialogue*. Albany, NY: State University of New York Press.

Condillac, E. B. de (2001). *Essay on the Origin of Human Knowledge*. Cambridge: Cambridge University Press.

Crary, A. and Read, R. (eds) (2000). The New Wittgenstein. London: Routledge.

Critchley, S. (2001). *Continental Philosophy: A Very Short Introduction*. Oxford: Oxford University Press.

Davey, N. (1993). 'Hermeneutics, language and science: Gadamer's distinction between discursive and propositional language', *Journal of the British Society for Phenomenology* **24**(3): 250–64.

Davidson, D. (1984). *Inquiries into Truth and Interpretation*. Oxford: Clarendon Press.

Derrida, J. (1978). *Writing and Difference*. London: Routledge & Kegan Paul.

Dostal, R. (ed.) (2002). *The Cambridge Companion to Gadamer*. Cambridge: Cambridge University Press.

Diamond, C. (1995). *The Realistic Spirit: Wittgenstein, Philosophy and the Mind*. Cambridge, MA: MIT Press.

Eagleton, T. (1983). *Literary Theory: An Introduction*, Oxford: Basil Blackwell.

Edmonds, D. and Eidinow, J. (2001). *Wittgenstein's Poker*. London: Faber and Faber.

Evans, M. (1981). *Lucien Goldmann: An Introduction*. Brighton: Harvester Press.

Finch, H. L. (1977). *Wittgenstein: The Later Philosophy*. Atlantic Highlands, NJ: Humanities Press.

Fiumara, G. C. (1990). *The Other Side of Language: A Philosophy of Listening*. London: Routledge.

Forster, M. N. (ed.) (2002). *Herder: Philosophical Writings*. Cambridge: Cambridge University Press.

Foucault, M. (1972). *The Archaeology of Knowledge*. London: Tavistock Publications.

Gadamer, H-G. (1970). 'The problem of language in Schleiermacher's Hermeneutic', in R. W. Funk (ed.) *Schleiermacher as Contemporary*. New York: Herder and Herder, pp. 68–95.

Gadamer, H-G. (1976a). *Philosophical Hermeneutics*. Berkeley, CA: University of California Press.

Gadamer, H-G. (1976b). *Hegel's Dialectic: Five Hermeneutical Studies*. New Haven, CT: Yale University Press.

Gadamer, H-G. (1980a). *Dialogue and Dialectic: Eight Hermeneutical Studies on Plato*, New Haven, CT: Yale University Press.

Gadamer, H-G. (1980b). 'The eminent text and its truth', *Bulletin Mid-Western Modern Language Association* 13(1): 3–23.

Gadamer, H-G. (1981). *Reason in the Age of Science*. Cambridge, MA: MIT Press.

Gadamer, H-G. (1986). *The Relevance of the Beautiful and Other Essays*, ed. R. Bernasconi. Cambridge: Cambridge University Press.

Gadamer, H-G. (1989). *Truth and Method* (revised second edition), trans. J. Weinsheimer and D. G. Marshall. London: Sheed and Ward.

Gadamer, H-G. (1991). *Plato's Dialectical Ethics: Phenomenological Interpretations relating to the 'Philebus'*. New Haven, CT: Yale University Press.

Gadamer, H-G. (1992). *Hans-Georg Gadamer on Education, Poetry, and History: Applied Hermeneutics*, ed. D. Misgeld and G. Nicholson. Albany, NY: State University of New York Press.

Gadamer, H-G. (1994a). *Heidegger's Ways*, trans. J. W. Stanley, Introduction by D. J. Schmidt. Albany, NY: State University of New York Press.

Gadamer, H-G. (1994b). *Literature and Philosophy in Dialogue: Essays in German Literary Theory*, trans. R. H. Paslick. Albany, NY: State University of New York Press.

Gadamer, H-G. (1996). *The Enigma of Health: The Art of Healing in a Scientific Age*. Cambridge: Polity Press.

Gadamer, H-G. (1997a). *Gadamer on Celan*. Albany, NY: State University of New York Press.

Gadamer, H-G. (1997b). 'Rhetoric and hermeneutics', in W. Jost and M. J. Hyde (eds) *Rhetoric and Hermeneutics in our Time*. New Haven, CT: Yale University Press.

Gallagher, K. T. (1982). 'Wittgenstein, Augustine, and language', *New Scholasticism* **56**: 462–70.

Genova, J. (1995). *Wittgenstein: A Way of Seeing*. London: Routledge.

Gibson, J. and Huemer, W. (eds) (2004). *The Literary Wittgenstein*. London: Routledge.

Gier, N. (1981). *Wittgenstein and Phenomenology: A Comparative Study of the Later Wittgenstein, Husserl, Heidegger, and Merleau-Ponty*. Albany, NY: State University of New York Press.

Gill, J. H. (1996). *Wittgenstein and Metaphor*, revised edition. Atlantic Highlands, NJ: Humanities Press.

Glendinning, S. (1998). *On Being with Others*. London: Routledge.

Glock, H-J. (2001). *Wittgenstein: A Critical Reader*. Oxford: Blackwell.

Goldmann, L. (1964). *The Hidden God*. London: Routledge & Kegan Paul.

Goldmann, L. (1992). 'Pascal and dialectical thought', *The Philosophical Forum* **XXIII**(1–02): 9–19.

Griffith-Dickson, G. (1995). *Johann Georg Hamann's Relational Metacriticism*. Berlin: Walter de Gruyter.

Griswold, C. L., Jr. (ed.) (1988). *Platonic Writings, Platonic Reading*. State College, PA: Pennsylvania State University Press.

Grondin, J. (1994). *Introduction to Philosophical Hermeneutics*. New Haven, CT: Yale University Press.

Grondin, J. (1995). *Sources of Hermeneutics*. Albany, NY: State University of New York Press.

Grondin, J. (2003a). *The Philosophy of Gadamer*. Chesham: Acumen.

Grondin, J. (2003b). *Hans-Georg Gadamer: A Biography*, New Haven, CT: Yale University Press.

Haase, U. (1991). 'The Providence of Language in Gadamer's *Truth and Method*', *Journal of the British Society for Phenomenology* **22**(3): 17–84.

Habermas, J. (1983). 'Hans-Georg Gadamer: Urbanizing the Heideggerian Province', in J. Habermas, *Philosophical-political profiles*. London: Heinemann.

Habermas, J. (1986). 'Review of Gadamer's *Truth and Method*', in Wachterhauser, B. R. (ed.), *Hermeneutics and Modern Philosophy*. Albany, NY: State University of New York Press, pp. 243–76.

Hahn, L. E. (ed.) (1997). *The Philosophy of Hans-Georg Gadamer*. The Library of Living Philosophers, Vol. XXIV. Chicago, IL: Open Court.

Hegel, G. W. F. (1977). *Phenomenonology of Spirit*. Oxford: Oxford University Press.

Heidegger, M. (1975). *Poetry, Language, Thought*. New York: Harper & Row.

Heidegger, M. (1977) *The Question concerning Technology and Other Essays*. New York: Harper Row.

Heidegger, M. (1982). *On the Way to Language*. New York: Harper & Row.

Heidegger, M. (1996). *Being and Time*, trans. J. Stambaugh. Albany, NY: State University of New York Press.

Hintikka, J. (2000). 'Gadamer: squaring the hermeneutical circle', *Revue Internationale de Philosophie* **3**: 487–97.

Hirsch, E. D., Jr (1967). *Validity in Interpretation*. New Haven, CT: Yale University Press.

Hobbes, T. (1968). *Leviathan*. Harmondsworth: Penguin.

Hogan, J. P. (1987). 'Hermeneutics and the logic of question and answer: Collingwood and Gadamer', *Heythrop Journal* **XXVIII**: 263–84.

Hollinger, R. (ed.) (1985). *Hermeneutics and Praxis*. Notre Dame, IN: University of Notre Dame Press.

Howard, R. J. (1982). *Three Faces of Hermeneutics*. Berkeley, CA: University of California Press.

Janik, A. and Toulmin, S. (1973). *Wittgenstein's Vienna*. New York, NY: Simon and Schuster.

Kahn, L. E. (ed.) (1997). *The Philosophy of Hans-Georg Gadamer*. Chicago, IL: Open Court.

Kearney, R. (1995). *Poetics of Modernity: Toward a Hermeneutic Imagination*. Atlantic Highlands, NJ: Humanities Press.

Kenny, A. (ed.) (1994). *The Wittgenstein Reader*. Oxford: Blackwell.

Kerr, F. (1997). *Theology after Wittgenstein* (revised edition). London: SPCK.

Kirwan, C. (1989). *Augustine*. London: Routledge.

Kirwan, C. (2001). 'Augustine's philosophy of language', in E. Stump and N. Kretzmann (eds) *The Cambridge Companion to Augustine*. Cambridge: Cambridge University Press, pp. 186–204.

Knox, T. M. and Miller, A. V. (trans.) (1985). *Hegel's Introduction to the Lectures on the History of Philosophy*, Oxford: Clarendon Press.

Kockelmans, J. J. (1972). *On Heidegger and Language*. Evanston, IL: Northwestern University Press.

Krell, D. F. (ed.) (1978). *Martin Heidegger: Basic Writings*. London: Routledge & Kegan Paul.

Kripke, S. A. (1982). *Wittgenstein on Rules and Private Language*. Oxford: Basil Blackwell.

Kusch, M. (1989). *Language as Calculus vs. Language as Universal Medium: A Study in Husserl, Heidegger and Gadamer*. Boston: Kluwer.

Lafont, C. (1999). *The Linguistic Turn in Hermeneutic Philosophy*. Cambridge, MA: MIT Press.

Lawn, C. (1996). 'Adventures of self-understanding: Gadamer, Oakeshott, and the question of education', *Journal of the British Society for Phenomenology* **27**(3): 267–77.

Lawn, C. (1997). 'Review of H-G. Gadamer's *The Enigma of Health*', *Milltown Studies* **39**: 142–7.

Lawn, C. (2001). 'Gadamer on poetic and ordinary language', *Philosophy and Literature* **25**: 113–26.

Lawn, C. (2002). 'Wittgenstein, history and hermeneutics', *Philosophy and Social Criticism* **29**(3): 281–95.

Levin, D. M. (ed.) (1997). *Sites of Vision: The discursive construction of sight in the history of philosophy*. Cambridge, MA: MIT Press.

Locke, J. (1924). *An Essay Concerning Human Understanding*. Oxford: Clarendon Press.

Losonsky, M. (ed.) (1999). *Humboldt: On Language*. Cambridge: Cambridge University Press.

Louth, A. (1989). 'Augustine on language', *Journal of Literature and Theology* **3**(2): 151–8.

Lyotard, J-F. (1984). *The Postmodern Condition: A report on Knowledge*. Manchester: Manchester University Press.

MacIntyre, A. (1971). *Against the Self-Images of the Age*. London: Duckworth.

Malcolm, N. (1984). *Ludwig Wittgenstein: A Memoir*. Oxford: Oxford University Press.

Malpas, J., Arnswald, U. and Kertscher, J. (eds) (2002). *Gadamer's Century: Essays in Honor of Hans-Georg Gadamer*. Cambridge, MA: MIT Press.

Margalit, E. and A. (eds) (1991). *Isaiah Berlin: A Celebration*. London: Hogarth Press.

Mendelson, J. (1979). 'The Habermas-Gadamer debate', *New German Critique* **18**: 44–73.

Michelfelder, D. P. and Palmer, R. E. (eds) (1989). *Dialogue and Deconstruction: The Gadamer-Derrida Encounter*. Albany, NY: State University of New York Press.

Misgeld, D. and Nicholson, G. (eds) (1992). *Hans-Georg Gadamer on Education, Poetry and History: Applied Hermeneutics*. Albany, NY: State University of New York Press.

Monk, R. (1990) *Wittgenstein: The Duty of Genius*. London: Jonathan Cape.

Moran, D. (2000). *Introduction to Phenomenology*. London: Routledge.

Mulhall, S. (1990). *On Being in the World: Wittgenstein and Heidegger on Seeing Aspects*. London: Routledge.

Mulhall, S. (ed.) (1996). *The Cavell Reader*. Oxford: Blackwell.

Mulhall, S. (2001). *Inheritance and Originality: Wittgenstein, Heidegger, Kierkegaard*. Oxford: Clarendon Press.

Nagl, L. and Mouffe, C. (eds) (2001). *The Legacy of Wittgenstein: Pragmatism or Deconstruction*. Frankfurt: Peter Lang.

Norman, R. (1976). *Hegel's Phenomenology: a Philosophical Introduction*. Brighton: University of Sussex Press.

Norris, C. (1983). *The Deconstructive Turn: Essays in the Rhetoric of Philosophy*. London: Methuen.

Oakeshott, M. (1991). *Rationalism in Politics and Other Essay*. Indianapolis, IN: Liberty Press.

Oates, W. J. (ed.) (1948). *Basic Writings of Saint Augustine*, Vol. 2. New York: Random House.

O'Neill, J. (ed.) (1976). *On Critical Theory*. New York: Seabury Press.

Palmer, R. (1969). *Hermeneutics: Interpretation Theory in Schleiermacher, Dilthey, Heidegger, and Gadamer*. Evanston, IL: Northwestern University Press.

Palmer, R. (ed.) (2001). *Gadamer in Conversation: Reflections and Commentary*. New Haven, CT: Yale University Press.

Pascal, B. (1966). *Pensées*, trans. A. J. Krailsheimer. Harmondsworth: Penguin Books.

Pascal, B. (1995). *Pensées and other writing*, trans. H. Levi. Oxford: Oxford University Press.

Perloff, M. (1996). *Wittgenstein's Ladder: Poetic Language and the Strangeness of the Ordinary*. Chicago, IL: University of Chicago Press.

Putnam, H. (1995). *Pragmatism*. Oxford: Basil Blackwell.

Reeder, H. P. (1989) 'Wittgenstein never was a phenomenologist', *Journal of the British Society for Phenomenology* **20**(3): 257–77.

Rhees, R. (ed.) (1984). *Recollections of Wittgenstein*. Oxford: Oxford University Press.

Rhees, R. (1998). *Wittgenstein and the Possibility of Discourse*, ed. D. Z. Phillips. Cambridge: Cambridge University Press.

Risser, J. (1997). *Hermeneutics and the Voice of the Other: Re-reading Gadamer's Philosophical Hermeneutics*. Albany, NY: State University of New York Press.

Rorty, R. (1980). *Philosophy and the Mirror of Nature*. Oxford: Basil Blackwell.

Rorty, R. (1989). *Contingency, Irony, and Solidarity*. Cambridge: Cambridge University Press.

Rorty, R. (2000). 'Being that can be understood is language: On Hans-Georg Gadamer and the philosophical conversation', *London Review of Books* 22(6): 23–5.

Saint Augustine (1961). *Confessions*. Harmondsworth: Penguin.

Saint Augustine (1997). *On Christian Doctrine*. Oxford: Oxford University Press.

Scheibler, I. (2000). *Gadamer: Between Heidegger and Habermas*. Lanham, MD: Rowman & Littlefield.

Schleiermacher, F. (1998). *'Hermeneutics and Criticism' and Other Writings*. Cambridge: Cambridge University Press.

Schmidt, L. K. (ed.) (1995). *The Specter of Relativism: Truth, Dialogue and Phronesis in Philosophical Hermeneutics*. Evanston, IL: Northwestern University Press.

Schmidt, L. K. (ed.) (2000). *Language and Linguisticality in Gadamer's Hermeneutics*. Lanham, MD: Lexington Books.

Silverman, H. (ed.) (1991). *Gadamer and Hermeneutics*. London: Routledge.

Sluga, H. D. and Stern, D. G. (eds) (1996). *The Cambridge Companion to Wittgenstein*. Cambridge: Cambridge University Press.

Smith, P. C. (1979). 'Gadamer's hermeneutics and ordinary language philosophy', *The Thomist* 43: 296–321.

Smith, P. Christopher (1991). *Hermeneutics and Human Finitude*. New York: Fordham University Press.

Staten, H. (1984). *Wittgenstein and Derrida*. Lincoln, NE: University of Nebraska Press.

Stern, J. P. (1963). *Lichtenberg: A Doctrine of Scattered Occasions*. London: Thames and Hudson.

Stump, E. and Kretzmann, N. (eds) (2001). *The Cambridge Companion to Augustine*. Cambridge: Cambridge University Press.

Taylor, C. (1985). *Human Agency and Language: Philosophical Papers 1*. Cambridge: Cambridge University Press.

Vattimo, G. (1997). *Beyond Interpretation: The Meaning of Hermeneutics for Philosophy*. Cambridge: Polity Press.

Vesey, G. (ed.) (1974). *Understanding Wittgenstein*. London: Macmillan.

Wachterhauser, B. R. (ed.) (1986). *Hermeneutics and Modern Philosophy*. Albany, NY: State University of New York Press.

Wachterhauser, B. R. (ed.) (1994). *Hermeneutics and Truth*. Albany, NY: State University of New York Press.

Wachterhauser, B. R. (1999). *Beyond Being: Gadamer's Post-Platonic Hermeneutical Ontology*. Evanston, IL: Northwestern University Press.

Warner, M. (1989). *Philosophical Finesse*. Oxford: Clarendon.

Warnke, G. (1987). *Gadamer: Hermeneutics, Tradition and Reason*. Cambridge: Polity Press.

Weinsheimer, J. (1985). *Gadamer's Hermeneutics: A Reading of 'Truth and Method'*. New Haven, CT: Yale University Press.

Weinsheimer, J. (1991). *Philosophical Hermeneutics and Literary Theory*. New Haven, CT: Yale University Press.

Wittgenstein, L. (1922). *Tractatus Logico-Philosophicus*, trans. C. K. Ogden. London: Routledge & Kegan Paul.

Wittgenstein, L. (1953). *Philosophical Investigations*. Oxford: Blackwell.

Wittgenstein, L. (1967). *Zettel*, ed. G. E. M. Anscombe. Oxford: Blackwell.

Wittgenstein, L. (1972). *Blue and Brown Books: Preliminary Studies for the 'Philosophical Investigations'*. Oxford: Basil Blackwell.

Wittgenstein, L. (1974a). *Philosophical Grammar*. Oxford: Basil Blackwell.

Wittgenstein, L. (1974b). *On Certainty*, trans. D. Pauland G. E. M. Anscombe. Oxford: Basil Blackwell.

Wittgenstein, L. (1979). *Notebooks: 1914–1916* (second edition) Oxford: Basil Blackwell.

Wittgenstein, L. (1980). *Culture and Value*. Oxford: Basil Blackwell.

Wittgenstein, L. (1993). *Philosophical Occasions: 1912–1951*. Indianapolis, IN: Hackett.

Wood, D. (ed.) (1981). *Heidegger and Language*. Coventry: University of Warwick Parousia Press.

Wright, G. H. von (1971). *Explanation and Understanding*. Ithaca, NY: Cornell University Press.

Wright, G. H. von (1982). *Wittgenstein*. Oxford: Basil Blackwell.

Wright, K. (1986). 'Gadamer: the speculative structure of language', in Wachterhauser, B. R. (ed.), Hermeneutics and Modern Philosophy. Albany, NY: State University of New York Press, pp. 193–218.

Index